FEMINISM, LAW, INCLUSION:
INTERSECTIONALITY IN ACTION

FEMINISM, LAW, INCLUSION:

INTERSECTIONALITY

IN ACTION

EDITED BY

Gayle MacDonald,
Rachel L. Osborne
& Charles C. Smith

SUMACH
PRESS

WOMEN'S ISSUES PUBLISHING PROGRAM

SERIES EDITOR: BETH MCAULEY

LIBRARY AND ARCHIVES CANADA CATALOGUING IN PUBLICATION

Feminism, law, inclusion : intersectionality in action / editors:
Gayle MacDonald, Rachel L. Osborne, Charles C. Smith.

Includes bibliographical references.

ISBN 1-894549-45-7

1. Women— Legal status, laws, etc. — Canada. I. MacDonald,
Gayle Michelle, 1957- II. Osborne, Rachel L., 1965- III. Smith,
Charles C., 1953-

KE450.W6F44 2005   349.71'082   C2005-900743-5
KF390.W6F44 2005

Edited by Beth McAuley
Design by Liz Martin

Maryka Omatsu, "The Fiction of Judicial Impartiality," *Canadian Journal of Women
and the Law* 9, no. 1 (1997). Reprinted by permission of University of
Toronto Press Incorporated (www.utpjournals.com).

Sherene Razack, "*R.D.S. v. Her Majesty The Queen*: A Case About Home,"
Scratching the Surface: Canadian Anti-Racist Feminist Thought, eds. Enakshi Dua
and Angela Robertson, 281–294. Reprinted by permission of Women's Press.

*Sumach Press acknowledges the support of the Canada Council
for the Arts and the Ontario Arts Council for our publishing program.
We acknowledge the financial suport of the Government of Canada through
the Book Publishing Industry Development Program (BPIDP)*

Printed and bound in Canada

Published by

SUMACH PRESS

1415 Bathurst Street #202
Toronto Ontario Canada
M5R 3H8
www.sumachpress.com

CONTENTS

ACKNOWLEDGEMENTS

The editors would like to thank Beth McAuley at Sumach Press for her patience and commitment to this book. We also wish to acknowledge the contribution Abby Bushby made to this project in its early stages. We especially acknowledge Yola Grant, Kim Bernhardt, Avvy Go, Arleen Huggins, Margaret Parsons, Kim Murray, Patricia Monture-Angus, Michele Williams and other Aboriginal women and women of colour fighting for justice and equality in the legal profession and, through law, in society. We thank our research assistants Twila Reid, Luanne Efford, Meagan Cameron, Mike Fleming and, more recently, Mary-Ellen Green. Anita Saunders provided excellent secretarial and editorial support.

We also wish to thank all the authors who have contributed to this collection. They have worked with us for quite some time, revising and editing on different occasions, and remaining engaged in this volume while otherwise working on so many other projects. We thank each of you for your patience and your commitment.

Gayle also wishes to thank Jonathan, Erls and Breagh who gave much and asked for less, in their patient wait for this book. Jo's sense of humour and balance kept things on track. Rachel would like to thank Margaret Froh for her thoughtful and challenging discussions and for her valuable suggestions on the content of this collection. Charles would like to acknowledge Tema and Asher for their ongoing love and support.

Surveying the Landscape: An Introduction to Feminism, Law, Inclusion

Rachel L. Osborne & Charles C. Smith

There have been so many developments concerning women and the law over the past three decades that the sheer accounting of activities — scholarship, advocacy, case law and legislative initiatives — is nothing short of astounding. From the initial impact of second-wave feminism in the early to mid-1970s, which focused on women's equality rights, up to the current actions and debates of 2005, which concern the interplay of gender and other elements of identities, there has been an explosion of ideas and initiatives that have challenged gendered norms. The challenge that the very notion of gender posed to law and legal discourse in the 1970s and 1980s was indeed revolutionary, much the same way that current legal discourse on women and law is challenged by our present-day conceptualizations of gender — now reflective of intersections of race, sexual identity, Aboriginal identity and disability. The mainstream conceptualizations of women's social, economic and political roles in the 1970s and 1980s were based on the gendered norms of white, heterosexual, able-bodied, class-privileged women. The degree to which such gendered norms could affect transformative change in law and legal discourse was limited by the exclusion of voices, perspectives and experiences of racialized women, Aboriginal women, lesbian and bisexual women and women with disabilities. The reconceptualization of gendered norms in current feminist discourse, which are inclusive of intersections of other aspects of identity, promise to push our understandings of women and the law to new levels.

In this context, the spirited attack against male-dominated laws and their institutional supports have become part of the everyday concerns among a growing number of feminist legal advocates who have taken their issues to the courts, of community activists who have become engaged in extra-parliamentary and parliamentary initiatives[1] and of legal scholars who have published their research and arguments and engaged in on-campus and in-classroom debates.[2] As well, feminists began to question the notion of gendered essentialism, which gave rise to concerns about the preponderance of a feminism concerned with white, heterosexual, able-bodied, economically advantaged and politically liberal and conservative women. Such a perspective, with its attempts to contain the discourse on gender within the bounds of a "universal womanhood," have been subject not only to critiques from men but also to critiques from women who have sensed that there are other aspects of identity that are critical to their being — such as race, economic status and sexual orientation.[3] Needless to say, these challenges have created tensions between women and men in society at large and between women within the women's movement. This tension between men and women in society has been perplexing in terms of the advancement of women's equality rights and the positioning of these challenges against patriarchal values and systems, including laws and institutional supports. This has been of particular concern during this time that many consider to be a significant retrenchment and re-establishment of heterosexist white male power and class privilege.

This disturbing threat of the retrenchment of women's rights was witnessed in the recent 2004 federal election in Canada and the 2004 U.S. presidential election, where commitments to re-examine laws governing women's reproductive rights were prominent in conservative party platforms. Promises to nullify the hard-fought legal victories won by gays and lesbians also played a significant role in conservative party politics in both elections.

Thus, the importance of exploring and articulating a praxis based on intersectionality as a challenge to the notion of universal womanhood has been offered as a more inclusive conceptualization. This has had a tremendous effect on feminist scholarship and on women's political organizing during the 1990s, which continues into the new millennium. The scholarship produced since the 1990s contrasts sharply to earlier efforts that were characterized by a narrowly contained discourse reliant on the notions of gendered essentialism and universal womanhood. Political activism was similarly hindered by these notions and often led to fragmentation and conflict within communities and within the women's movement as marginalized women grew increasingly frustrated and discontented with the continued silencing of their voices.

However, through political action in communities, in classrooms and in the legal profession itself, those previously marginalized voices began to weave themselves into discourse, effectively reconstructing our understandings of gender and increasing the relevance and applicability of gender analyses. As a consequence, intersectionality influenced and shaped feminist activism and political organizing. In the Canadian context of legal activism, for example, the most significant women's legal advocacy organization — the Women's Legal Education and Action Fund (LEAF) — responded to the challenges posed by this demand for a broader and more inclusive understanding of women's experiences. LEAF came to realize that, prior to 1990, because of the composition of its founding board the legal work it had undertaken had failed to address women's inequality in all its complexity and diversity. Gender analyses that excluded the voices and experiences of all but white, heterosexual, class-privileged women proved to be limiting when taking on cases that demanded a more inclusive and relevant understanding of women's lives. In addition to noting the inadequacy of gender analysis, LEAF also recognized that its founding board and staff fit into the concept of "universal womanhood": they were white, middle-class professional women.

Based on this realization, LEAF acknowledged that the skepticism that existed concerning the organization's ability to respond to and incorporate the interests and experiences of diverse women did, in fact, have foundation.[4] Once it understood the limitations of relying on a narrow conceptualization of woman, LEAF adopted a Diversification Policy which forced it "to confront the barriers to diversity posed by LEAF's commitment to litigation, an activity that relies upon skills and qualifications obtainable only through privileged processes." Furthermore, the policy mandated that the organization actively pursue a broad representation of women throughout the organization, recognize the importance of inclusiveness and accountability in its administration and governance processes, and select cases that would involve and affect the greatest possible number and range of women.[5] With a broader, more inclusive gender analysis, LEAF was in a better position to advocate on behalf of women in cases involving the deportation of women with Canadian-born children, spousal support for same-sex couples and access to legal aid for economically disadvantaged women.

The shifts that can come about in organizational and governance structures as a result of adopting more inclusive and broader conceptualizations is also reflected in the changes made to the committee structures and mandates of bar associations. The Law Society of Upper Canada, for example, which is the governing body of lawyers in Ontario, responded to the growing number of women joining the ranks of the legal profession during the 1970s and 1980s by establishing a committee to address issues of gender equality. In 1990, the Society mandated its "Women in the Legal Profession Committee" to be responsible for all of the research relating to gender issues. It is interesting to note that two of the main research projects undertaken by the Society in 1989 and 1991 which examined women's experiences in the legal profession did not address any other aspect of identity other than gender. In both the 1989 study of *Women in the Legal Profession* and the 1990/91 report *Transitions in Ontario Legal Profession*, Aboriginal lawyers, lesbian and bisexual lawyers, racialized lawyers and lawyers with disabilities were invisible. The construct of gender appeared to be absent of race, sexual identity, Aboriginal identity and certainly did not reflect women with disabilities or women who were economically challenged.

It wasn't until 1992 that the Law Society of Upper Canada undertook research that focused on racial discrimination, and that was done so at the request of the Black Law Students' Association of Canada (BLSAC). Over the following two years, in response to concerns raised by articling students, the Society conducted surveys to capture the extent to which articling students experienced discriminatory questions during articling interviews; students reported offensive remarks and inappropriate questions relating to sexual identity, country of origin, sex and family status. As noted in the Society's 1997 *Bicentennial Report* on equity and diversity in the legal profession, the Society merged its Women in the Legal Profession Committee and its Equity in Legal Education and Practice Committee in 1996. This move allowed the

Society to examine issues of gender equality alongside other equality issues being raised by racialized and Aboriginal lawyers. While the merging of these committees was attributed to a shift in the policy governance model that the Society adopted in 1996, it can also be explained by the increasing currency of notions of intersectionality that began to permeate discussions of women in the legal profession at that time.[6]

Similarly, the Canadian Bar Association established a task force led by former Supreme Court Justice Bertha Wilson. In 1993, this task force produced a comprehensive report on women in the practice of law entitled *Touchstones for Change: Equality, Diversity and Accountability*. Based on this report, numerous resolutions were adopted by the Association, including setting up a Standing Committee on Equality (now the Standing Committee on Equity) to implement these resolutions and to promote change within the legal profession. Shortly after this, the Association set up a Racial Equality Committee Working Group, which produced a report in 2000 entitled *Racial Equality in the Canadian Legal Profession*. While examining either gender or race, both of these reports explored relationships between the two and brought forward analysis and recommendations to address these in tandem.

In addition to the influence that intersectionality has had on feminist legal activism and the restructuring of organizations, notions of intersectionality have also affected feminist legal theorizing and scholarship. As intersectionality began to shape feminist legal scholarship in the 1990s, there was a shift away from the gender essentialist and universal notions of woman, which is reflected in the body of literature produced since then. In a bibliography on Canadian feminist legal literature produced between 1980 and 1998, the editors observed that diversity was a key theme in much feminist literature after 1988, and that current scholarship was characterized by a "serious focus on identifying the role of identities and structures related to race and sexuality as they interact with gender-based identities and structures."[7] Similarly, the editors of the 1999 "Women and Justice" issue of the *Canadian Woman Studies* journal insisted that contemporary understandings of "woman" required an understanding of intersectionality. The editors to that volume wrote, "It is essential to remember that all women are not the same nor are their lives, concerns, and choices the same. This is often profoundly influenced by who they are as racialized women, lesbians, or Aboriginal women ... [I]ssues of class and access to economic opportunity are important aspects which impact on the experiences that women have."[8]

As the 1990s unfolded, the voices of Aboriginal women, racialized women, lesbian and bisexual women and women with disabilities challenged gender essentialist notions even further, and had a decisive influence on the way we thought about and organized around women's issues and, in particular, how we interacted with legal institutions. Feminist scholars and political activists were shifting their attention away from the confines of the narrowly constructed discourse underlain by notions of universal womanhood and were instead grounding their theorizing and activism in the richer and more inclusive understandings of intersectionality. Legal scholar Martha Minnow cautioned in the early 1990s that when feminist analyses assume that a white, middle-class, heterosexual, Christian, able-bodied person is the norm behind "women's experience," we are simply recreating the very problem feminist analyses seek to address, that is, "the adoption of unstated reference points that hide from view a preferred position [that] shields it from challenge by other plausible alternatives."[9] By the end of the 1990s, the notion of intersectionality had become an important and constant component of meaningful feminist analyses, whether in the context of political activism or legal scholarship. Sherene Razack, for example, insisted that feminist analyses must take into account the interlocking systems of domination if we are to fully understand women's experiences in meaningful ways, and she maintained that "it is vitally important to explore in a historical and site-specific way the meaning of race, economic status, class, disability, sexuality, and gender as they come together to structure women in different and shifting positions of power and privilege."[10]

It is for these reasons that we sought to create a discourse on women and law in the new millennium. We were concerned about the way in which the discourse was being shaped and felt it was important to bring together women from various perspectives and social locations to discuss where women were heading and how issues of personal and community intersections were being addressed, particularly in how these intersections were influencing law. This led us to organize a series of seminars in Toronto that were held over three days in March 2000, and to the publication of this collection. Many of the essays included here were inspired by the presentations and discussions of the academics, practitioners and community activists who participated. It is worth exploring here some of the diverse issues that were presented as they illustrate the depth and complexity of inclusivity as conceptualized in theories of intersectionality.

For example, Patricia Monture-Angus focused on the definition of Aboriginal rights and the case for equity in education, particularly as these influence how lawyers understand and act on behalf of Aboriginal clients. She argued that such lawyers need to understand Aboriginal legal systems, social orders and traditions. Cynthia Petersen explored the case of *Little Sisters v. Canada: Challenging the Definition of "Obscene,"* a case which involved a constitutional challenge to the prohibited entry of "obscene" materials (that is, lesbian and gay literature) into Canada. In addition to addressing the freedom of expression rights under section 7 in the Charter of Rights and Freedoms, it challenged the discriminatory impact of the legislation on gays and lesbians as well. Interestingly enough, her discussion rekindled a dialogue about pornography, art and the responsibility of the state to sequester activity that may contribute or lead to the degradation of, or violence against, women.

Karen Mock spoke of her experiences within the Jewish community of building coalitions with other communities to address issues of racism and anti-Semitism. Margaret Parsons discussed the reluctance of the courts to respond to the concerns of African-Canadian women, particularly in such cases as *Baker*. Avvy Go addressed the number of times the issue of intersectionality has been the focal point for discourse within feminist conferences. She was particularly concerned that issues of intersectionality have not been adopted by the legal profession and within courtrooms across Canada. Carole Curtis addressed the failure of the legal aid program in New Brunswick to provide support for a state-funded lawyer to take on the case of a mother facing a temporary wardship case. The Supreme Court of Canada found that this infringed on the mother's rights under section 7 of the Charter wherein both the National Association of Women and the Law and LEAF intervened.

Yola Grant, who has taken on many challenging cases as intervenor for LEAF and the African Canadian Legal Clinic, addressed issues concerning workplace harassment and discrimination as they have been addressed by the courts since *Bliss* under the Canadian Bill of Rights up to the recent Supreme Court decision in *Meiron v. BCGSEU.* Patricia McDermott discussed how the concept of gender has been developed in Canadian jurisprudence since the 1970s, particularly to demonstrate that shaping legal arguments in terms of gender has helped provide the jurisprudence needed for development in related concepts of race and sexual orientation.

INTERSECTIONALITY AND ACTION

We have attempted in this collection to illustrate how intersectionality has been integrated into legal scholarship and activism. The themes discussed in the essays presented here are truly like a "living tree"[11] and the dialogue sparked at the seminar and continued here continues to shape contemporary discourse regarding women and law in Canadian society.

In terms of the essays in this collection, we thought it would be important to open with a commentary on "Theorizing the Intersections." In this chapter, Rebecca Johnson articulates a sense of intersectionality that is both contemporary and challenging, beginning with the notions of intersectionality as they have been constructed through the discourse of individual and group identity formation, as well as the emerging notions of self and group categories. As the initial foray into this collection, Johnson makes an excellent case for the role that identity formation plays in individual and social life and the importance of identity formation for individuals and groups, bringing into focus the multiple notions of identity that are needed in the formation of self.

Following the Commentary is the first section entitled "Theory in Action." The chapters in this section address perspectives as diverse as community mobilization, the social construction of sexuality, notions of judicial impartiality and issues concerning sexual orientation. Some essays begin to unpack the challenges of discussing intersectionality, while others actually address intersectionality directly. Erica Lawson and Amanda Hotrum discuss the importance of bringing a critical perspective to victims of hate crimes and human rights violations. Gayle MacDonald focuses on women's sexuality and argues that it is constructed as deviant in a variety of social contexts, which leads to an oppression of women's reality in particularized ways. Judge Maryka Omatsu discusses the fiction of judicial impartiality and points to the importance of analyzing the gender and racial characteristics of the judiciary. Lori G. Beaman comments on the Supreme Court of Canada case *Trinity Western University v. British Columbia College of Teachers*. In doing so, she looks at recent legal history regarding sexual orientation and its protection under human rights legislation and the Charter of Rights and Freedoms. She argues that the Supreme Court is able to minimize the perceived harm to gays and lesbians and to frame the issues so as to avoid dealing with the continuing discrimination faced by gays, lesbians, bisexual and transgendered persons through a series of discursive techniques.

The second section, "Organizations in Action," includes chapters that discuss various women-led initiatives that support women's challenges to man-made laws and looks at women's place in the legal profession. This section opens with Jan Kainer's discussion of the development of the educational video *In the Face of Justice*, a project that was supported by the Equity Initiatives Department at the Law Society of Upper Canada. In doing so she looks at the issues that formed the ways of thinking of how to frame the video, which include the relationship of law to society, and the nature of legal decision making. Marilou McPhedran discusses the critical roles that LEAF, the Canadian-based International Women's Rights Project, international NGOs and the United Nations have played in the development of women's international rights. Daina Green focuses on the ways that the advocacy organization known as the Alliance for Employment Equity organized to protest the dismantling of the *Employment Equity Law* in Ontario that was intended to prevent discriminatory practices in the workplace surrounding gender, race and sexual orientation.

The final section, "Law in Action," begins with a critique by Beverley Jacobs of the historical and legal summary of the 1985 amendments to the *Indian Act* (Bill C-31), which were intended to remove from the Act the sexually discriminating sections. In doing so, Jacobs discusses existing cases that have been reported along with those that are currently in litigation. Sherene Razack looks at the case of *R.D.S. v. Her Majesty The Queen* and discusses the problems associated with naming racism, specifically gender racism, in the court and the "will not to know" on the part of whites. In closing, Martha McCarthy and Joanna Radbord review the case *M. v. H.*, which was the first high court case to recognize the spousal status of gays and lesbians. In this chapter, they discuss how this case was supposed to provide substantive equality rights to deal with sex-orientation discrimination; however, they argue that such a concept is more easily written about than it is to actualize.

The works compiled in *Feminism, Law, Inclusion* are written by legal advocates, community activists and legal scholars whose research and scholarship represent a diverse pool of knowledge on the issues of gender, sexual orientation and racial bias within Canada. This is but a sampling of the struggles for justice and equality that women within Canadian society have overcome and of the battles that are yet to be fought.

NOTES

1. The establishment of the Royal Commission on the Status of Women in 1967, which was set up to address women's equality and make recommendations to the federal government, was likely the most significant effort in this context. The Royal Commission was followed by a number of other initiatives engaging women as catalysts for constitutional, legislative, bureaucratic and social change, including advocacy work addressing the equality sections of the Charter of Rights and Freedoms; the Royal Commission on Employment Equity headed by Justice Rosalie Abella; the establishment of the Federal Advisory Committee on the Status of Women, the Ontario Women's Directorate and the Secretary of State Status of Women Canada; the Royal Commission on Reproductive Technology; and other initiatives addressing pay equity, sexual harassment in the workplace and promoting gender equality.

2. For example, see Katherine Bartlett and Roseanne Kennedy, eds., *Feminist Legal Theory: Readings in Law and Gender* (Boulder, CO: Westview, 1991); Women's Legal Education and Action Fund (LEAF), *Equality and the Charter: Ten Years of Feminist Advocacy before the Supreme Court of Canada* (Toronto: Emond Montgomery Publications, 1996); Josée Bouchard, Susan Boyd and Elizabeth Sheehy, *Canadian Feminist Literature on Law: An Annotated Bibliography / Recherches Féministes en Droit au Canada: Une Bibliographie Annotée* (Toronto: University of Toronto Press, 1999).

3. See, for example, Hazel Carby, "White Women Listen! Black Feminism and the Boundaries of Sisterhood," in R. Hennessey and C. Ingraham, eds., *Materialist Feminism* (London: Routledge, 1997); Roxanne Ng, "Racism, Sexism and

NationBuilding in Canada," in C. McCarthy and W. Crichlow, eds., *Race, Identity and Representation in Education* (New York: Routledge, 1993); Tania Das Gupta, "Political Economy of Gender, Race and Class: Looking at South Asian Immigrant Women in Canada," in *Canadian Ethnic Studies* 26, no. 1 (1994); Elizabeth Abell, "Black Writing, White Reading," in K. Appiah and H.L. Gates, Jr., eds., *Identities* (Chicago: University of Chicago Press, 1995); Kimberlé Crenshaw, "Mapping the Margins: Intersectionality, Identity Politics, and Violence Against Women of Color," in Kimberlé Crenshaw et al., eds., *Critical Race Theory: The Key Writings that Formed the Movement* (New York: The New Press, 1995).

4. Women's Legal Education and Action Fund (LEAF), *Equality and the Charter,* xxi. Occurring within the same time frame, a similar phenomenon had a marked impact on the National Action Committee on the Status of Women.

5. Ibid., xxii.

6. The Law Society of Upper Canada, *Bicentennial Report and Recommendations on Equity Issues in the Legal Profession* (Toronto: The Law Society of Upper Canada, 1997), 5–6.

7. Bouchard, Boyd and Sheehy, *Canadian Feminist Literature on Law / Recherches Féministes en Droit au Canada,* xx.

8. Brenda Cranney, Christine Dearing, Darlene Jamieson et al., "Editorial," *Canadian Woman Studies/les cahiers de la femme* 19, no. 1/2 (1999), 3.

9. Martha Minnow, "A Feminist Reason: Getting and Losing It," in Bartlett and Kennedy, eds., *Feminist Legal Theory,* 358.

10. Sherene Razack, *Looking White People in the Eye: Gender, Race, and Culture in Courtrooms and Classrooms* (Toronto: University of Toronto Press, 1998), 11–12. See also Patricia Monture-Angus, "Standing Against Canadian Law: Naming Omissions of Race, Culture and Gender," in Elizabeth Comack, ed., *Locating Law: Race/Class/Gender Connections* (Halifax: Fernwood, 1999), in which she has written, "It is very difficult for me to separate what happens to me because of my race and culture. My world is not experienced in a linear and compartmentalized way. I experience the world simultaneously as a Mohawk and as a woman" (177–178).

11. This was the term used by the Privy Council in the Person's Case. See *Edwards v. A.G. Canada* [1930] AC 123 (PC).

GENDER, RACE, CLASS AND SEXUAL ORIENTATION: THEORIZING THE INTERSECTIONS

Rebecca Johnson

[One can't conceal one's past or parents.] They inevitably come along for the ride and are part of a shadow government that always occupies part of our being. They are, like the aspects of our fate that arrive before we know they are there, residues that we either learn how to make use of or else allow to poison us in one way or another. They cannot be expunged, for they are part of our fate, part of what made us what we are.

— James S. Hans, *The Fate of Desire*[1]

The term "intersectionality" has recently become prominent in critical literature.[2] However, feminist attention to intersections is not a new phenomenon. As Angela Miles points out, many feminists have long been attending to intersections in an attempt to construct an integrative vision of feminism.[3] Like Hans in the epigraph above, Miles reminds readers of the importance of attending to the past. Too often, she argues, feminist theorizing ignores its own past, minimizing the complexity of debates within feminism about the need to work constructively and creatively with the tension between difference and specificity — a tension often arising from the intersections of privilege and disadvantage.

Taking Miles's observation to heart, I will attempt to sketch the foundation of intersectional theory by commenting on some moments in the history of feminist thought, scholarship and practice — moments which are part of the shadow government that has made us what we are. Here, following Foucault, my goal is to attempt a genealogy of moves that have been made in the development of intersectional theory. That is, I propose a conceptual "history of the present" in feminist intersectional scholarship, rather than a comprehensive history of the women's movement.[4] The point is to provide a brief introductory description of the contours of intersectional theory, a description drawing in large measure on a history of discussions in the feminist community about essentialism and identity.

I preface this discussion with the following observation: activists have often confronted quite different kinds of arguments about essentialism and identity depending on the "public" or "private" nature of both their concerns and of the arenas in which those concerns have been articulated. As such, I would like to first offer a few reflections on the public/private divide, as this divide is an important part of the background scenery against which intersectional theory has unfolded.

THE INTERSECTIONAL ACTIVIST AND THE PUBLIC/PRIVATE DIVIDE

At the heart of social and political life in any modern liberal state is the notion that important distinctions must be drawn between public and private domains. The public/private divide provides a conceptual framework for drawing the boundary between these different domains and the activities that occur within them. On the one side, fall those activities or matters appropriate to public or political concern. On the other side, fall those activities or matters appropriate to private or personal concern.

Of course, it can be argued that activities themselves do not have an ontological "publicness" or "privateness": "public" and "private," like beauty, can be said to exist only in the eye of the beholder. And the eye of the beholder often views the world through the lens of some dominant ideology.[5] Although standards for beauty may vary with time and place, and though there may be individuals with unusual visions or preferences, there can be generally widespread social agreement as to what is beautiful.[6] So too there is often widespread social agreement as to what is public and what is private. This agreement reveals less about the nature of the activity in question than it does about the influence of a dominant ideology on how people conceptualize the world in which they live.

Now, to call the public/private divide "ideological" is *not* to say that the divide is *only* a mental construct: it *is* a mental construct but with significant material consequences. The divide involves the allocation of tasks and responsibilities in both ideological *and physical terms*. Significantly, even those who do not subscribe to the ideological framework justifying a given allocation of tasks will find themselves nonetheless subjected to it. Even the most cursory review of women's activism reveals a persistent concern with *how* tasks and responsibilities have been allocated under various manifestations of the private/public divide.[7] The divide has been drawn, women have often argued, using the pen of gender: men have claimed the public for their own concerns, relegating women's concerns to the private.[8] Men's concerns have not only dominated but have also defined the political realm. Women's concerns, to the extent that they have diverged from men's, have been characterized as personal. As Ruth Gavison puts it, the labelling of something as private or personal has had far reaching material (that is, social, economic and political) consequences:

> One of the functions of dubbing something "personal" is to define that activity, decision, or complaint outside of the social, political, or public arena, and to connect it with the particular circumstances and responsibilities of the individual or individuals concerned. This definition, in turn, identifies the proper way to address the complaint or problem: The individual suffering from personal difficulties may need aid or therapy. Although the general availability of such help may be a social concern, the particular problem is of no public interest or concern.[9]

Thus, it is no surprise that activists have often drawn heavily on the famous rallying cry, "the personal is the political." This classic statement has always served to challenge those manifestations of the public/private divide that suggest that women's problems are personal or private ones. As Carol Hanisch argues, "personal problems *are* political problems."[10] But while the rallying cry has been effective at foregrounding the politics inherent in any drawing of the public/private divide, it has not resolved complicated questions arising from challenges to those drawings. Some challenges have come in the form of internal critiques of the divide. Internal critiques generally argue that the divide has been drawn in the wrong place. External critiques, however, question or challenge the legitimacy of the distinction itself, suggesting that no distinction can be drawn, or rather, that the process of dividing things between an allegedly public and private world is so unremittingly harmful or discriminatory in the resulting distribution of benefits and burdens, that the distinction itself should be dissolved.[11]

Both internal and external challenges to the divide raise pressing questions in a context where it is becoming increasingly clear that the implications of labelling something as private or public can vary significantly to the extent that gender intersects with class, race, sexual orientation and physical ability. Indeed, if some women are disadvantaged through their relegation to the private, others are harmed through a denial of access to any sphere of privacy.[12] Neither the public nor private realm is necessarily better for women. Rather, these realms function in contradictory ways. Further, the benefits or burdens attached to any given division seem to be historically contingent and contested.

Thus, statements like "the personal is the political" are not simply assertions that given issues should fall to the public rather than private side of the line. Rather, they are assertions that the drawing of the line is itself political. Their greatest value lies in their ability to trouble the obviousness of the division, and to force a social articulation of the rationale for drawing the line in any given place. The important point may be that, while there is perhaps little in life that is inherently "public" or "private," important implications flow from the ways in which the boundaries are drawn. And whether launching internal or external critiques to the divide, we can see how intersectional theorists have consistently reminded us of the concrete ways in which gender, race, class and sexual orientation have played a part in the differential distribution of benefits and burdens in both the so-called public and private worlds. Let us then turn to our conceptual history of the present.

INTERSECTIONAL THEORY:
ACKNOWLEDGING THE SHADOW GOVERNMENT

One of the main concerns of early second-wave feminism[13] was with the widespread exclusion of women from positions of power in public life. This exclusion, they argued, was revealed not only by the numerical absence of women in politics and the professions but also in the partiality of society's written records of its history and its knowledge. That written record, feminists argued, was "his" story, a story that purported to be universal, but which was in truth partial. Dale Spender put it thus:

> Males, as the dominant sex, have only a *partial* view of the world and yet they are in a position to insist that their view and values are the *"real"* and *only* values; and they are in a position to impose their version on other human beings who do not share their experience. This is one of the crucial features of dominance ... it is the means by which one half of the human population is able to insist that the other half sees things its way.[14]

Women's experiences, feminists argued, were not reflected in the records of supposedly universal human knowledge. Women were sometimes completely absent from the record, and at other times were represented in terms that did not accord with women's often unrecorded experiences of themselves or their lives.

In the face of this partial universality, women began articulating their differences from men. Feminists argued that women shared common experiences of oppression and exclusion. Women from a wide number of disciplines began exploring and documenting these exclusions. The exclusion of women was not simply a physical absence of women in certain professions, though it was that as well. It was also an absence of women and their perspectives in the construction of knowledge across a wide body of disciplines: philosophy, history, science, the arts, law, religion, linguistics, politics, psychology. Slogans like "sisterhood is global" asserted a common female identity and became the rallying cry for united political activism designed to bring about political change, and to end a history of gender-based exclusion.[15]

But if there was widespread agreement that women were absent in many fields of human endeavour, there was less agreement about what that absence meant and how it should be rectified. One can see this in what has commonly been referred to as the "sameness/difference" debates.[16] The problem involved theorizing the meaning of women's difference. What difference should those differences make? Historically, women's "difference" had been one excuse for women's exclusion from the public world of work and politics. Arguing that women's difference should not be made the source of their oppression, one strand of thought was that the best strategy was to assert that men and women were similar in the most relevant (legal) ways. That is, women's difference could not provide a justification for exclusion. Here, the strategy was to remove the barriers that excluded women by labelling them "different." The false universality would be resolved by simply adding women into the mix. Once women were represented in power, professions and politics, their presence would make a difference. Women would transform the structures of power from within.[17]

However, a second strand of thought suggested that this strategy might not resolve the problem of false universality. While, given a chance, women might well be able to be successful on the terms of the male world, what if the problem was with the terms themselves? Perhaps the add and stir method could only accommodate women through assimilation, erasing differences that really did matter. That is, the system could adjust itself to allow women to compete with men, but only on the already established terms. What if one significance of women's difference lay in the ability it gave women to see the need for radical restructuring? Perhaps a strategy of inclusion would lead only to assimilation, leaving the deeper structures of oppression and exclusion untouched.[18] The better strategy, some argued, was to affirm and value women's differences from men.

In the midst of these ontological and political debates within feminism, cautionary notes began to sound. In particular, women of colour began speaking up within the feminist community, warning that feminism was replicating some of the very errors it had identified in "male-stream" thought. Audre Lorde warned that feminists tended to speak of women's oppression in universal ways, and that this language of universality sometimes effaced the experiences of women of colour. Asking that feminists be more attentive to the presence of difference not just between men and women, but also between women themselves, she said:

> ... differences expose all women to various forms and degrees of patriarchal oppression, some of which we share, and some of which we do

not ... The oppression of women knows no ethnic nor racial boundaries, true, but that does not mean it is identical within those boundaries.[19]

Indeed, women of colour began speaking up about the specificity of their oppression, of their feelings of exclusion within the feminist community, and of the ways in which claims of universal sisterhood often seemed premised on an unspoken norm of white sisterhood. And, based on their history, women of colour had good reasons to be cautious of feminism's claims of a global sisterhood. In both Canada and the U.S., nineteenth-century discourses of women's emancipation had dovetailed with other discourses about race and class.[20] Racist assumptions and strategies were deeply implicated in much of the reproductive and sexual politics of the early feminist movements. For many women of that time, reproduction was seen as inextricable from racial and imperial politics: women reproduced the race. The suffrage movement was often the call for votes only for specific kinds (and colours) of women.[21] One only had to look at the history of the birth control movement, Angela Davis argued, to understand why women of colour were nervous about joining the fight for "women's" abortion rights.[22] Of course, if problems of race were not easily addressed within feminist communities, neither were questions of gender easily addressed within communities of colour.[23] Women of colour were often high-centred on the rocks of racism and sexism.

But women of colour were not the only ones questioning the false unity in sisterhood. Other women were articulating concerns with the heterosexual presumptions embedded in the description of "the woman" at the centre of the women's movement. Lesbian women, in spite of their important contributions, were often marginalized in both feminist scholarship and activism.[24] And this was true across racial lines. Cherrie Moraga and Gloria Anzaldúa suggested that homophobia had been one of the biggest sources of separation among women of colour.[25] To the extent that women's activism was articulated in the shadow of "compulsory heterosexuality," lesbian experience was rendered invisible.[26] Charlotte Bunch argued that, because it had failed "to understand the importance of heterosexuality in maintaining male supremacy," the women's liberation movement lacked direction.[27] She and others suggested that until straight women could deal with their own homophobia, radical separation was a better option for lesbian survival.[28] Other women rejected separatism as a strategy, admonishing heterosexual feminists to resist the urge to disclaim their lesbian sisters — to instead confront their own emotional fear and prejudice and be accepting of lesbian activism within the women's movement.[29] These debates about inclusion and exclusion were further complicated by voices from the bisexual and transgendered communities.[30]

While Bunch also indicted the straight women's movement for its inattention to questions of race and class, similar reminders would come from women of colour within the lesbian community. Certainly, many women found their activism stymied because of their membership across multiple categories. As Elandria Henderson put it:

> We are Black, we are gay, we are women, we are Black Gay Women. We cannot split ourselves. We cannot fight against heterosexual bias and be subjected to racism. We cannot fight racism and be subjected to sexism. We cannot battle sexism and be subjected to heterosexual bias ... Do we have to become completely separate in our revolution? Do we have to break off from our gay white sisters and brothers? Is there no place for us in Gay Liberation, in Black Liberation, in society?[31]

Cheryl Clarke challenged women to remember that differences needed to be accounted for, but that it was crucial to move across these boundaries, to join in common cause based on politics, not on the basis of sexual orientation or skin colour.[32]

The issue of difference among women continued to percolate to the surface, and claims of exclusion proliferated. Many groups of women — Aboriginal, Francophone, Third World — articulated their sense of marginalization within mainstream feminism. Feminists began applying the essentialist critique to feminism itself, even to its "mother" texts. Elizabeth Spelman, for example, noted that Simone de Beauvoir's rightly famous work proceeded as if the viewpoint of a white Western middle-class heterosexual woman was the viewpoint of all women.[33] Just as Aristotle's discussions of the nature and equality of men did *not* include women or slaves, de Beauvoir's discussion of woman was similarly, if unintentionally, partial. In taking this position, Spelman did not dismiss the insights contained in de Beauvoir's work. She did warn, however, against false essentialism, an essentialism which would leave feminism without the tools to dismantle structures of oppression.

While this "anti-essentialist" critique provided an important avenue for the exploration of differences between women, some feminists worried that the flight from false unity was leading feminism towards the equally dangerous trap of false difference.[34] Feminists needed to remember that the goal of attending to the particular was to identify commonalities that crossed the borders of different experiences. As Kimberlé Crenshaw argues:

> When we pierce the veil of race and class and look to find women's issues behind that veil we will find unexpected opportunities to better women's lives and to build a coalition ... When we begin to see that a problem initially conceived somewhat narrowly has broader manifestations, we also see that problems we thought unrelated are actually somewhat familiar and that in fact feminism might have some conceptual tools to address them.[35]

While feminism needed to be wary of essentialism, it also needed to remember that essentialism was not always a tool of oppression and exclusion. As Debbie Epstein noted, "essentialising slogans have played a necessary part in the construction of positive identities by people in subordinated groups and the development of oppositional strategies has often rested on these identities."[36] Essentialism was a double-edged sword, which could be part of a strategy of resistance and necessary in certain political contexts. The point was, intersectionality theorists reminded, that anti-essentialism for its own purpose was a weak insight. As Sherene Razack put it, to have any political value, the critique had to be combined with a strategy of anti-subordination.[37]

Intersectional theory attempts to do just that. It does so by focusing on the very specific ways that gender intersects with a number of other dimensions in the lives of women. Often, this has meant focusing on the lives of women who had been at the margins of mainstream theorizing. The point of this focus has not simply been to document difference, nor to encourage guilt amongst the groups at the centre of the theory — though guilt and denial have been common responses to intersectional critiques. The point of intersectional analysis is to see whether or not the experiences of those located at the intersections can provide insights crucial to the construction of better theories.

The increased attention to the concrete experiences of women who have been caught between multiple systems of oppression has generated some important insights. One is the importance of focusing not only on the specific kinds of victimization that occur at these intersections but also on the unique strategies of resistance that emerge there. A view that focuses only on the double victimization of women often fails to reveal the ways in which these women have crafted innovative strategies of resistance. A view that reveals both the victimization and the resistance reminds us of Adrienne Rich's insight that power may come from the same location as wound.[38] A second related insight concerns the need to connect a study of exclusion with a study of privilege.[39] In what ways have the privileges of some women been implicated in the marginalization and exclusion of other women? And further, how can one distinguish between privileges that needed to be extended to more people and privileges that needed to be dismantled?

Patricia Hill Collins has woven these two insights together in her work examining the ties that bind different forms of oppression together.[40] Her focus is on violence as one of the mechanisms, and her study concentrates on the ways this mechanism functions at the intersection of privilege and disadvantage. The Collins approach emphasizes the importance of paying as much attention to the ways that women are privileged as to the ways that they are disadvantaged. That is, one needs to examine not simply Black women but also Black men, white men and white women in order to understand how the various patterns of oppression, resistance and benefits combine to hold these systems of disadvantage in place. She argues that each of these groups experiences specialized kinds of harm and develops specialized traditions of resistance. The implication is that we should focus on the kinds of resistance that may be possible in specific locations. This shifts attention from a search for universal strategies towards attention to particular locations to discover the specific strategies that might be available, different kinds of resistance available to people who are inflected by varying currents of advantage and disadvantage. That is, it is useful to look at those who are marked by multiple axes of disadvantage and equally necessary to theorize those who are pulled by and pull on the threads of both disadvantage and privilege.

Since modern theories of power have been influenced by the work of Foucault, a few observations on Foucault's approach to power may be in order. Foucault argued that many theories of power were riven through with reifying metaphors, metaphors which spoke of power as if it were something that could be held, accumulated, possessed or found. He argued that the use of such metaphors allowed "an extremely complex configuration of realities ... to escape."[41] Foucault, attempting to avoid the use of these metaphors, laid out his theory of power in five propositions. The five propositions are (1) power is not something that is held but is something that is exercised in relations; (2) relations of power are not exterior to other types of relationships but are immanent and productive of those relationship; (3) power comes from below and is rooted in the social nexus; (4) power relations are both intentional and non-subjective; and (5) where there is power, there is resistance.[42]

The propositions combine to generate two important insights. First, Foucault argued that if the powerless are produced by the operations of power, so too are the powerful. Second, power is not a capacity owned so much as a process shared. While individuals (whether we label them the powerful or the powerless) are the effects of power, they are at the same time the element of its articulation. All individuals both enact power and are acted upon by it. Power is not a commodity possessed only by some, wielded against others. It is a property of a system of social relations, a shared resource that can be activated from many different positions within that system. The implication is that the search for the unitary opponent is misguided. So too the search for the unitary victim.

Some critics have argued that this view tends to erase inequalities by suggesting that all people are similarly situated with respect to power. This rests on a misreading of the insight. To say that power is a process shared is *not* to say that all individuals are equally situated with respect to their abilities to act. The costs of acting are *not* distributed evenly throughout society, and the costs of participation are much higher for some than for others. However, to acknowledge that there are important differential costs is not to imply that only some selves have agency, or the power to act.

Foucault's approach centres the focus on a different problem. The issue is not to figure out "who has power" but to examine different options for action available to different people at different locations, the costs associated with those options and the ways in which these options are connected to other locations and options. In Patricia Hill Collins's terms, it becomes crucial to pay attention to the connections, in order to gain a sense of the ways in which specifically located individuals both benefit from current configurations of power and can avail themselves of specific opportunities to resist or reconfigure current patterns. Of particular importance is Foucault's insistence on attention to the local mechanisms through which power is enacted. The crucial insight involves a decentring of the search for "who is responsible" and a focus instead on the processes which give meaning to encounters.

This decentring of the question "Who is responsible?" does not mean that there are no actors or that choice becomes a meaningless concept. On the contrary. This view accepts that individuals are agents and must take responsibility for their actions, but responsibility becomes a weaker notion. All people are situated at such locations, having variable potential for effective resistance and variable abilities to benefit from the actions of (even unknown) others. Further, it suggests that metaphors of power and wound should reflect the primacy of exactly this kind of experience.

These Foucauldian insights on power and the self are reflected in the work of intersectional theorist Patricia Mann. Mann argues that one of the pressing challenges for feminists is the crafting of new terms to represent a struggle without the unitary political subject "Woman," and without the unitary political opponent "Patriarchy."[43] This focus is part of her attempt to create a theory of individual agency that better responds to gendered social transformations. Current social and political frameworks of modernism, she argues, are "exhausted and incapable of making sense of most important contemporary problems."[44] Indeed, as the debate above about the essential nature of woman has revealed to many, the modern notion of a unified self no longer seems plausible. To modern sensibilities, the self seems to have fragmented, to have dissolved. At the same time, the sense of dissolution is coupled with the lingering conviction that there is something at the core. As Hans puts it, "To dissolve the self completely is obviously an absurdity, for we clearly *are* in some sense, even if *how* we are and what it means to *be* are problematic."[45]

Mann suggests that one of the first important steps is to take the focus off the self and put it instead on action. As she puts it:

> Insofar as social identities are presently unstable we should stop focussing so intently upon these fragile notions of selfhood. Instead, I suggest we think more about the quality of our actions ... We should think of ourselves as conflicted actors rather than as fragmented selves.[46]

Rather than seeing individuals as fragmented selves, her approach views individuals as conflicted actors, involved in site-specific embodied struggles over issues of race, class and sexual preference as well as gender. Any approach to oppositional politics, she asserts, must begin with the reality of this embodiment. Under her theory, the relevant questions deal less with who we *are*, than with what we *do*. The concern is with the significance and meaning of the actions available to us. An embodied focus is crucial to such questioning, since embodiment takes seriously the colour, sex, class, sexual orientation and physical ability of specific bodies in specific contexts. This focus also emphasizes the crucial nature of attention to the conjuncture of multiple dimensions of both oppression and agency within concrete institutional settings.

Current intersectional theory is best understood as part of feminism's ongoing dialogue with the past that gave it birth. Indeed, the theory carries the visible markings of a very specific kind of past, a past in which women have grappled with issues of power, essentialism and identity. At its best, intersectional theory represents a valiant effort to prevent some of the painful parts of feminism's past from poisoning its present and future.

NOTES

Portions of this chapter have appeared elsewhere in different form. I would like to thank University of British Columbia Press for permission to make use of material in chapter 2 of my book *Taxing Choices: The Intersection of Class, Gender, Parenthood and the Law* (Vancouver: UBC Press, 2002).

1. James S. Hans, *The Fate of Desire* (New York: State University of New York Press, 1990), 147.

2. Articles explicitly referring to intersectionality include Kimberlé Crenshaw, "Demarginalizing the Intersection of Race and Sex: A Black Feminist Critique of Antidiscrimination Doctrine, Feminist Theory and Antiracist Politics," *University of Chicago Legal Forum* 139 (1989), 139–167; Darlene Clark Hine, "'In the Kingdom of Culture': Black Women and the Intersection of Race, Gender, and Class," in Gerald Early, ed., *Lure and Loathing: Essays on Race, Identity, and the Ambivalence of Assimilation* (New York: The Penguin Press, 1993), 337–351;

Trina Grillo, "Anti-Essentialism and Intersectionality: Tools to Dismantle the Master's House," *Berkeley Women's Law Journal* 10 (1995), 16–30; Marie-Claire Belleau, "L'intersectionalité: Feminisms in a Divided World (Quebec–Canada)," in Dany Lacombe and Dorothy Chunn, eds., *Law as a Gendering Practice* (London: Oxford University Press, 1999), 19–37.

3. See Angela Miles, *Integrative Feminisms: Building Global Visions, 1960s–1990s* (New York: Routledge, 1996).

4. See Michel Foucault, "Nietzsche, Genealogy, History," in Donald F. Bouchard, ed., *Language, Countermemory, Practice: Selected Essays and Interviews* (Ithaca: Cornell University Press, 1977), 139–164.

5. This point is powerfully made in Frank P. Tomasulo, "'I'll See It When I Believe It': Rodney King and the Prison-House of Video," in Vivian Sobchack, ed., *The Persistence of History: Cinema, Television, and the Modern Event* (New York: Routledge, 1996), 69–88.

6. Marilyn Yalom makes this point with respect to the breast, noting the distinctions between the valued "little breasts" of the Middle Ages, and the often silicon-enhanced "supersized" breasts so valued in our own century. See particularly chapter 2, "The Erotic Breast" in her book, *A History of the Breast* (New York: Alfred Knopf, 1997).

7. For a valuable collection of articles exploring some of this history, see Susan B. Boyd, ed., *Challenging the Public/Private Divide* (Toronto: University of Toronto Press, 1997).

8. See, for example, Jean Bethke Elshtain, *Public Man, Private Woman: Women in Social and Political Thought* (Princeton, NJ: Princeton University Press, 1981).

9. Ruth Gavison, "Feminism and the Public/Private Distinction," *Stanford Law Review* 45 (1992), 1–45.

10. Carol Hanisch, "The Personal Is Political," in Barbara A. Crow, ed., *Radical Feminism: A Documentary Reader* (New York: New York University Press, 2000), 114.

11. For a more thorough discussion of these critiques, see Gavison, "Feminism and the Public/Private Distinction."

12. See, for example, Anita Allen, who argues that Black women have often been denied the privacy that has been the source of suffocation for many white middle-class women. Anita L. Allen, "Women and Their Privacy: What is at Stake?" in Carol Gould, ed., *Beyond Domination: New Perspectives on Women and Philosophy* (Totowa, NJ: Rowman and Littlefield, 1984), 233–249.

13. "Second-wave feminism" is a phrase used to discuss women's activism that began growing out of the social foment of the 1960s. References to "first-wave feminism" are generally to late nineteenth- and early-twentieth-century activism that often focused on issues of suffrage and married women's property regimes. A classic Canadian text on first-wave feminism is Catherine L. Cleverdon, *The*

Woman Suffrage Movement in Canada (Toronto: University of Toronto Press, 1950).

14. Dale Spender, *Man Made Language* (London: Routledge and Kegan Paul, 1985), 1–2.

15. For a collection of broadsides, cartoons, manifestos and other writings documenting the many dimensions of second-wave thinking in the U.S., see Rosalyn Baxandall and Linda Gordon, eds., *Dear Sisters: Dispatches from the Women's Liberation Movement* (New York: Basic Books, 2000). For Canada, see Ruth Roach Pierson, Marjorie Griffin Cohen, Paula Bourne and Philinda Masters, eds., *Canadian Women's Issues*, vol. 1, *Strong Voices* (Toronto: James Lorimer, 1993), and Ruth Roach Pierson and Marjorie Griffin Cohen, eds., *Canadian Women's Issues*, vol. 2, *Bold Visions* (Toronto: James Lorimer, 1995). For a collection of more theoretically based writings from this period, see Crow, ed., *Radical Feminism*.

16. On the sameness/difference debates generally, see Joan C. Williams, "Dissolving the Sameness/Difference Debate: A Post-Modern Path Beyond Essentialism in Feminist and Critical Race Theory," *Duke Law Journal* (1991), 296–323.

17. Indeed, this was the rather modest argument made by Canada's first female Supreme Court Justice, Bertha Wilson, in "Will Women Judges Really Make a Difference?" *Osgoode Hall Law Journal* 28 (1990), 507–522. Her argument remains controversial in some camps. Indeed, the right-wing conservative women's group REAL Women (the acronym stands for Realistic, Equal, Active for Life) made a formal complaint to the Canadian Judicial Council about the "feminist" attitudes expressed in Justice Wilson's speech. See REAL Women, Letter to the Editor, *The Toronto Star*, 24 February 1990.

18. Taking this approach, Kathy Ferguson argued that bureaucracy could not be reformed from within. Women were in a position to see that the system itself was flawed. The liberal strategy of inclusion, while admirable, was simply unable to confront the magnitude of the problem. Kathy E. Ferguson, *The Feminist Case against Bureaucracy* (Philadelphia: Temple University Press, 1984).

19. Audre Lorde, "An Open Letter to Mary Daly," in *Sister/Outsider: Essays & Speeches by Audre Lorde* (Freedom, CA: The Crossing Press, 1984), 70.

20. Angus McLaren, *Our Own Master Race: Eugenics in Canada, 1885–1945* (Toronto: McClelland and Stewart, 1990). See also Mariana Valverde, "'When the Mother of the Race Is Free': Race, Reproduction, and Sexuality in First-Wave Feminism," in Franca Iacovetta and Mariana Valverde, eds., *Gender Conflicts: New Essays in Women's History* (Toronto: University of Toronto Press, 1992), 3–26.

21. In Canada, the vote was first given to married women of British descent. See Cleverdon, *The Woman Suffrage Movement in Canada*. See also Glenda Elizabeth Gilmore, *Gender and Jim Crow: Women and the Politics of White Supremacy in North Carolina, 1896–1920* (Chapel Hill: University of North Carolina Press, 1996).

22. Angela Davis, "Racism, Birth Control, and Reproductive Rights," in Marlene Gerber Fried, ed., *From Abortion to Reproductive Freedom: Transforming a Movement* (Boston: South End Press, 1990), 15–25.

23. See, for example Frances E. White, "Africa on My Mind: Gender, Counter Discourse and African-American Nationalism," *Journal of Women's History* 2 (1990), 73–97.

24. Leigh Megan Leonard, "A Missing Voice in Feminist Legal Theory: The Heterosexual Presumption," *Women's Rights Law Review* 12 (1990–91), 39, 41–42.

25. Cherrie Moraga and Gloria Anzaldúa, eds., *This Bridge Called My Back: Writing by Radical Women of Color* (New York: Kitchen Table Women of Color Press, 1981), 105.

26. Adrienne Rich, *Compulsory Heterosexuality and Lesbian Existence* (London: Only-Women Press, 1983).

27. Charlotte Bunch, "Lesbians in Revolt," in Crow, ed., *Radical Feminism*, 335.

28. See, for example, Jill Johnstone, *Lesbian Nation: The Feminist Solution* (New York: Simon and Schuster, 1974); and Frances, "The Soul Selects: A New Separate Way," in Crow, ed., *Radical Feminism*, 328–331.

29. Sidney Abbott and Barbara Love, "Is Women's Liberation a Lesbian Plot?" in Crow, ed., *Radical Feminism*, 310–324.

30. There were certainly those within the feminist movement who argued strongly against the inclusion of transgendered women within the community. See, for example, the controversial work by Janice Raymond, *The Transsexual Empire: The Making of the She-Male* (Boston: Beacon Press, 1979). Other feminist scholars have had a more complicated view of the radical challenge posed by the "Bi" category. See, for example, Ruth Colker, "Bi: Race, Sexual Orientation, Gender and Disability," *Ohio State Law Journal* 56 (1995), 1–67.

31. Elandria V. Henderson, "The Black Lesbian," in Crow, ed., *Radical Feminism*, 325–326.

32. Cheryl Clarke, "Lesbianism: An Act of Resistance," in Moraga and Anzaldúa, eds., *This Bridge Called My Back,* 128–137.

33. Elizabeth V. Spelman, *Inessential Woman: Problems of Exclusion in Feminist Thought* (Boston: Beacon Press, 1988).

34. For example, see Jane Roland Martin, "Methodological Essentialism, False Difference, and Other Dangerous Traps," *Signs* 19 (1994), 630–657.

35. Crenshaw, "Demarginalizing the Intersection of Race and Sex," 1474–1475.

36. Debbie Epstein, *Changing Classroom Cultures: Anti-Racism, Politics and Schools* (Stoke-on-Trent: Trentham Books, 1993), 17.

37. Sherene Razack, "Beyond Universal Women: Reflections on Theorizing

Differences among Women," *University of New Brunswick Law Journal* 45 (1996), 209–227.

38. See her poem "Power," in *Dream of a Common Language: Poems 1974-1977* (New York: Norton, 1978), 3.

39. A good primer to the problem of privilege is provided in Peggy McIntosh, "White Privilege: Unpacking the Invisible Knapsack," *Peace & Freedom* (July/ August 1989), 10–12.

40. Patricia Hill Collins, "The Tie That Binds: Rethinking Racism, Sexism and Violence," public lecture presented at the University of Michigan, 25 October 1994. The insights are summarized in Rebecca Johnson, "Power & Wounds: Diversity and the Transformative Potential of Legal Practice," *University of New Brunswick Law Journal* 45 (1995), 265–277, see especially 274–276.

41. Michel Foucault, *The History of Sexuality,* vol. 1, *An Introduction (1978)* (New York: Vintage Books, 1990), 217.

42. As summarized in Steven L. Winter, "The 'Power' Thing," *Virginia Law Review* 82 (1996), 721–835.

43. Patricia S. Mann, *Micro-Politics: Agency in a Post-Feminist Era* (Minneapolis: University of Minnesota Press, 1994), 159.

44. Ibid., 1.

45. Hans, *The Fate of Desire,* 67.

46. Mann, *Micro-Politics,* 4.

PART I

THEORY IN ACTION

CHAPTER 1

EQUITY FOR COMMUNITIES: INTEGRATING LEGAL COUNSEL AND CRITICAL RACE THEORY

Erica Lawson & Amanda Hotrum

The authors of this paper are anti-racism educators in Toronto.[1] While co-ordinating an anti-racism support and advocacy program in 1999, we observed that racialized clients were experiencing great difficulty securing the legal assistance that they required to properly assert their rights. In an attempt to address this gap in legal services, a collaborative initiative was developed between a number of community-based organizations and the Equity Initiatives Department of the Law Society of Upper Canada, and the Connecting Communities with Counsel (CCWC) project was created. The CCWC sought to connect individuals from equity-seeking communities with pro bono legal counsel that they would not otherwise be able to access.

Using the CCWC as a site of interrogation, this chapter argues for centring equity in the delivery of legal services and considers how this can be done from the critical race theory perspective. The first section offers a cursory examination of the historical context in which critical legal services must be grounded. The aim of this section is not to provide an exhaustive overview of racism in the Canadian legal system but to provide a snapshot of the body of knowledge that must inform critical legal service delivery. The second section sets out the analytical framework of critical race theory. Section three offers a critical analysis of the CCWC, commenting on what it means to contextualize and contest knowledge. The final section considers integrative and de-colonizing approaches to the delivery of legal services. While this chapter discusses critical race theory in the context of legal services, it is our hope that it will offer service providers in general with an analytical framework that can assist them in centring equity in their services and organizations.

RACISM AND THE LEGAL SYSTEM

The practice of exclusion and disenfranchisement on the basis of race is central to Canada's nation-building project. Historically, Euro-Canadians embraced the typology of racial superiority and inferiority that pervaded European consciousness. They believed that non-white races were innately unsuitable to participate in the country's government and institutions on the basis of phenotypical characteristics and perceived cultural deficiencies. Further, it was widely accepted that "unsuitable" races that could not easily assimilate would lead to the demise of the emerging Dominion.[2] Today, it is widely accepted that race has no scientific or biological basis, but is rather a social signifier that influences who has access to power and resources.[3] The centrality of racist discourses and practices in nation-building has led to the entrenchment of institutionalized and systemic racism. Both have resulted in the granting of unearned privileges on the basis of whiteness and are defended in discourses of denial, innocence and colour-blindness. Racism also affects the psyche of individual Canadians who, having been socialized in predominantly Eurocentric institutions, internalize racist perceptions and attitudes. In this way, racism permeates Canadian society at the macro and micro levels, socializing individuals to have a vested interest in racism while denying its existence.

As an institution, the justice system has played a key role in legitimizing racist practices. These practices have flourished despite claims to colour-blindness and racelessness in the deliberation and delivery of justice. Constance Backhouse captures the connection between racism and the legal system by arguing that

> legislators and judges working in combination nipped, kneaded and squeezed artificial classifications into rigid, congealed definitions of race under Canadian law. They jointly erected hierarchies of racial grouping

and delineated segregated boundaries based on race. In their hands, the law functioned as a systemic instrument of oppression against racialized communities.[4]

What Backhouse describes is most evident in the treatment of Aboriginal peoples in this country. For example, she argues that in 1884, the Canadian government moved to pass criminal laws prohibiting the ceremonial dances of Aboriginal peoples and later extended these laws to encompass all festivals, dancing and ceremonies involving giving away goods or money or the wounding of humans or animals.[5] These types of laws were grounded in white supremacist beliefs that viewed Aboriginal peoples as primitive. They also lent justification to the theft of Aboriginal lands and supported missionary and patronizing attitudes. Moreover, the exclusion and criminalization of specific racialized communities was also reflected in labour, immigration and education laws.[6]

Racism in Canada's courts and legislative bodies is not confined to the annals of history, although today's contentions can be traced to legalized historical wrongs. Everyday, across this country, courtrooms become sites of encounter between predominantly white judges and racialized peoples.[7] These encounters are lessons in how racism persists in Canada's legal institutions and the ways in which it is normalized. Racialized perceptions held by judges are pre-scripted since the systems of privilege in which they are socialized and educated perpetuate problematic ideas about racialized communities.[8] In courtrooms, there is an emphasis on the use of a "cultural" discourse to understand racialized peoples who appear before white judges.[9] That is, racialized victims and perpetrators of violence are seen in the context of a static and unchanging culture. Thus the narratives of violence and suffering are heard in terms of what can be expected from "traditional" people "who don't know any better." This attitude is an example of the shift from the articulation of racism on the basis of biological stereotypes to one that relies on mapping racialized bodies with culturalized meanings. However, the apparent demise of biologically based discourses of racial superiority and inferiority is deceptive. Not only are cultural discourses racialized but they also result in dire material and social consequences for racialized peoples.

Of course, "culture" also intersects with other oppressive markers. For example, during the trial of a Black man accused of transporting illegal migrants, the judge demanded that male spectators wearing hats should take them off. What followed next illuminates the intersection between race, religion and culture to compound oppression.

> One individual ... protested that he was wearing a head covering for religious reasons. The fracas in the courtroom led to a formal ruling by Judge Whealy ... that "a presiding judge not only has the authority but also the duty to oversee the demeanor, solemnity and dignity which must prevail in a superior court of law" ... Recognizing that head coverings may be required in some religions, the judge was prepared to grant this right to major, recognized religions but warned that "self-proclaimed and unrecognized forms of religion or cults claiming to be religious," would receive limited protection under the Charter of Rights and Freedoms.[10]

In this case, the religion in question is the world's largest religion. Sherene Razack reminds us that it is not difficult to see why the defense would argue that the barring of Muslim men wearing headdress, all of whom were African Canadian, indicated a reasonable apprehension of bias. The above incident is an example of culturalized racism whereby Black inferiority is attributed to cultural deficiency, social inadequacy and technological underdevelopment in a social climate that is officially pluralist. The attitude displayed by the judge is also indicative of the new social markers of difference that are evident in references to language, politics, culture and religion. These types of encounters foster the view that the judiciary does not represent society and is biased or insensitive to racialized communities.[11]

CRITICAL RACE THEORY

Critical race theory was forged in response to inadequate or absent visions of race, racism and law that were dominant in the post-civil rights period of the 1970s.[12] The values and principles that inform this movement emerged out of a collective struggle to shape a legal theory and practice reflective of the realities of oppressed communities. The gradual development of critical race theory marked a shift from positing law as a set of abstract ideas to one that centres voice, context and experience. It also marked a formidable challenge to Eurocentric notions of justice that seek to deny complicity and privilege and erase histories of genocide and colonialism.

As a political project, critical race theory embraces subjectivity of perspective and offers a course of action characterized as both pragmatic and utopian.[13] That is, critical race theorists seek to respond to the immediate needs of those who are marginalized while developing a vision of a world that embraces inclusivity, humanity and equality. As critical race theory requires a contextual and historical analysis of existing circumstances, it critiques the role of liberal-capitalist ideology and legal definitions of merit, fault and causation in maintaining a system of white dominance. Unlike multicultural perspectives on "difference," critical race theory does not posit inequality or injustice as isolated acts of bigotry or cultural ignorance. Rather, racism is understood as an organized system of dominance that supports white privilege.

CONTEXTUALIZING AND CONTESTING KNOWLEDGE IN THE CCWC

The Connecting Communities with Counsel (CCWC) aimed to collaborate with lawyers to situate legal work in a historical context, to view the client as an embodied subject in her own right with an understanding of her situation, and to understand that the acquisition of legal knowledge is partial and contestable. This approach was particularly crucial because legal rules and conventions suppress the stories of marginalized groups and promote a fiction of objectivity.[14] By way of example, Razack states:

> Judges who do not see the harm of rape or of racist speech are considered to be simply interpreting what is before them. They are not seen to possess norms and values that derive directly from their social location and that are sustained by such practices as considering individuals outside of their social contexts.[15]

From its inception, the CCWC project provided legal services to African-Canadian clients who experienced physical violence and strip searches by the police. As such, it was important to connect these clients with lawyers who understood the connections between organized state violence towards African Canadians and the daily overpolicing of this community under the guise of law and order. Further it was important to connect clients with lawyers who understood the connection among the violation of Black bodies under systems of white supremacy (e.g., slavery), the extent to which strip searches are both racialized and racializing, the highly sexualized nature of strip-search encounters and the pervasive myths about Black male and female sexuality in dominant North American culture. Finally, it was important to connect clients with a lawyer who, in the process of uncovering facts, would not dismiss or attempt to justify violence towards African Canadians. This is not to suggest that a subject's story is above question. Rather, it is an acknowledgement that legal practitioners must listen and dialogue "while emphasizing the significance of the authority of experience."[16]

AN INTEGRATIVE AND DE-COLONIZING APPROACH TO THE CCWC

In addition to encouraging lawyers to fully consider issues of race and racism, the CCWC also challenged lawyers to approach their work from a perspective that acknowledged the multiple and often contradictory identities and subjectivities of individuals.[17] This perspective requires an examination of the ways in which race is mediated with other forms of social marginality. Anne McClintock reminds us that race, gender and class are not distinct realms of experience, existing in privileged isolation from one another. Nor can they be simply yoked together. They come into existence in and through their relations to one another, if in contradictory and conflictual ways. McClintock also explains that race and gender are not simply questions of skin colour and sexuality, but also questions of subdued labour and imperial plunder.[18] Thus colonialism and imperialism must be viewed as fundamental aspects of Western industrial modernity and race, gender, sexuality, class and ability must be considered within this context.

Missionary or charitable attitudes towards subordinated peoples characterized the European colonial project. Even as they performed violence through genocide and slavery, colonizing forces framed their actions in terms of saving the "uncivilized" from themselves. The abolishment of slavery led to an increased mobilization of religious, educational and other institutions to modernize the "uncivilized" through the inculcation of European norms of values. In this process, indigenous and cultural knowledge forms of oppressed peoples have been devalued or appropriated. Today, the dominance of Eurocentric systems of law and education ensure that racialized peoples are not seen as creators of knowledge or experts in their own right.

With this colonial context in mind, it was crucial for the CCWC to challenge lawyers to interrogate their own motivations for providing pro bono legal services and to move away from narratives of "adopting a community in need." In addition to being patronizing, missionary and charitable approaches to legal services prevent an analysis of how individual cases of racism are connected to historical patterns of racial violence and fail to implicate the legal system in these patterns. Colonial practices can also be reproduced by missionary or charitable approaches by perpetuating the myth that the dominant group is required to intervene on behalf of racialized communities. Finally, narratives of charity prevent legal practitioners from being held accountable for the services that they deliver by creating an expectation of gratitude. At the initial stages of the CCWC, clients indicated that they were hesitant to seek clarification or provide feedback on the direction of their cases given that they were receiving legal services on a pro bono basis.

***

Despite the widespread denial of racism in Canada, raced and colonial hierarchies continue to be embedded in Canadian institutions, structures, policies and practices. Given this reality, it was imperative that a pro bono legal service for equity-seeking communities was conceptualized, developed and implemented in transformative ways. In the CCWC this meant establishing a service that remained grounded in a historical context that drew on the central tenets of critical race theory, that contextualized and contested knowledge and that moved towards an integrative de-colonizing approach to legal services. As the CCWC developed, a number of tensions emerged as the project struggled to stay true to its community roots, to centre equity in all aspects of its development, and to maintain a sense of political clarity. Indeed, the greatest challenge was to locate the CCWC within the broader critical race theory movement: a movement that is advocating for a radical critique and transformation of the existing legal system.

NOTES

1. We define anti-racism as an action-oriented educational and political strategy for institutional and systemic change that addresses the issues of racism and the interlocking systems of social oppression (sexism, heterosexism, ableism, classism). Thus, we take an integrative approach that recognizes the multiple identities in the reproduction of power and social difference. This definition is defined by the work of George Dei, *Anti-racism Education: Theory and Practice* (Halifax: Fernwood, 1996), and George Dei and Agnes Calliste, eds., *Power, Knowledge and Anti-Racism Education* (Halifax: Fernwood, 2000).

2. J. St. G. Walker, *"Race," Rights and the Law in the Supreme Court of Canada: Historical Case Studies* (Toronto: The Osgoode Society for Canadian Legal History, and Waterloo: Wilfrid Laurier University Press, 1997); D. Statsiulis and R. Jhappan, "The Fractious Politics of a Settler Society: Canada," in D. Statsiulis and N. Yuval Davis, eds., *Unsettling Settler Societies: Articulations of Gender, Race, Ethnicity and Class* (London: Sage, 1995), 95–131.

3. Dei, *Anti-racism Education;* Dei and Calliste, eds., *Power, Knowledge and Anti-racism Education;* R. Miles and R. Torres, "Does Race Matter? Transatlantic Perspectives on Racism after Race Relations," in V. Amit-Talao and C. Knowles, eds., *Re-Situating Identities: The Politics of Race, Ethnicity and Culture* (Peterborough: Broadview, 1996), 24–46.

4. Constance Backhouse, *Color-Coded: A Legal History of Racism in Canada, 1900–1950* (Toronto: Osgoode Society for Canadian Legal History, 1999), 15.

5. Ibid., 63.

6. In 1912 the Saskatchewan legislature passed *An Act to Prevent the Employment of Female Labour in Certain Capacities,* also known as the "White Women's Labour Law." The purpose of the law was to prevent "Chinamen," constructed as dangerous and untrustworthy, from supervising or managing white female workers. The law was based on the racist fear that Chinese men were likely to rape white women. (See Backhouse, *Color-Coded,* 136–146). In 1914, in the House of Commons, Sir Wilfrid Laurier declared that "the people of Canada want to have a white country." Further, Canadian immigration policy has consistently placed restrictions on the entry of people who are not white. (See St. G. Walker *"Race," Rights and the Law in the Supreme Court of Canada,* 246–247.) In 1836, the *Education Act* was passed in Nova Scotia permitting commissioners to set up segregated schools for Black students. Due to the widely held belief that Black people were inferior to whites and incapable of learning, schools for Black children were underfunded and the quality of education was extremely poor. (Ibid., 128.)

7. Sherene Razack, *Looking White People in the Eye: Gender, Race and Culture in Courtrooms and Classrooms* (Toronto: University of Toronto Press, 1998); and Sherene Razack, *"R.D.S v. Her Majesty The Queen:* A Case About Home," in this volume.

8. The terms "people of colour" and "racialized people or communities" are used in this chapter in reference to those who are subjected to unequal and differential access to power, privilege and resources on the basis of their skin colour and physical characteristics.

9. Razack, *Looking White People in the Eye.*

10. Razack, *R.D.S v. Her Majesty The Queen,* 209–210, in this volume.

11. Maryka Omatsu, "The Fiction of Judicial Impartiality," in this volume.

12. M.J. Matsuda, C.R. Lawrence III, R. Delgado and K.W. Crenshaw, *Words that Wound: Critical Race Theory, Assaultive Speech, and the First Amendment* (San Francisco: Westview, 1993).

13. Ibid.

14. Razack, *Looking White People in the Eye,* 36.

15. Ibid., 38.

16. bell hooks, *Yearning: Race, Class Gender and Cultural Politics* (Toronto: Between the Lines, 1990), 29.

17. Dei, *Anti-racism Education.*

18. Anne McClintock, *Imperial Leather: Race, Gender and Sexuality in the Colonial Contest* (New York: Routledge, 1995).

CHAPTER 2

IN ABSENTIA:
WOMEN AND THE SEXUAL AS A SOCIAL
CONSTRUCT IN LAW

Gayle MacDonald

In this chapter, I argue that women's sexuality is constructed as deviant in a variety of social contexts, and that this construction leads to an oppression of women's reality in particularized ways. This oppression is manifest, both discursively and in praxis, in explicit patterns when analyzed through a sociological lens. Loosely categorized, these patterns can be represented as the three typologies of sameness, difference and absence, each of which I explore here. I take the position that the construction of women's sexuality as deviant is both socially constructed and hegemonically maintained through legal process, and further, that feminist sociology has much to contribute that can reveal this hegemonic maintenance.

The chapter begins with a general analysis of how the three patterns of sameness, difference and absence emerge and how they are used in the legal analysis of women's sexuality. It appears that "woman" is a problematic classification on a variety of counts: as definition, as sex, as legal entity and even as body.[1] Sexuality, it appears, is even more problematic. To trace the discursive spaces in which women's sexuality are delineated in law reveals specific patterns of oppression, most of which have an ominously familiar resonance to feminist sociology. Within sociological thought, social constructionist arguments can enable an understanding of how these patterns operate to (mis)represent fundamental aspects of women's sexuality and lives in courts of law. Yet arguments about the embodiment of women's sexuality offer equal strength in the analysis of law.

THE SOCIO-LEGAL CONSTRUCTION OF SEXUALITY

I define sexuality as a social practice, constituted and reconstituted as a reaction to other social practices, taking many forms, places and contexts for women, but always reflective of the embodiment of desire. I argue, as does Margrit Shildrick, that women need to begin with an embodiment as a given, that women live in their bodies materially, sexually and emotionally.[2] Despite my earlier suggestion that deviance around women's sexuality is socially constructed, women's bodies, simply put, are *not* social constructions,[3] and any conceptualization that does not address that reality does not recognize that power relations around the female body tend to be obscured or blurred. Such blurring tends to disservice the more problematic arenas of women and sexuality, such as desire, violence or abuse. Foucault's analysis of power, although illuminating, does not distinguish adequately between male and female power, in any real way.[4] Power might be embodied according to Foucault, but men and women carry that embodiment very differently.[5]

However, that being said, it is clear that social constructions of women, of their sexuality and of their lives, are constructed almost as surely as the Lacanian "gaze" occurs with female body builders. Sociologists have long recognized that feminist thought has successfully analyzed the body.[6] Feminist thought in jurisprudence, in particular, has produced a number of interesting analyses of the body, although many focus on either sexual assault or reproduction.[7] Law has often had an uneasy partnership with women's sexuality, which reflects the unease with which women's bodies are received, socially. The ways through which women's bodies do not fit social proscription are evident historically. The "messiness" of female bodies or the ways in which the female body births, bleeds, lactates, menopauses, aborts fetuses, gets ill and the diseases of which women die have been historically subject to a variety of processes, interventions and male definitions.[8] The medicalization of women's bodies began as a reaction to midwifery, and the corresponding rise of the medical profession was linked to legislative initiatives intended to outlaw women helping women birth. Therein lies the first legally enabled insult to women's body integrity.[9]

Women have been most often defined socially "as a lack," in Luce Irigaray's phrasing,[10] or which could read in Freudian terms as not quite a man, or as the opposite of man (in which "man" remains the dominant signifier), or not quite an adult but infantile. In law, woman is defined as absence, she is either not there at all or is defined as the "unreasonable" man[11] of legal discourse. The enabling of absence as a defining concept for women, the contrariness of categorizations that deem women as "other," has not surprisingly been particularly disabling in dealing with women's sexuality. Indeed, the sexuality of women as manifest through women's bodies and the corresponding treatment in law, has been rendered "other" discursively.[12] Nowhere is this more true than in the very categories of law in which one would expect to feel women's "presence," that is, in cases involving sexual assault, abortion and reproduction.

In sexual assault, women's bodies are absent from a discourse that is focused on a male point of view. The female bodily integrity that is present in the conferring or denying of consent to an act, it appears, is irrelevant. In law, sex begins and ends when a man says it does. Similarly if a man says the action is not assault but sex, then the definition of what is sex and what is not becomes the question, rather than the intention of either party or the interpretation of each. If a man does not/did not intend for an action to become assault, then most assuredly it is not. Most reading this would assume that all of the debates over the years regarding the issue of the presence or absence of consent would settle this argument once and for all. However, the recent case of *R. v. Ewanchuk* presents this analysis quite clearly.[13]

Action alone often constitutes a crime in other circumstances. If a body is discovered dead and the death is ruled neither natural nor accidental, then murder might be suspected. The intention to murder determines the degree of the charge, not whether or not the result (the death of a person) actually occurred. Although we know a murder can be "a rose by any other name" (manslaughter or criminal negligence, for example) sexual assault is often a case in which the degree of assault is not in question (as in the original intention of the legislation), but the *nature* of the action is. Is the action criminal (sexual assault) or consensual (just sex)? These questions, and therefore these legal problems, have their roots in a society that does not clearly name its premise in such arguments — that a clear definition of what constitutes sex deviantized is more about views of women's sexuality/bodies than it is about criminal actions committed in the name of women's sexuality.

Absence is also a feature of another legal event involving sexuality and women, that of abortion. Here, it is the "virtual" absence of the fetus that overlaps and interplays with a projected absence, that of mother-hood. The woman's body disappears in such an analysis. A woman seeking an abortion becomes an absence, is defined for what she is not, a non-mother so to speak or, as the right wing would have it, a "murderer" of children. Law dances around these categories with great weight, like an ungainly buffoon cast in a ballet. However, even when motherhood is desired, some uncertainty remains, especially when conception is difficult or artificially induced. The "good mother" is the reproducing woman, the all-nurturing woman, a proscription for us all (even those of us without children). Yet reproduction has an uneasy relationship with law. Law itself is uncertain here, definitions of motherhood and surrogacy are elusive, contradictory and bound to ideas of property. For example, the surrogate mother is often the biological mother, a blood relative by any other name. In law, she can be designated as one who must hand over her child, in the name and in the interests of upper-middle-class property owners. Children and women both become property in these arenas, dis/embodied conceptual beings who are defined and matter only in relational terms to someone else. After all, "mother" implies child, "child" implies parent. They do not, therefore, exist as a "woman" or as a "young person." They exist through and for others.

But postmodern descriptions around and about the body fail to capture the ways in which the law systematically absents or reifies the female body in an attempt to get that body to "fit" normative, patriarchal legal proscriptions. How does this happen? Power might be dispersed in the social body, according to Foucault, but it is actualized and located there, for women. What does this mean? It means that women live in their bodies but do not always have control over them, especially in matters of law. It means, as we all know, that law was written for and is practised in the name of white, male, able-bodied, economically privileged, propertied men. We knew that before we started any type of analysis.

What I'm getting at here is that sociology as a discipline has something to offer the postmodern reader, as postmodernism cannot explain the disruptive spaces that allow women to occasionally "win" in court or to redefine law.[14]

It is not necessarily sexuality, so to speak, that determines whether or not women can enter into legal process. It is the way in which women's sexuality is socially constructed as deviant that explains how one "mom" (an abused heterosexual mother, for example) can win in court and not another (an abused lesbian mother); how a propertied and/or monied woman can sue for surrogacy rights to a child, but the biological mother who has contractually agreed to birth said child cannot. It explains how one woman can attempt to claim nanny expenses as business expenses[15] and how "other" and/or immigrant women work as nannies.[16] It is the proximity to normativeness that is operational here; in other words, "all women" are most certainly not diserviced by law, whereas as "others," such as lesbian mothers and immigrant women, most certainly are.[17]

The closer one's social practices are to normative boundaries, the easier it is to recognize such practices as more easily legally enabled. In other words, the closer one's experiences are to normative boundaries, the easier it is for law to universalize those experiences as a category: women's experiences only "fit" such categorizations as approximations to a norm, which is usually a male-defined norm. Lesbian mothers, for example, fit as approximations to heterosexual married mothers. The approximation that law does when it is working with the details of people's lives is a type of universalizing. This is an active social practice that law repeats, this universalizing of women's experiences, a problem I argue more fully elsewhere.[18] Universality can lead to highly essentialist arguments as to the "nature" of womanhood, arguments which are then used to discredit feminist analysis.[19] Such universalization of women's experience is merely reflected by and in law. Simply put, women's experiences are neither socially contextualized nor affirmed by law. They are either approximations to a norm, a category of expected behaviours or they are exceptions to a rule.

However, simply "adding women's experiences and stirring"[20] will not vastly improve the situation. For women's experiences themselves are diverse, something that new sociologies, such as ethnomethodology, gloss over. If women's experiences and the social processes by which they are constructed are taken as "givens" by feminist researchers, for example, there may be an implicit danger of not recognizing that such experiences and processes may themselves be hegemonically created and maintained. I agree with the caution expressed by Jeffrey Weeks and Janet Holland:

> Feminist academics who take cultural accounts as "factual," for example, or personal experience as a prime ground for validating knowledge, are in danger of ignoring the social processes by which interpretations are reached and knowledge is produced ... respecting and being informed by

experience is a beginning not the end of feminist scholarship. Analysis of cultural phenomena is one part of sociology. It is not the whole, and trying to make it so is a large step backwards.[21]

It is to these social processes through which interpretations of women's sexuality are reached and knowledge is produced that sociology must be applied if any real sense is to be made of the systematic nature of misrepresentation of women's sexuality in law. These processes often have specific patterns of demarcation, which can be grouped for classificatory purposes, in categories which may help to explain what it is happening in legal analysis involving women and sexuality. I argue that three patterns emerge in any cursory analysis of legal process which are, as pointed out above, sameness, difference and absence. I will deal with each of these in turn.

SAMENESS

Part of the reason that women's sexuality becomes so fragmented in legal process is that women, as a group, are treated "the same." Although this is not a new concept in law,[22] it renders the diversity of women's experiences invisible. What this means in practical ways is that women are characterized as "the same" as each other, regardless of material means, race identity or sexual preference. In some cases women are also infantilized or depicted as "the same" as children. Aside from the obvious biological differences from men or children, which one would expect are the most obvious and easiest for law to deal with, this similitude is voiced in very real ways in legal process. This sameness, by definition, creates "othering," that is, it creates women's experiences that are not normative; indeed, women's sexuality itself is deviantized. This is revealed as law's feeble attempt to come to grips with the real life situations of women, however sexuality is defined, exercised and lived. Pregnancy proves, as always, to be a good example of this in law.

Zillah Eisenstein has argued in *The Female Body and the Law* that law has difficulty with pregnancy, as not all women are pregnant at the same time, or are in the same stage at the same time.[23] Similarly, not all women are fertile, nor do all women desire to bear children, nor do all women experience pregnancy the same way. Pregnancy is mediated by materiality and dominant perceptions of race and ability, and it is a particularly useful example of sexual "deviance" under law — as, apart from the constructionist arguments, it is real, actual, tangible and has specific results. Pregnancy alters the meaning/identity constructs for women, because it changes women's experiences socially, emotionally, physiologically and financially. Pregnancy, while very real and actual in the corporeal body of a woman, has social meanings as well, which are constructed and reconstructed to suit dominant ideology. Some pregnancies are simply more "acceptable" than others, such as heterosexual monogamously produced pregnancies as opposed to, say, sperm-bank fathered, "artificially induced" lesbian creations.[24] The "deviance" practised here, then, is not the pregnancy but the process by which pregnancy is obtained.

It is the adherence to normative, socially constructed proscriptions of the "good" mother as we all know her that benefit most from legal process. The "good" mother, as an archetype, devotes her life to her children, is devoted to them, is heterosexual, is married, is probably middle class and is most often white. The "bad" mother, in contrast, could be the professional/working mother who leaves the "rearing" of her children to childcare centres; she may be single, poor and most probably not white. Indeed, Sandra Wachholz outlines how the concept of child neglect is a construction of the "bad" mother's ability to reconcile poverty, rather than any overt behaviour on her part. In other words, a mother who neglects her children as a direct result of a paucity of material means is constructed in custody equations as "unfit."[25] It is she who is disserviced by law, not the *stabat mater* or the "good" mother as Julia Kristeva would probably argue.[26]

But that is the similitude argument. Women are to be "the same" as men, which, of course, the ability to bear children immediately disrupts; "the same" as each other, which materiality, sexual orientation and perceptions of race disrupt; or "the same," in fact, as children, which is obviously mediated by age and ability. The "docile bodies" of Foucault's powerful imagery are useful here. His work reveals that those points of power enacted through the body are the most volatile of all.[27] But if power is "all and nothing," where indeed are those bodies? How do we explain the direct results of power enacted on women's bodies? How do we explain rape and other forms of violence against women?[28] If we argue, as feminists, that sexual assault is a crime of power enactment, then how does Foucault explain the gendered context of that power, given that most victims of sexual assault are *women?*

An analysis that is useful here comes to us from interpretive sociology.[29] Interpretive sociology is a branch of the discipline that is more concerned with interactive social processes and explanations of social meaning than it is with explanations of the workings of social structures, such as the economy or the state. Interpretive sociology is interested in how people work through a structure, how they create understanding to make their way through social structure and what meaning is ascribed to that journey. Simply put, the process of how people do this is of more interest than the structure itself. One way of doing interpretive work is to pay attention to the minutiae, the conversational twists and turns that alter meaning and create boundaries. One such work describes best "what happens" in a rape case by analyzing the "court talk" around a case, the discursive creation of hegemonic meaning. I refer here to the work of Gregory Matoesian who, following the tradition of Garfinkel and others in interpretive work, demonstrates that "talk" has real power over the bodies of women as victims. Matoesian argues that the speech act is not merely words but an act of reciprocity, the "uptake" of which is constructed socially.[30] To talk, then, is to be heard. Silencing, therefore, can take many forms, "to not hear" is but one.

Although Matoesian's work goes on to minutely analyze turn-taking, interruptions and use of language, his claim is that this revisionism, this "talk" about rape, takes place within an institutional setting that is far more indicative of systemic bias rather than individual agency.

As he points out, "The rape trial is generated through an institutionally anchored and patriarchally driven system of power, a two-tiered, socially structured mode of domination that is both a resource for, and a product of, talk in action."[31] To capture Matoesian's claim of how institutional power is manifest, it is useful to turn to the work of Dorothy E. Smith, as she has long argued that institutional practices come to "take on a life of their own" and that those same practices are organized in specific ways to disable, to not reflect or reconstitute the everyday, mundane practices within the life worlds of women. One of her more useful techniques is to explore the process of record keeping as institutional practice, as evidence of the organizing relations of institutional power.[32] When her concept of organizing the "relations of ruling" is applied to the institution of law, we begin to see, conceptually, how discursive practices silence women:

The practice and organization of ideological circles ... coordinate and transpose actualities and the subject's experience of those actualities into the textual forms of the discursive and institutional consciousness. Ideological practices organize the interchangeability of actual events, the treatment of individuals (whether persons or events) as equivalent "for all practical purposes," and the coordination of processes and events occurring in different places and at different times. They bring them into a coherent relation to the objectives, interests, and relevances vested in a given discursive form.[33]

What is operative here is Smith's principle of "documentary text as reality." In other words, the textual representation of a woman — her sexual assault, the definition of who and "how" she is and what she does — is a reality created by text instead of the other way around. Record keeping, particularly in legal process, reflects a reality, but this is rarely the reality of women's embodiment; it is, rather, the "organizational form" to which she has been reduced. This, then, is how legal process can systemically oppress women's sexuality. The deviance can be constructed rather than actual, so to speak, demonstrated rather than proven, and the entire accounting of a woman's victimization, including any definition of her sexuality, is done from a specific set of ideological circumstances that are most assuredly patriarchal in nature. It is in this way that all women's stories can sound "the same" to a court of law.

Difference

The most disruptive space in law for the social construction of women's sexuality as deviant is, of course, prostitution. The prostitute often constitutes the "other" woman, the greatest "difference" or "difference from" both men and most white middle-class older women. Women in the sex trade have an uneasy "fit" with feminist theory on victimization,[34] and an even uneasier "fit" with the legal category of offender (is she a victim or a perpetrator?). A fairly routine practice in textbooks on deviance is to label prostitutes as deviant. It is an interesting teachable moment for the feminist sociologist, a perfect example of the "slippery slope" categorization of deviant sexuality and women. The social construction of prostitutes, as we know, limits our understanding of the criminalization of women to women as offenders and men as clients, rather than women as service providers and men as offenders. It also creates a space for some interesting questions around the presenting of prostitution in argument or in text.[35]

John Lowman's work reveals some interesting ideas around the question of who the offender is. In his fieldwork in Vancouver in the late 1980s, he argued that even progressive legal policies became problematic, for example those enacted by Vancouver's lower mainland to target the arrests of both prostitutes and johns, which was a move away from the typical depiction of prostitutes as offenders. Lowman demonstrated that the arrest patterns were mediated by both class and race, as street hookers and their clients — particularly when those clients were white working-class men or Aboriginal men — were more likely to be arrested than were their madame counterparts or men of higher socio-economic status.[36] (This could also be explained much as other street-crime arrest patterns are, that visibility for arrest can also be mediated by class.)

Fran Shaver goes beyond the offender/victim dichotomy to argue that prostitution is work and, as such, needs to be compared with that of other service workers such as hospital technicians to be fully understood. Not surprisingly, she found similar complaints related to work — boredom, repetitive stress injury and leg/back problems from standing so long in one place — as common to both groups. Although Shaver is not the first academic to construct prostitution as work,[37] overall she offers an interesting point of view when she argues that workers' compensation needs to be considered as a possible remedy for prostitutes.

Leslie Jeffrey demonstrates how the sex trade industry in Thailand has come to be seen as "work" and how it is benefiting from legal practices that both allow female prostitution to exist and that relax restrictions on arrest. These regulations recognize prostitution's contribution to the state's gross national product through tourism dollars.[38] The relationship of this situation in Thailand to Canada becomes apparent through the importation of sex-trade workers to cities like Toronto. Such economic transactions — that is, the importation of Thai women to work in the trade — offer challenges to feminist researchers exploring either the intersection of law and immigration or examining how legal definitions of work pertain to the sex trade. Sex-trade workers in many countries are themselves arguing for legal rights and status as workers, contrary to all legal proscriptions that define who they are and how they are to engage with the law.[39]

Legal categories that have far more slippage than actual meaning are those of gender, race and class. I have argued elsewhere that such categorizations are social constructions, based on normative meanings/

understandings and not necessarily useful as stable concepts for use in legal process.[40] Race, for example, is often confused with ethnicity and can have inappropriate, inaccurate and problematic usage, dependent on historical and social contexts.[41] Similarly, "class" is equally nebulous, as it is usually reflective of one spectrum of socio-economic positioning that is completely consistent with dominant social control processes of state-invested legal action. Nowhere is this more aptly demonstrated than in Chris Doran's excellent piece on workers' compensation boards, in which he argues that class bias is persistent in workers' compensation board decisions. Doran conducts his analysis using Foucauldian and feminist conceptions of power, tracing how language itself can be the form through which power is dispersed.[42] Arguably, gender is the most problematic category of all, as it is assumed to be socially acquired, subsumed with female identity and heterosexist, to boot.[43] That ontological premise leads to a faulty demise, conceptually, as gender cannot by definition be a stable category for use in legal discourse. There are situations in which gender may be a useful category for legal discourse but only if that category is an embodied one, rooted in the "everydayness," as in Smith's analysis, of women's sexual practices. It might also lead one to believe that women's sexuality cannot be used as a category for analysis in law. As Margrit Shildrick puts it: "The endless metaphors of woman may serve some discursive purpose, but if we are to enter into the ethical and political, then it is my contention that we must insist on the materiality of women's bodies, and on the specificity of our sexual otherness."[44] Difference, then, is truly in the eyes of the beholder, as those defining "difference" or "other" are by definition themselves in positions of power.

Bifurcated Absence

The pattern of bifurcated absence refers to the myriad fissures in both the ideology and practice of legal process in dealing with women's sexuality that fit neither the sameness nor difference proscriptions illustrated above. It could be constructed as the great Canadian compromise, as we always seem to come up with at least three solutions for every political problem. If law were a theatre play, then this principle would refer to the "absent" scene or the ways in which women's sexuality is written completely out of the script. Nevertheless, such a manoeuvre is useful for the patriarchy to uphold. It is here that postmodernism has its greatest hour.

Shildrick argues, in an innovative book on the subject of postmodernism and bio-ethics:

> Quite simply, women are deemed to live their bodies in ways that men are not, and this constraint on transcendence is alone sufficient to disqualify them from full subjectivity. The absent body characterizes male/ moral discourse, and women, being all too solid, are paradoxically situated in that absence.[45]

There are a number of "absences" that women go through in the course of legal process. A good example is the issue of lesbians who procreate and who may at some point seek custody of their children.[46] It is here that a woman who has sex for "her" own pleasure rather than according to the male definition of pleasure, and who dares to have children in this context becomes the bifurcated "other" in law. There simply is no place to "put" the bodily existence of lesbians or to deal with their desire to have or raise children. As Didi Herman has so aptly pointed out in an analysis of one of the first gay rights cases in Canada, the *Mossop* case, it is the definition of "family" that first comes under attack in legal process.[47] Basically, the "deviant" rule here reads: Women don't have sex with other women because a straight man doesn't recognize sexual pleasure "for her," but "for him." The manner in which law has dealt with these issues, up until now, is a matter of erasure or denial of the non-biological "other" parent. If there is an absent body in a court of law, it is that of the lesbian mother.

In what other ways is women's sexuality bifurcated, split if you will, between bodily presence and abstracting absence? In what other ways is women's sexuality constructed as deviant in law? This is where the property principles upon which rape clauses were initially constructed raise their ugly heads once again. Nowhere are these issues more clear than in cases of reproductive technology cases, surrogacy and abortion. What these issues have in common, in legal process, is the "cyborg" approach to their existence, à la Donna Haraway. Haraway contends that the world is full of cyborgs and patented life forms, an interesting claim in current arenas where Dolly the cloned sheep is used as a basis to make media arguments about the same ability in humans.[48]

Even when women are not in danger of becoming the "cyborgs" of Haraway's imagination, of becoming half person/half machine, law still determines (or attempts to determine) definitions of life itself. Debates in reproductive knowledge around the beginnings of life are usually tied to property arguments (as all children and women are) and are usually centred around times when women's sexuality is barely necessary to the reproductive process. Women may disappear into surrogacy, into a "rentable" womb. The biological mother may be rendered a surrogate in the neatly inverted discursive state of media language or she may, indeed, be depicted as a cyborg. The non-sexual futuristic scenario of a sterile petrie-dish clone, which is "re-birthed" in a woman's womb, should give us pause. To rethink what it is we mean by conception is to rethink what we mean by birth. To rethink birth is to rethink motherhood and mothering. (This is not entirely new to women, elite classes have always had wet nurses who suckled their babes, often for a fee.) But do we want law to perceive all of these situations as sameness debates? As difference or absence debates?

Advances in reproductive technology are not the only grounds for Haraway's cyborg arguments. Abortion debates are also fraught with definitions of the beginning, means and ending of life. What is most often absent from all of these debates, of course, is what mothering actually means. In its struggle to define the rights of a fetus, or of a melded sperm and egg, women are yet again absent in the legal discourse. The "balance of rights" argument, wherein competing groups are weighed in law to determine who has rights, when and under what circumstances, can often lead to further patronizing women. The comparator in the debates above is the unborn fetus. One can only wonder who would "win" the argument if a man's rights were weighted against those of the unborn fetus.

It is clear that law's strategies for incorporating the female (identified here as sameness, difference and absence) work as well as linear logic does; that is, the strategies work well to make a legal argument or to come up with a specific remedy. Linear logic implies a normativeness of experience, which law always attempts to approximate.

The test of reasonableness, for example, gets to this experience. What would a "reasonable" person do in a similar fact situation? What would the "reasonable" course of action be, given these same set of circumstances? This is not a facile question. For years this test of "reasonableness" was gendered. The test used to read what a reasonable "man" would do in the same set of circumstances, and it was applied in cases of domestic violence, wherien what a reasonable man might do were someone beating him up would be to "fight back." If a woman in a similar circumstance did not do so, then this was taken into account. What is missing from this scenario, though, is everything we know now (and knew then) about what the patterns of domestic violence represent: the cyclical and escalating nature of the beatings and the correlated plummeting of the women's self-esteem and ability to "fight back." This test was eventually challenged and the "man" removed. Although this was a significant step forward in the letter of the law, it remains one of those spaces in law in which ghosts can wander.

The "man" may have disappeared from the test but his presence can still be felt. Without a long explanation here of why fundamental logic arguments always feel and sound male to women, suffice it to say it is the very nature of "reasonableness" that gets at what is critical here. Who, in the end, is the reasonable woman? Against whom is the woman of difference, the bifurcated woman, compared? The married woman who stays married most of her adult life? The divorced woman with children whose family may blend with another family? The lesbian stepparent of children not biologically hers? The transgendered person who wants to identify as female? Clearly, some examples or cases in law are simply easier to adjudicate than others. Even without the additional complexity of children in the mix, however, it is still not clear to me just exactly who this "reasonable" woman is.

For example, is this reasonable woman a white professional woman? How would reasonable for a white professional woman compare with reasonable for a Native professional woman? A Native woman who has suffered the layered oppression of assault, substance abuse and abandonment is going to look at life, love and children very differently than does a white woman, even if she is in the same class status as a white woman and of a similar age. Most Native women in professional careers have more than just their career to carry through life. They often carry the weight of a community behind them and have more constituencies to answer to than do most politicians. What is reasonable to a Native woman in terms of voluntary commitments, responses to children and women in their communities and lobbying governments in their spare time may look like overkill to a white woman, who may not understand the social location of a first generation professional Native woman.[49]

Cases that challenge predetermined linear normativeness, represented here by the sameness/difference duality, often fall into the bifurcation category, which splits women into categories to suit legal arguments rather than a deeper explanation of personal experience. Sex workers who are abused by common-law husbands, for example, can have their cases thrown out because of the assumption that the common-law husband must be her pimp. This conflation of category is the true bifurcation of women. It denies women agency in the identification of the problem at hand (in this case, abuse) and at the same time re-identifies the nature of her relationship with her partner.

Questions remain for law and for women. Who will law recognize, in the end, as the woman of its legal question? Is she raced, sexed and classed? Is she straight or queer or transgendered? Is she a biological mother, a stepmother or a mother of a "blended" family? But the most important question raised here is, Is she present at all in the discourse of law? Or does she continue to be absent? Absence in this argument does not make the heart grow fonder. It barely recognizes the heart at all.

NOTES

An earlier version of this paper, entitled "(In)Difference: Women, Sexuality, Deviance and Law," was presented at the Gender, Sexuality and the Law Conference, Keele University, Stoke-on-Trent, UK, June 19–21, 1998.

1. See, respectively, Denise Riley, *"Am I That Name?" Feminism and the Category of "Women" in History* (Minneapolis: University of Minnesota Press, 1988); Judith Butler, *Gender Trouble: Feminism and the Subversion of Identity* (London: Routledge, 1990); Zillah Eisenstein, *The Female Body and the Law* (Berkeley: University of California Press, 1988); and Doug Aoki, "Sex and Muscle: The Female Bodybuilder Meets Lacan," *Body and Society* 2, no. 4 (1996), 59–74.

2. Margrit Shildrick, *Leaky Bodies and Boundaries: Feminism, Postmodernism and Bio-Ethics* (London: Routledge, 1997).

3. Caroline Ramazanoglu and Janet Holland, "Women's Sexuality and Men's Appropriation of Desire," in Caroline Ramazanoglu, ed., *Up against Foucault: Explorations of Some Tensions between Foucault and Feminism* (London: Routledge, 1993), 239–264.

4. Foucault's work on power discussed it as an embodied concept, as actualized within, rather than external to, the human subject. Power/knowledge operated on an inseparable nexus for Foucault, evident through disciplinary techniques such as ranking, ordering, separating and, most importantly, through surveillance. To say his work revolutionized the thinking on punishment and educational regimes is an understatement.

5. See Ramazanoglu, ed., *Up against Foucault.*

6. For more on the "gaze," see Akoi, "Sex and Muscle." For more on feminist thought analyzing the body, see Dawn H. Currie and Valerie Raoul, eds., *Anatomy of Gender: Women's Struggle for the Body* (Ottawa: Carleton University Press, 1992); and Chris Shilling, *The Body and Social Theory* (London: Sage, 1993).

7. Martha Albertson Fineman and Nancy Sweet Thomadsen, eds., *At the Boundaries of Law: Feminism and Legal Theory* (London: Routledge, 1992); and Patricia Smith, ed., *Feminist Jurisprudence* (New York: Oxford University Press, 1993). *The Canadian Journal of Women and the Law,* since its inception in 1985, has taken up numerous issues around women and legal process. I would particularly recommend "Legal Theory Legal Practice I: Contemporary Approaches," *CJWL* 5, no. 1 (1992), "Legal Theory Legal Practice II: Historical Connections," *CJWL* 5, no. 2 (1992), and "Feminism in Transition," *CJWL* 9, no. 1 (1997).

8. Constance Backhouse, *Petticoats & Prejudice: Women and Law in Nineteenth-Century Canada* (Toronto: Women's Press, 1991); and Shildrick, *Leaky Bodies and Boundaries.*

9. Sheila Noonan, "Of Death, Desire and Knowledge: Law and Social Control of Witches in Renaissance Europe," in Gayle MacDonald, ed. *Social Context and Social Location in Sociology of Law* (Guelph, ON: Broadview Press, 2002).

10. In the essay "And the One Doesn't Stir without the Other" (trans. Helene Vivienne Wenzel), Luce Irigaray contemplates the relationship of the mother–daughter and the confusion of identities of/for both. She would very much like both identities to stand independently of each other and of man. See Diana Tietjens Meyers, ed., *Feminist Social Thought: A Reader* (New York: Routledge, 1997), 320–327.

11. What is currently known as the "test of reasonableness" in law had its origins as the "test of the reasonable man." Facile arguments in law, such as what the "reasonable man" might do if hit by (his) husband, were often used to determine whether or not women were "reasonable" in their actions in situations of abuse, especially if they did not leave the man in question or did not "appear" to resist. Similar arguments were used to construct a discourse around victims of sexual assault, by determining what the "reasonable man" might assume from a woman's actions, an inferral of meaning, in other words, rather than a confirmation of meaning.

12. Sheila Duncan, "Disrupting the Surface of Order and Innocence: Towards a Theory of Sexuality and the Law," *Feminist Legal Studies* 2, no. 1 (1994), 1–28.

13. See Rebecca Johnson, "Leaving Normal: Constructing the Family at the Movies and in Law," in Lori G. Beaman, ed., *New Perspectives on Deviance: The Construction of Deviance in Everyday Life* (Scarborough, ON: Prentice Hall Allyn and Bacon Canada, 2000), 163–179.

14. Occasionally, women do win in court. The most concentrated efforts on break-

ing through barriers in law to women's realities has been achieved, in some instances, through equality cases, which are cases that are mounted as challenges to
government practices under section 15 of the Charter of Rights and Freedoms.
As an organization, the Women's Legal Education and Action Fund (LEAF) is
dedicated to this purpose.

15. For an interesting discussion on the question of "choice" that is omnipresent
in the *Symes* case, a fairly controversial case in which a woman sues for nanny
expenses as business expenses, see Rebecca Johnson, "If Choice is the Answer,
What is the Question? Spelunking in *Symes v. Canada,*" in Dorothy Chunn
and Dany Lacombe, eds., *Law as a Gendering Practice* (Don Mills, ON: Oxford
University Press, 2000), 199–222. Johnson delicately weaves how the rhetoric
of choice undermines the more subterranean theme of responsibility and blame
that lay, she claims, just under the surface of questions of "choice" in law.

16. For an analysis of immigrant women as domestic workers, see Sedef Arat-Koc,
"Good Enough to Work but not Good Enough to Stay: Foreign Domestic
Workers and the Law," in Elizabeth Comack, ed., *Locating Law: Race/Class/
Gender Connections* (Halifax: Fernwood, 1999), 125–151.

17. Karlene Faith, *Unruly Women: The Politics of Confinement & Resistance*
(Vancouver: Press Gang Publishers, 1993).

18. Gayle MacDonald, "The Body Inscribed, Described and Divided," paper
presented at a joint session of the Canadian Sociology and Anthropology
Association and the Canadian Law and Society Association meetings, Memorial
University, St. John's, Newfoundland, June 1997.

19. Dianne L. Brooks, "A Commentary on the Essence of Anti-Essentialist in
Feminist Legal Theory," *Feminist Legal Studies* 2, no. 2 (1994), 115–132.

20. For a critique of this point, see Didi Herman, "'Socially Speaking': Law,
Sexuality and Social Change," in Dawn Currie and Brian MacLean, eds.,
Rethinking the Administration of Justice (Halifax: Fernwood, 1991), 150–168.

21. Jeffrey Weeks and Janet Holland, eds., *Sexual Cultures: Communities, Values and
Intimacy* (New York: St. Martin's Press, 1996), 29.

22. Canadian sex equality cases under the Charter embody Aristotelian notions of
equality as being the same. See Sherene Razack, *Canadian Feminism and the
Law: The Women's Legal Education and Action Fund and the Pursuit of Equality*
(Toronto: Second Story Press, 1991; now available from Sumach Press, Toronto).

23. Eisenstein, *The Female Body and the Law.*

24. Although Shelley Gavigan (see note 46) probably created the most prolific
academic critique of the lesbian custody issue, other Canadian writers, notably
Didi Herman, have contributed widely and extensively towards the formulation
of a lesbian/gay jurisprudence in Canada. Rebecca Johnston's intervention at the
Supreme Court of Canada on the *Egan* case and Lori Beaman's commentary on
same are also interesting examples. See Didi Herman, "'Sociologically Speaking':
Law, Sexuality and Social Change," *Journal of Human Justice* 2, no. 2 (1991),

57–76. Lori Beaman's commentary provides another interesting example in "Sexual Orientation and Legal Discourse," *Canadian Journal of Law and Society* 14, no. 2 (1999), 173–201.

25. Sandra Wachholz, "Confronting the Construct of Child Neglect as Maternal Failure: In Search of Peacemaking Alternatives," in MacDonald, ed., *Social Context and Social Location* 14, no. 2 (1999), 181.

26. Julia Kristeva, *"Stabat Mater,"* in Diana Tietjens Meyers, ed., *Feminist Social Thought: A Reader* (New York: Routledge, 1997), 302–319.

27. Michel Foucault, *Discipline and Punish: The Birth of the Prison* (New York: Pantheon Books, 1977).

28. For an analysis of just how law "works" relative to sexual assault, see Karen Busby, "Not a Victim Until a Conviction Is Entered: Sexual Violence Prosecutions and Legal 'Truth,'" in Comack, *Locating Law*, 260–288. For an interesting analysis of the connections between women abuse and subsequent offending, see Elizabeth Comack, *Women in Trouble: Connecting Women's Law Violations to Their Histories of Abuse* (Halifax: Fernwood Publishing, 1996). For an international perspective, see Radhika Coomaraswamy, "Some Reflections on Violence against Women," in Nuzhat Amin, Francis Beer, Kathryn McPherson et al., eds., *Canadian Women's Studies: An Introductory Reader* (Toronto: Inanna Publications, 1999), 253–274.

29. Peter Berger and Thomas Luckman, *The Social Construction of Reality* (New York: Anchor Books, 1967).

30. Gregory Matoesian, *Reproducing Rape: Domination Through Talk in the Courtroom* (Chicago: The University of Chicago Press, 1993).

31. Ibid.

32. Dorothy E. Smith, *The Everyday World as Problematic* (Toronto: University of Toronto Press, 1987). See also Dorothy E. Smith, *Writing the Social: Critique, Theory, and Investigations* (Toronto: University of Toronto Press, 1999).

33. Smith, *The Everyday World as Problematic,* 173.

34. For the finest argument I've seen to date on this point, see Linda LeMoncheck, *Loose Women, Lecherous Men: A Feminist Philosophy of Sex* (New York: Oxford University Press, 1997), chap. 4, "I Only Do It for the Money: Pornography, Prostitution, and the Business of Sex."

35. Frances Shaver, "The Regulation of Prostitution: Avoiding the Morality Traps," *Canadian Journal of Law and Society* 9, no. 1 (1994), 123–146; John Lowman, "Notions of Formal Equality before the Law: The Experience of Street Prostitutes and Their Customers," *The Journal of Human Justice* (Spring 1990), 55–76; Faith, *Unruly Women,* 72–85; and Christine Overall, "What's Wrong with Prostitution? Evaluating Sex Work," in Debra Shogan, ed., *A Reader in Feminist Ethics* (Toronto: Canadian Scholars' Press, 1993), 563–586.

36. Lowman, "Notions of Formal Equality before the Law."

37. Shaver, *The Regulation of Prostitution,* and Backhouse, *Petticoats & Prejudice.*

38. Leslie Jeffrey, "Sex and Borders: Gender National Identity and the 'Prostitution Problem' in Thailand" (PhD diss., York University, 1999).

39. Laurie Bell, ed., *Good Girls/Bad Girls: Sex trade Workers & Feminists Face to Face* (Toronto: Women's Press, 1987); and Gail Pheterson, ed., *A Vindication of the Rights of Whores* (Seattle: Seal Press, 1989).

40. MacDonald, "The Body Inscribed, Described and Divided."

41. Vic Satzewich and Li Zong, "Social Control and the Historical Construction of 'Race,'" in Bernard Schissel and Linda Mahood, eds., *Social Control in Canada: Issues in the Social Construction of Deviance* (Toronto: Oxford University Press, 1996), 263–287.

42. Chris Doran, "Medico-Legal Expertise and Industrial Disease Compensation: Discipline, Surveillance and Disqualification," in MacDonald, ed., *Social Context and Social Location,* 159–180.

43. Butler, *Gender Trouble;* Janet Holland, Caroline Ramazanoglu, Sue Sharpe and Rachel Thomson, "Power and Desire: The Embodiment of Female Sexuality," *Feminist Review* 46 (1994), 21–38; Judith C. Daniluck, "The Meaning and Experience of Female Sexuality," *Psychology of Women Quarterly* 17 (1993), 53–69.

44. Shildrick, *Leaky Bodies and Boundaries,* 164.

45. Ibid., 168.

46. Shelley Gavigan differs with me on this point. When I presented a version of this paper to the International Conference on Gender, Sexuality and Law at Keele University in Stoke-on-Trent, she challenged my construction of lesbian mothers. In the paper she presented at the conference ("Legal Form, Family Forms, Gender Norms: What Is a Spouse?"), she argued that lesbian parents are indeed winning more cases in Canada and that the lesbian spouse is beginning to receive some acknowledgement as the "good parent" in the custody cases she examined. With all due respect to my Canadian colleague, where I differ is on the point that lesbian parents win for exactly that reason, because they approximate a heterosexual norm, not because they are being recognized in their own rights as parents.

47. See note 11 for an explanation of how the "test of the reasonable man" is applied. See also Genevieve Lloyd, *The Man of Reason* (Minneapolis: University of Minnesota Press, 1984).

48. Donna J. Haraway, *Modest_Witness@Second_Millennium.FemaleMan_Meets OncoMouse: Feminism and Technoscience* (New York: Routledge, 1997); CBC, *The Journal,* 14 July 1998. In *Simians, Cyborgs and Women: Reinventing Nature* (New York: Routledge, 1991), Haraway queries the relationship between what

it is to be human and what it is to be "half-human" as the interpellation of humans with technology is created with the cyborg. As a professor of history of consciousness at the University of California at Santa Cruz, Haraway is interested in critical and feminist readings of advances in science/technology that examine our humanness relative to technology. Her ideas have proven to be not far-fetched at all. For example, in 1998, a University of Reading professor had a chip implant placed in his forearm that allowed him to open doors at will. Retreived 30 May 2002 from http://www.kevinwarwick. com/info. The ontological questions of course are, What/whom is next? And what legal rights might more advanced "blending" of technology and humanity claim?

49. By first generation I mean the first generation after the residential school experience. For most Native professional women today, their mothers and grandmothers are actually the first generation survivors of residential schools. But this generation is the first to rise above the damages of the experience, to see their careers reach a potential only dreamed of by their mothers.

CHAPTER 3

THE FICTION OF JUDICIAL IMPARTIALITY

Maryka Omatsu

The Canadian judiciary is a homogenous institution. It has been ar-gued that this homogeneity has resulted in a certain myopia of vision. In response to recent public criticism about a powerful tenured insti-tution that is overwhelmingly middle-class, white and male (87 per cent white male), governments have begun to increase the numbers of women and minority judges. The judicial maxim of a fair and public hearing by an independent and impartial tribunal is now enshrined in section 11(d) of the Canadian Charter of Rights and Freedoms. *It is believed that greater diversity on the bench will increase sensitivity and awareness to the people and issues before the court, thereby promot-ing public confidence and legitimacy. However, less homogeneity may result, ironically, in the women and minority judges being scrutinized more closely for bias for the very characteristics that they are said to bring to the bench, rather than a reconsideration of the concept of im-partiality.*

ON MY APPOINTMENT

In the July 17th 1992 edition of the Ontario Reports, I read a notice that changed my life. It invited applications from lawyers of ten years standing for two vacancies on the provincial bench, criminal division. The advertisement concluded, "In order to improve the representation of traditionally under-represented groups in the judiciary, applications are particularly encouraged from aboriginal peoples, francophones, persons with disabilities, racial minorities and women."[1] For several years, I had been aware that business was not as usual in the appoint-ment of Ontario provincial judges.

The system of judicial selection, introduced in 1989 by the then Attorney General Ian Scott, is the first of its kind in Canada. Scott, a legal maverick and innovator, declared a moratorium of sorts on the political appointment of provincial judges in Ontario. He established a ten-person committee to recruit and select candidates for the judiciary. The committee was for a time referred to as the "Peter Russell Committee," after the University of Toronto political scientist.[2] In 1990, I received a provincial judge advertisement with a letter attached from then Attorney General Howard Hampton, encouraging all women lawyers of ten years standing to apply.[3] Although I thanked him for the initiative, I declined his invitation.

Born an outsider,[4] I had spent sixteen years as an activist lawyer. However, having most recently been chair and an adjudicator for the Ontario Human Rights Boards of Inquiry and a Law Society Referee, hearing compensation claims by clients against their lawyers, I viewed the job of sitting in judgement with less disdain and with greater respect. After some soul searching, I responded, little expecting the letter that arrived several months later requesting me to attend for an interview with the Judicial Appointments Advisory Committee.

The secretary of the Committee informed me that hundreds of applications had been received in response to the advertisement. The Committee's mandate is to paper screen, run background audits on aspirants and then interview a smaller pool. Additional follow-up checks are conducted on successful candidates, whose names are forwarded onto the attorney general's office, and then to the Ontario Judicial Council[5] for a final interview. Any survivors are forwarded to Cabinet for final consideration and affirmation.

On November 2, 1992, I had a one-hour interview with the Committee. From my perspective, it was a friendly discussion regarding my views about societal changes and the law. On November 30, the attorney general's office called advising me that I had been "passed by the Committee and the A.G." On Friday, December 11, I met with the Provincial Chief Judge and the Senior Regional Judge for Toronto to discuss where I might sit, a conversation that seemed premature as my interview with the Ontario Judicial Council (OJC) loomed ahead. I had been warned that the OJC was most impressed with one's appellate experience and had been critical of women with eclectic experience or administrative law backgrounds. On December 14, I was ushered into a private room at Osgoode Hall where the members of the Judicial Council engaged me in a ten-minute, perfunctory interview. I received in the mail Order-in-Council (OIC) #3751-92 dated two days later, appointing me as a provincial judge.

Since my "elevation" had seemed unlikely, I had viewed the entire process as somewhat unreal. It was not until I held the OIC in my hands that I began to seriously contemplate what being a judge might entail. Previously an advocate for the disadvantaged, my concerns were echoed by my brother, who on hearing the news of my appointment, declared sarcastically, "She's gone and done it, she's joined the Establishment." I was aware that I was being admitted into a "club," albeit at the ground floor, previously closed to Asian women. I wondered whether I could feel at home on a bench that demanded near monastic silence and withdrawal from community affairs.

DEMOGRAPHICS AND "ALLEGIANCES"

Told I would stick out like a wart on a hog's back, I was aware of the statistics compiled by political scientists Peter McCormick and Ian Greene[6] that support the analogy. They point out that judges as a group are married,[7] overwhelmingly male,[8] of British or French ancestry,[9] in their mid-fifties,[10] Judeo-Christian,[11] born into the middle or upper-middle classes,[12] were successful lawyers,[13] and had limited trial experience.[14]

There are approximately 2,500 judges in Canada: 1,000 are federally appointed and 1,500 are provincially appointed. The subset to which I belong demographically is one of 263 women judges (women make up approximately 10.5 per cent of the bench);[15] one of a small percentage of visible minority judges (about 2 per cent); and, to date, Canada's first and only East Asian Canadian woman judge.

In recognition of these demographics. Ontario introduced an employment equity recruitment policy for judicial appointments. This initiative was continued by the NDP when it replaced the Liberals in 1990. An intention to adopt a similar approach was expressed by federal Justice Minister Allan Rock on taking office in 1994. Rock announced that the federal government would undertake a system of public advertisements; create independent councils of lawyers and citizens to review and recommend applicants; and establish new criteria for determining suitability. He hoped to thereby increase the number of women and minorities on the federal bench so that it is more reflective of the society that appears before it.[16]

In the remainder of this chapter, I shall briefly address the justification for increasing diversity on the bench. Then I shall turn to examine worrisome evidence of a backlash.

JUSTIFICATION

In thinking about the justification for judicial diversity, it seems to me that the initiative to appoint traditionally excluded groups to the bench is designed to address the following issues: (1) the necessity in a liberal democratic society that the judiciary maintain political legitimacy and public respect; and (2) a concern that the administration of justice is being undermined because of a widespread perception that the judiciary does not represent society and is thus biased or insensitive to certain groups and issues. Further to the belief that the bench should come much closer than at present to reflecting society in order to maintain public confidence and legitimacy, one must distinguish two related but distinct claims: first, that, at least in the case of women, their presence on the bench will bring with it a special-uniform perspective; and second, that increased representation will correct existing biases.

With respect to the first justification, there seem to be two schools of thought. Madam Justice Bertha Wilson wrote that two decades of feminist Canadian scholarship is premised on the proposition that

> women view the world and what goes on in it from a different perspective from men; and that women judges, by bringing that perspective to bear on the cases they hear, can play a major role in introducing judicial neutrality and impartiality into the justice system.[17]

Accordingly, feminist theorists such as Catharine MacKinnon observe that (male) judges have not traditionally been sensitive to gender issues involved in cases of rape, abortion, pregnancy and pornography.[18] Professors Isabel Grant and Lynn Smith point to landmark decisions such as *Murdoch, Morgentaler* and *Daigle* that have a greater impact on women's lives than on men's lives,[19] and to the "extensive literature about the existence of gender bias in existing legal doctrine and judicial decisions."[20] They define "gender bias" as the "built-in tilt of the legal system resulting from the exclusion or near-exclusion of women from the formation of its principles."[21]

Shortly, I shall indicate how the observations of Madam Justice Wilson and Professors Grant and Smith might be interpreted in a way compatible with the first justification for judicial diversity mentioned above. To the extent, however, that some feminist theorists may suppose that women bring a uniform insight to the bench, I think they are subject to criticism. Grant and Smith caution that "women do not have a monopoly on caring and compassion nor do men have a monopoly on cold detachment and mistaken reliance on conclusions dictated by abstract reasoning."[22] Professor Martha Minow maintains,

> Women fall into every category of race, religion, class and ethnicity, and vary in sexual orientation, handicapping conditions and other sources of assigned difference. Claims to speak from women's point of view, or to use women as a reference point, threaten to obscure this multiplicity and install a particular view to stand for the views of all.[23]

My admittedly limited experience on the bench, where I have interacted with both male and female judges, leads me to side with Grant, Smith and Minow on this question. However, a theory about the special or uniform insight of women, or of any other demographic group is not the same thing as the claim that the presence on the bench of heretofore under-represented people can help to balance an existing tilt.

I take it that a judge is biased when he or she is disposed to make unjustified judgements either of fact or of law to the disadvantage or to the advantage of specific individuals or categories of individuals. Bias is obviously something to be avoided, and when it is deliberate, to be condemned on moral grounds as well. No doubt there are examples of biased judges among all the demographic groups represented on the bench. If this is so, then judicial diversity cannot be justified on the ground that it will replace biased judges with unbiased ones. However, not all bias is deliberate and based on prejudice. The more systemic biases of the bench are unconscious and derive from the paucity of relevant life experiences on the part of judges. As Lord Justice Scrutton observed on the issue of class:

> This is rather difficult to attain in any system. I am not speaking of conscious impartiality, but the habits you are trained in, the people with

whom you mix, lead to your having a certain class of ideas of such a nature that, when you have to deal with other ideas, you do not give as sound and accurate judgments as you would wish. This is one of the great difficulties at present with Labour. Labour says: "Where are your impartial judges? They all move in the same circle as the employers and they are all educated and nursed in the same ideas as the employers. How can a labour man or a trade unionist get impartial justice?" It is very difficult sometimes to be sure that you have put yourself into a thoroughly impartial position between two disputants, one of your own class and one not of your class. Even in matters outside trade-unionist cases ... it is sometimes difficult to be sure, hard as you have tried, that you have put yourself in a perfectly impartial position between the two litigants.[24]

More recently, Professor McCormick, in his study of 4,000 decisions of the Supreme Court of Canada (from 1949 to 1992), said, "There's no suggestion that the underdog always loses — it's just that they tend to lose, on balance over the long run." McCormick's conclusion is that the courts, "rather than acting as a check on the rich and powerful, in fact have privilege-reinforcing tendencies."[25]

The lesson I draw from these observations is not that middle- and upper-class judges set out to twist laws and misrepresent facts prejudicially to advantage institutions and individuals with whom they identify on class grounds (though this may sometimes happen). Rather, their lack of experience of the daily lives of working-class people and the circumstances and functioning of specifically working-class institutions, such as trade unions, deprives them of potentially relevant information on which to make impartial judgements. This lack of experience will especially be apparent regarding findings of fact and judgements of motive, but perhaps it may also sometimes create blind spots affecting findings of law as well. The presence on the bench of more people from working-class origins would help to correct for this sort of systemic blind spot.

Similar considerations justify complementing the judiciary with people from other under-represented groups. Women judges, for example, are likely to be more sensitive to all aspects of situations involving sexual harassment and its effects than those who have never personally experienced harassment.[26] People who have encountered racial or ethnic prejudice will be better able to identify its various manifestations than those who have not. To the extent that gender, class, race or ethnicity affect one's behaviour on the stand, direct experience will also help judges to interpret a witness's demeanour, for instance to assess credibility.[27]

The strongest argument for judicial diversity, in my view, pertains to Lord Hewart's often quoted dictum that the law requires "justice should not only be done but should be seen to be done." Always good advice, this principle creates a special burden for the judiciary in today's world where people are aware of the challenges of diversity and where it is increasingly recognized that, as [then] Ontario Court of Appeal Madam Justice Rosalie Abella put it, "every decision maker who walks into a courtroom to hear a case is armed not only with the relevant legal texts, but with a set of values, experiences and assumptions that are thoroughly embedded."[28] Social commentators have long remarked on the ties between the judiciary, business, and the major political parties. Now there is also an increasing adverse popular response in a pluralistic society to a powerful, tenured institution that is overwhelmingly white, male and upper-middle class.

In this climate, governments are moving towards greater representation on the bench, in recognition that increasing public respect for the law requires a judiciary that is more reflective, aware and sensitive to the people and issues before the court. In agreement with this policy, it seems to me that proactive measures are justified precisely to maintain public confidence that one can receive justice in a diverse society. I therefore find it distressing that such proactive measures, even though slight to date, bring with them an unexpected cost.

BACKLASH

Professor Constance Backhouse was appointed in November 1991, by the then Ontario Minister of Citizenship, to adjudicate a protracted Ontario human rights complaint.[29] In 1985, Diane Gale, head deli clerk at Miracle Food Mart (a division of Steinberg's, some of whose assets were later bought by the Great Atlantic and Pacific Company of Canada Limited) alleged that her employer and her union, the United Food and Commercial Food Workers International Union, locals 175 and 633, discriminated against her in pay and promotion on the basis of her sex.

The complaint had potentially serious repercussions for the respondents. During the administrative tribunal hearing of the "A & P" case, the respondents brought a motion before the Ontario General Division for judicial review. The respondents argued that there "exists a real and reasonable apprehension of bias and perhaps acts of bias on the part of Professor Backhouse, based both on her background as an advocate in matters and issues involving sex discrimination and the fact of her being a party in proceedings outstanding before the Commission in which that issue is raised."[30]

The latter was a reference to Professor Backhouse's being one of 121 women law students, law professors and lawyers who had filed a complaint against Osgoode Hall Law School and York University, referred to as the *Osgoode* complaint. The *Osgoode* complaint alleged direct sex discrimination and systemic sex discrimination in failing to appoint Mary Jane Mossman as Dean of Law. Professor Backhouse had been elected by the other complainants as one of a twelve-person steering committee to direct the complaint. Although in August 1989 there was a Memorandum of Agreement setting out the parameters for settlement, the complaint continued to be classified as "outstanding." Professor Backhouse received no material benefit as a result of any of the terms of settlement. In April 1992, Professor Backhouse wrote to the Ontario Human Rights Commission (OHRC) to withdraw her name from the list of complainants and, in March 1993, the OHRC acceded to her request.

All parties to the judicial review proceeding agreed that the appropriate test to determine reasonable apprehension of bias was set out in Mr. Justice de Grandpré's dissenting opinion in the *Committee for Justice and Liberty v. National Energy Board*.[31] The test required "an analysis of the relevant facts by a reasonable and right-minded person who was well informed as to the issues."[32] In a decision, 7 June 1993, the Divisional Court in the "A & P" case disqualified Professor Backhouse as a Human Rights Board of Inquiry adjudicator on the grounds of a "reasonable apprehension of bias." The court held that:

> We did not think it necessary to decide whether Miss Backhouse's public advocacy in favour of the same position advanced before her by the Commission in relation to systemic sex discrimination went so far as to create a reasonable apprehension of bias in relation to this case. Rather we told counsel that, for the purposes of determining this issue, our attention was focused only upon the fact of Miss Backhouse's involvement

in the proceedings outstanding before the Commission in which she was, at the relevant times, one of the complainants.[33]

The court held that: "In our view, the unique aspect of this case is that Miss Backhouse went beyond the position of an advocate and descended personally, as a party, into the very arena over which she has been appointed to preside in relation to the very same issues she has to decide."[34] The court ordered costs in the amount of $10,000 to both the Union and to "A & P" against both the Ontario Human Rights Commission and the Board (i.e., Professor Backhouse) on a joint and several basis.

The OHRC sought leave to appeal to the Ontario Court of Appeal. In its factum, the Commission noted that the only commonalities between the *Osgoode* and "A & P" complaints were that "(i) the complaints involve women, albeit different women; and (ii) an analysis of the complaints would require the application of the same legal test for systemic discrimination,"[35] albeit to completely different facts and parties.[36] The General Division decision was upheld by the Ontario Court of Appeal, which refused to grant leave to appeal.[37]

Traditionally, judicial impartiality has been tied to judicial independence. Professor Martin Friedland in his recent report for the Canadian Judicial Council devoted several pages to the topic of impartiality and the balance of his book to judicial independence. He quoted, with approval, Chief Justice Antonio Lamer, who said:

> The rule of law, interpreted and applied by impartial judges, is the guarantee of everyone's rights and freedoms ... Judicial independence is, at its root, concerned with impartiality in appearance and in fact! And these, of course, are elements essential to an effective judiciary. Independence is not a perk of judicial office. It is a guarantee of the institutional conditions of impartiality.[38]

In the past, scant attention has been paid to judicial bias and challenges have been narrowly limited to financial interest, close personal friendship or relationship, or previous partisanship on issues. In circumstances where a judge disclosed political party membership or personal activities, parties were generally content to abandon allegations of partiality. However, following on the heels of the "A & P" decision, respondent counsel have been quick to raise allegations of bias in other Ontario administrative hearings.

In *Dulmage v. Ontario (Police Complaints Commissioner)*,[39] Audrey Smith, an African-Canadian woman, complained to the tri-partite Complaints Board that she had been strip-searched by police officers on Queen Street, in Toronto. The Ontario Divisional Court, on a judicial review application by the officers, held that there was a reasonable apprehension of bias on the part of African-Canadian adjudicator Frederica Douglas. Douglas was president of the Congress of Black Women, Mississauga chapter, when the vice-president of the Toronto chapter of the Congress of Black Women commented publicly to the media on the case. The court directed that a new panel be struck to rehear the matter and awarded costs to the police officers.

Recent cases suggest a pattern, in *Re Masters and the Queen in right of Ontario, Tory, Tory, DesLauriers and Binnington et al., Intervenors,*[40] Carleton Masters brought a wrongful dismissal action upon his resignation as Ontario Agent General in New York after being investigated for sexual harassment. He alleged that the government's inquiry conducted by the law firm of Tory, Tory, DesLauriers and Binnington was biased because Mary Eberts, a well-known feminist firm lawyer, had been involved in the investigation. In reply, Ms. Eberts filed an affidavit and was cross-examined on it; the allegations of bias against Eberts, Lillian Pan and Mayo Moran were dropped in the final factum.

The case of the *United Church of Canada et al. v. Thompson, Elmhurst and Symons*[41] involved allegations of sexual harassment. Early on, one of the respondents, Elmhurst, alleged that a member of the tri-partite panel struck by the United Church, law professor Mary Jane Mossman, was biased because of her "well known feminist views on sexual harassment" and because she was a complainant in the *Osgoode* complaint, mentioned previously.[42] In response to the pleadings, Mossman filed an affidavit and was cross-examined on it. Although the hearing panel's bias was argued before the Ontario General Division Court, it made no mention of this issue in its short decision dismissing the appeal. Costs were awarded to the United Church.

In a sexual orientation and housing case before the human rights tribunal, disabled Board of Inquiry adjudicator Ron MacInnis was challenged for bias because he had filed a human rights complaint alleging wheelchair access discrimination against a theatre. Like Backhouse, MacInnis was a complainant and was sitting as an adjudicator on a human rights case; however, unlike Backhouse the issues before him for adjudication were different. MacInnis dismissed the application against himself and it was not appealed.

AMERICAN JURISPRUDENCE

In the mid-1970s, President Carter jolted the American legal community with an outspoken and widely publicized affirmative action policy directed at placing women, racial and ethnic minorities on the federal bench. Recent research on the results of Carter's appointment strategy concludes that this policy, far from undermining merit selection, on balance improved the quality of appointments.[43] However, shortly after Carter's initiative, American defendants began challenging their minority judges for bias. American jurists appear to have followed the traditionally restrictive approach to bias allegations as the following cases indicate.

In *Menora v. Illinois High School Association*,[44] U.S. District Court Judge Shadur, who is Jewish, denied a motion that he recuse[45] himself. The case had been brought by Orthodox Jews, represented by the American Jewish Congress (AJC), who challenged the defendant's rule prohibiting the wearing of headgear during basketball games. Judge Shadur, formerly a member of the AJC for whom he had done "pro bono" work as a volunteer lawyer, held that the defendants did not demonstrate that he had a personal bias or prejudice against them. Judge Shadur cited the case of *State of Idaho v. Freeman*,[46] in which Judge Marion Callister, a member of the Mormon Church, refused to recuse himself in an Equal Rights Amendment (ERA) case. Callister's decision was not appealed, even though the Mormon Church had taken a strong formal position opposing the ERA, while Judge Callister was serving as a Regional Representative for the Church when the suit was filed.[47]

There was a flurry of cases questioning whether African-American judges should be disqualified per se from adjudicating cases involving claims of racial discrimination.[48] Judge Higginbotham, in *Commonwealth of Pennsylvania v. Local Union 542, International Union of Operating Engineers*, responded eloquently when he wrote:

[R]equiring black judges to recuse themselves from racial discrimination cases would result in a double standard within the federal judiciary ...
In fact, until 1961, white litigants in the United States District Courts

never had to ponder the subtle issue which defendants now raise, because no President had ever appointed a black as a United States District Judge. If blacks could accept the fact of their manifest absence from the federal judicial process for almost two centuries, the plain truth is that white litigants are now going to have to accept the new day where the judiciary will not be entirely white and where some black judges will adjudicate cases involving race relations.[49]

In the *United States v. State of Alabama*,[50] the U.S. federal government brought an action against the state of Alabama and its institutions of higher learning, alleging that they were maintaining and perpetuating racial segregation. The defendants moved to disqualify presiding Judge Clemons, an African-American, who had dismissed the defendants' bias application. On appeal, District Court Senior Circuit Judge Dyer reheard the recusal proceedings. Judge Dyer upheld the original dismissal.

The defendants argued bias because, first, it was alleged that Judge Clemons' children were potentially members of a class of African-American children seeking to intervene. It was decided by Judge Dyer that the judge's personal interest in the outcome was too remote. Second, it was claimed that, while in private practice, Judge Clemons had been the lawyer for the plaintiffs in a statewide desegregation case. Judge Dyer held that this earlier contact provided no prior knowledge of the facts involved in the present case. Third, it was asserted that Judge Clemons had had a previous association with former Senator Stewart, who was a member of a firm representing a patty in a segregation action against the state of Alabama. Judge Dyer found that this association "created the possibility of appearance of personal bias but was insufficient to support the disqualification of a judge."[51] Fourth, it was claimed that Judge Clemons had represented plaintiffs in an action against one university on the grounds that it was failing to recruit African-American athletes and was not awarding them scholarships. Judge Dyer found that "the present case challenged vestiges of *de jure* segregation currently existing, [but the] theories and relevant facts pertaining to the cases were different"; thus, Judge Clemons' disqualification was not warranted as the "same matter was not in controversy."[52] Finally, the defendants argued that Judge Clemons had participated in adversary proceedings involving charges of racial discrimination in the state's educational system. On this final point, Judge Dyer found that the defendants were different in the two cases.

In his decision, Judge Dyer referred to *U.S. v. Haldeman*,[53] which had set out detailed stringent requirements for recusal allegations.[54] The court had held that 28 U.S.C. section 144 was

> designed to guard against groundless claims [of judicial bias] and the impositions they would inflict on the judicial process ... Assertions merely of a conclusionary nature are not enough, nor are opinions or rumours. [There must be evidence that] "... give(s) fair support to the charge of a bent of mind that may prevent or impede impartiality of judgment."[55]

A final American case on the point is *Laird v. Tatum*, decided by the U.S. Supreme Court. Although Justice Rehnquist had been a witness for the Justice Department in Senate hearings inquiring into the same subject matter as the issue before him, Justice Rehnquist dismissed a recusal motion against himself. He noted that none of the Supreme Court Justices since 1911 had followed a practice of recusing themselves in cases involving points of law with respect to which they had expressed an opinion or formulated a policy prior to ascending the bench.[56] Similarly, in *Morgentaler v. R.*,[57] then Laskin C.J.C. observed that prior partisanship on the subject now in litigation does not lead to disqualification. The Chief Justice then decided that Mr. Justice de Grandpré could remain on the panel to hear an abortion case, despite having made a personal statement on the subject the year before at a 1973 national meeting of the Canadian Bar Association.

***

The values conventionally thought essential to good judgement — impartiality, objectivity and neutrality — nonetheless remain sacrosanct despite a shift in the players, changes in state policy and challenges from social scientists and feminist and critical race legal theorists about new interpretations of the concepts of "good judgment" and "impartiality."[58] Certainly, there can be no dispute that objectionable bias and close-minded prejudgement are to be avoided. One would also expect unanimous support for the requirement that a judge put aside preconceptions and approach each case with an open mind. The appointment of women and minorities to the judiciary appears, however, to have resulted in initial unease with the new faces on the bench and a wider interpretation of the principle of impartiality.

The legal theorist, K.C. Davis asked: "Do we want unbiased judges, or do we want judges with the right biases?" He somewhat cynically responded to his own question:

> Anyone's initial answer is likely to be that of course we want unbiased ... objective and neutral judges ... Almost any intelligent person will initially assert that he wants objectivity, but by that he means biases that coincide with his [or her] own.[59]

Certainly, I agree that we want a more diverse bench and impartial judges. It was partly for these reasons that I welcomed the new judicial appointments' policies and procedures in my province and that I accepted a call to the bench. A one-sided homogeneity of the judiciary cannot help but carry with it a narrowness of vision and of life experiences that is bound to create unconscious biases. How ironic, indeed how sad, if the potential of an expanded bench is impeded by allegations of the very shortcomings in our judicial system that the appointments were meant to correct.[60]

NOTES

Earlier versions of this paper were presented as the Lansdowne Lecture, at the University of Victoria, BC, 24 January 1995 and at Queen's University, Faculty of Law, 10 March 1995. Thanks are due to the participants at these events for their helpful comments and criticisms. Thanks are also due to Constance Backhouse, Mary Eberts, Harry Glasbeek, Kathy Laird, Mary Jane Mossman, Peter Russell, Gary Yee and my judicial colleagues in Toronto North Court for reading a draft of this paper.

1. Ontario Reports, Law Society of Upper Canada, 17 July 1992.

2. For background information on a socially representative judiciary, see Peter H. Russell, *The Judiciary in Canada: The Third Branch of Government* (Toronto: McGraw-Hill Ryerson, 1987), 164–166.

3. Letter of Howard Hampton (27 November 1990). On file with the author.

4. Although my mother and I were born in Canada, we were both denied the rights of Canadian citizenship on our birth, which were only granted to Japanese

Canadians in 1949. I recount this history and my community's ultimately successful campaign for redress in my book, *Bittersweet Passage: Redress and the Japanese Canadian Experience* (Toronto: Between the Lines, 1992).

5. In 1992, the Ontario Judicial Council was composed of the Chief and Associate Chief Justice, the Chief and Associate Chief Justice of the Ontario Court, the Chief Judge of the Provincial Division, the Treasurer or the Law Society, and two lay members.

6. Peter McCormick and Ian Green, *Judges and Judging: Inside the Canadian Judicial System* (Toronto: James Lorimer, 1990).

7. Ibid., 68.

8. See also Madam Justice Bertha Wilson, *Touchstones for Change: Equality, Diversity and Accountability* (Toronto: Canadian Bar Association, 1993), chap. 10, "The Judiciary." Known as the Wilson Report, it states at p. 186 that "approximately 12 per cent of the federally-appointed judges and 13 per cent of the provincially-appointed judges were women."

9. McCormick and Green, *Judges and Judging*, 61. The authors conclude that minority ethnicities are "significantly under-represented among the senior judiciary." The authors cite Professor Peter Russell's observation that visible minorities are "especially under-represented on the judiciary in all the provinces."

10. Ibid., 64. The average age of federally appointed judges is 59 and provincially appointed judges is 53. Both serve, on average, ten years on the bench.

11. Ibid., 65. Judges are members of "main-line religious groups ... with a heavy skewing toward the more prestigious and established affiliations ... Roman Catholic, Anglican, United and Jewish."

12. Ibid., 66–67. The authors conclude that "socially, judges come disproportionately from upper-class backgrounds." George Adams and Paul Cavalluzzo, "The Supreme Court of Canada: A Biographical Study," (1969) 7 *Osgoode Hall Law Journal* 61, found that only two of the first fifty Supreme Court of Canada judges were born into working-class families.

13. Ibid., 70. Table 3.4 indicates that judges as a group are inclined to be "high achievers."

14. Ibid., 69. "About one-fifth ... considered themselves to be primarily trial lawyers before appointment."

15. In 1994, there were 263 female judges in Canada: 125 federally appointed and 138 provincially appointed. But see Wilson Report (note 8) at 136 for slightly different statistics.

16. Ross Howard, "Judicial Process Opened Up," *The (Toronto) Globe and Mail*, 29 April 1994, A5. The federal government has been slow to follow up on this promise.

17. Madam Justice Bertha Wilson, "Will Women Judges Really Make a Difference?"

(1990) 28 *Osgoode Hall Law Journal* 507.

18. See generally, Catharine MacKinnon, *Feminism Unmodified: Discourses on Life and Law* (Cambridge, MA: Harvard University Press, 1987).

19. *Murdoch v. Murdoch,* [1975] 1 S.C.R. 423, on division of family property; *Morgentaler et al. v. R.,* [1988] 1 S.C.R. 30, on abortion rights; *Tremblay v. Daigle* (1989), 62 O.L.R. (4th) 634 (S.C.C.), on abortion rights.

20. Isabel Grant and Lynn Smith, "Gender Representation in the Canadian Judiciary," in Law Reform Commission of Ontario, *Appointing Judges: Philosophy, Politics and Practice* (Toronto: Queen's Printer, 1991) 58 at 76. See also, Norma Juliet Wilder, "On the Judicial Agenda for the 80s: Equal Treatment for Men and Women in the Courts, (November 1980) 645 *Judicature* 202.

21. Grant and Smith, "Gender Representation in the Canadian Judiciary."

22. Ibid., 72.

23. Martha Minow, "Foreword: Justice Engendered," (1987) 501 *Harvard Law Review* 10 at 62–63.

24. Lord Justice Scrutton "The Work of the Commercial Courts," (1921) 1 *Cambridge Law Journal* 6 at 8, as quoted in Madam Justice Bertha Wilson, "Will Women Judges Really Make a Difference?" at 509.

25. Peter McCormick's study on 4,000 Supreme Court of Canada decisions from 1949 to 1992, as discussed in *The (Toronto) Globe and Mail,* 6 November 1993, A1.

26. But see Sean Fine, "Different Styles on the Bench," *The (Toronto) Globe and Mail,* 25 October 1993, A9. This article on judicial differences between Canada's two women Supreme Court of Canada justices (Justices Claire L'Heureux-Dubé and Beverley McLachlin) might seem to contradict this point: "... the two women have some deep divisions in how they view law and society. They are unlikely to become joint champions of women's rights in family-law disputes ... Judge L'Heureux-Dubé ... is reform-minded, following in the tradition of Bertha Wilson ... Judge McLachlin is a coolly methodical thinker ... she prides herself on objectivity." This argument pertains to the thesis that I earlier rejected that there is a uniform female perspective on the law, but it does not contradict the claim that women's life experiences will make them sensitive to ranges of relevant facts. How they choose to weigh these facts will depend on a variety of factors, including the legal philosophies they favour.

27. In endorsing this justification for judicial diversity, I am abstracting from a more theoretical debate about the nature, possibility and desirability of judicial "impartiality," "neutrality" or "objectivity." Some legal theorists, like Hudson Janisch, question the possibility of neutrality. See Hudson Janisch, "Case Comment: *Nfld. Light & Power Co. v. P.U.C. (Bd.),*" (1987) 25 *Administrative Law Reports* 196 at 198. Others, such as Professors Grant and Smith, note that what counts as objectivity itself depends on whose perspective is dominant. See

Grant and Smith, "Gender Representation in the Canadian Judiciary," 67 and 79. See also Jennifer Nedelsky, Book Review of *Inessential Woman: Problems of Exclusion in Feminist Thought*, by Elizabeth Spelman, (1991) 89 *Michigan Law Review* 1591 at1607.

In lieu of entering into these debates, I shall limit myself to commenting on the following view of Mr. Justice Brian Dickson, (formerly C.J.C.) that "Judges are human. They have been moulded by all they have experienced prior to elevation to the bench. They may hold strong views on many issues; yet when presiding at a trial, those views must be cast aside." "The Role and Function of Judges," (1980) 14 *Law Society Gazette (Law Society of Upper Canada)* 138 at 113. I agree with Mr. Justice Dickson's assumption that judicial impartiality or objectivity is a desirable goal, but I question whether the perceptions moulded by all that one has experienced in a pre-bench life can be so easily set aside. It is thus important that the judiciary include people from the widest possible range of life experiences.

28. Madam Justice Rosalie Abella, "The Dynamic Nature of Equality," in Sheilah Martin and Kathleen Mahoney, eds., *Equality and Judicial Neutrality* (Toronto: Carswell, 1987) 3 at 8–9.

29. *Great Atlantic & Pacific Co. of Canada v. Ontario (Human Rights Commission)* (1993), 13 O.R. (3d) 824 (Gen. Div.) (hereafter the "A & P" case).

30. Ibid., 832–833.

31. (1976), 68 D.LR. (3d) 716 (S.C.C.).

32. "A & P" case, at 834.

33. Ibid., 833–834.

34. Ibid., 834.

35. The test is set out in *Action Travail Des Femmes v. C.N.R. Co.* (1987), 40 D.LR. (4th) 193 at 210 (S.C.C.). The Supreme Court of Canada there wrote: "Systemic discrimination in an employment context is discrimination that results from the simple operation of established procedures of recruitment, hiring and promotion, none of which is necessarily designed to promote discrimination. The discrimination is then reinforced by the very exclusion of the disadvantaged group because the exclusion fosters the belief, both within and outside the group, that the exclusion is the result of 'natural' forces, for example, that women 'just can't do the job.' To combat systemic discrimination, it is essential to create a climate in which both negative practices and negative attitudes can be challenged and discouraged." See also, *Ontario Human Rights Commission and O'Malley v. Simpson-Sears*, [1985] 2 S.C.R. 536 at 546–547.

36. Ontario Human Rights Commission factum, leave to appeal the "A & P" decision, Court File No. M10959 at 8.

37. Diane Gale had abandoned her complaint. [See Jan Kainer, *Cashing In On Pay Equity? Supermarket Restructuring and Gender Equality* (Toronto: Sumach Press, 2002), 246–250.]

38. Cited in Martin Friedland, *A Place Apart: Judicial Independence and Accountability in Canada* (Ottawa: Canadian Judicial Council, 1995), 1.

39. (1994), 21 OR. (3d) 356 (Ont. Gen. Div.).

40. (1994), 18 O.R (3d) 551 (Ont. Div. Ct), at 575.

41. (2 May 1994). (Ont. Gen. Div.) [unreported].

42. Interestingly, Professor Mossman had never published on the topic of sexual harassment nor was she a complainant in the *Osgoode* complaint. Both Professors Mossman and Backhouse note that there has been a "chilling" as a result of bias challenges.

43. Sheldon Goldman, "Reagan's Judicial Appointments at Mid-term: Shaping the Bench in His Own Image," (March 1983) 66:8 *Judicature* 335 at 340–343.

44. 527 F. Supp. 632 (ND. Ill. 1981) (hereinafter *Menora*).

45. *Black's Law Dictionary* defines "recusation" as "A species of exception or plea to the jurisdiction, to the effect that the particular judge is disqualified from hearing the cause by reason of interest or prejudice."

46. 507 F. Supp. 706 (D. Idaho 1981).

47. *Menora* at 634.

48. *Vietnamese Fishermen's Association et al. v. Knights of the Ku Klux Klan*, 513 F. Supp. 1017 (S.D. Texas 1981).

49. 388 F. Supp. 155 at 165, 177 (E.D. Penn. 1974). Justice Higginbotham also reviewed American cases in which judges declined to sit, for a variety of reasons.

50. 582 F. Supp. 1197 (N.D. Ala. 1984).

51. Ibid. at 1198.

52. Ibid.

53. 559 F. 2d 31 at 134 (D.C. Cir. 1976).

54. 28 U.S.C. 144 (1988).

55. 582 F. Supp. 1197 (N.D. Ala. 1984) at 1200–1201.

56. 409 U.S. 824 at 831 (1972).

57. (2 October 1974) Motion No. 13504 (S.C.C.) [unreported]. This judgement is not reported in any official law reports. It is, however, reproduced as an appendix to an article by Jeremy Webber, "The Berger Affair," (1984) 29 *McGill Law Journal* 369 at 405. It can also be found at [1974] S.C.J. No. 1.

58. See Iris Young, *Justice and the Politics of Difference* (Princeton: Princeton University Press, 1990), chap. 4.

59. Kenneth C. Davis, *Administrative Law Treatise,* 2d ed. (San Diego: K.C. Davis), 377–378.

60. Richard Devlin, "We Can't Go On Together with Suspicious Minds: Judicial Bias and Racialized Perspective in *R. v. R.D.S.*," (1995) 18 *Dalhousie Law Journal* 408. In 1994 when I wrote this paper, the only challenges for bias against the "new faces" were at the administrative tribunal level. Unfortunately, as I feared, Canada is following the American precedent and Devlin's article discusses higher court findings of racial bias by Canada's first African-Canadian woman judge, Judge Corrine Sparks.

CHAPTER 4

PRESERVERVING HETERONORMATIVITY: TRINITY WESTERN UNIVERSITY v. BRITISH COLUMBIA COLLEGE OF TEACHERS

Lori G. Beaman

In May 2001, the Supreme Court of Canada decided that the anti-gay and lesbian "moral" policy of Trinity Western University, an evangelical school in western Canada, did not constitute a "harm" that would warrant keeping Trinity graduates in its teaching program out of the public school system. The Court was able to minimize the harm by, first, reshaping the case as a misapplication of human rights law by an unqualified tribunal and, secondly, by framing the issues around the premise that evangelical Christians can separate their beliefs from their practices, and therefore gay, lesbian, bisexual and transgendered (GLBT) students[1] in the public school system were not at risk of harm.

In its decision, the Court ignored a fundamental tenet of evangelical Christian teachings, that in fact belief and practice are impossible to separate and that those with a Christian commitment should live their beliefs in the course of their everyday lives. *Trinity Western* is an important example of the ways in which "the facts" are characterized in law so as to both highlight and minimize particular aspects of the narratives of different groups. A strictly instrumentalist view of law is too simplistic, however, to help to understand the process by which various interests become privileged in law. Rather, law is a terrain on which struggles for recognition occur. Balances shift and change according to the ways in which issues are characterized and voices are privileged, whether those voices be homophobic, mainstream religious or, occasionally, on the margins.

In this chapter, I briefly outline recent legal history in relation to sexual orientation and its protection under human rights legislation and, more specifically, the Charter of Rights and Freedoms. After setting out the facts of *Trinity Western* and an analytical framework inspired by Mary Jane Mossman, Hermer and Hunt, Carol Smart and Michel Foucault,[2] I argue that through a series of discursive techniques the Supreme Court is able to minimize the perceived harm to gays and lesbians and to frame the issues so as to avoid dealing with the continuing discrimination faced by GLBT persons. In the conclusion, I link this to the idea of governance and regulation.

A Brief Legal History

The legal history of this case involves a collision course between two separate bodies of rights discourse emerging from the Charter of Rights and Freedoms. The first involves sexual orientation and the fight for equality primarily under section 15 of the Charter, although human rights legislation has generally been used as well. The second body of rights discourse involves the interpretation of religious freedom, which is protected primarily under section 2(a) of the Charter ("freedom of religion"), but receives a mention in the preamble of the Charter (where God is recognized), section 15 (discrimination on the basis of religion) and is alluded to in the Charter's recognition of Canada's multicultural heritage. As is the case with sexual orientation, religious freedom is also mentioned in various pieces of human rights legislation at the provincial level.

The issues around sexual orientation have been varied, and the battle for equality has been fought on a number of fronts, including the protection of gays and lesbians under marital property legislation, the right to marry,[3] the right to participate in military service, equal employment benefits, the public celebration of Gay Pride Week and adoption, custody and access to children.[4] The law varies from province to province, and from issue to issue.

While complex (and confusing) in its legal reasoning, the *Egan* case (1995) was an important landmark in the rights struggle for gays and lesbians.[5] In that case, the Supreme Court of Canada "read in" sexual orientation as an analogous ground under section 15 of the Charter. However, legal victories have not been without their costs. As Miriam Smith points out,

Rights talk is a specific type of political discourse that has stemmed from the entrenchment of the Charter. As a type of political discourse, it privileges the law and the courts as the mechanism for the resolution and processing of political problems such as conflict of interest and values between groups or conflicts between groups and the state.[6]

The problem with this approach is that law shapes and frames claims in ways that are not always intended by those who make rights claims. Smith argues that the "gay liberation" movement has been transformed by rights discourse that has resulted in a substantial narrowing of goals and the reframing of a social movement into one that is situated primarily in law. On this theme, Carol Smart calls for a decentring of law, recognizing that the situation of social problems within the discourse of law can sometimes have negative effects on the group seeking to alleviate the problem.[7] According to Smith, then, the gay liberation movement has moved in the opposite direction; it has become more, rather than less, "centred" in law, perhaps to its detriment.

On a similar note, Kathleen Lahey argues that the law perpetuates the notion that gays and lesbians are less than full citizens even as it holds out the promise of full citizenship through "guarantees" of equality. Lahey also points out that "every 'rights' decision implicitly ranks rights."[8] Arguably, it is religious freedom that ranks over equality for gays and lesbians in *Trinity Western*. But this is too simplistic a characterization of the result, and begs the question of how courts should cope with competing rights, if indeed what happens in cases like *Trinity* is aptly characterized as a "competition," either because there is no competition — that is, sexual orientation is disadvantaged from the outset — or because to frame the rights as competing rights is setting up the legal discussion in ways that are not particularly useful. In some measure, Charter interpretation is always about balancing competing interests, whether those explicitly named in the Charter as rights or those that are couched as "community" or "social" interests.

Like the rights discourse that has emerged around sexual orientation, religious freedom has undergone some interesting post-Charter shifts as well. From the dramatically broad interpretation of religious freedom offered in *Big M. Drugmart* to the reining in of those parameters in *Edwards Books*, the status of religious freedom in Canada is transformed from a broadly interpreted right to a somewhat ambiguous privilege. In *Big M.*, the Supreme Court states: "What may appear good and true to a majoritarian religious group, or the State acting at their behest, may not, for religious reasons, be imposed upon citizens who take a contrary view. The Charter safeguards religious minorities from the threat of the 'tyranny of the majority.'"[9] In somewhat stark contrast, the Court appears to have shifted its position considerably in *Edwards Books*, where it states: "Section 2(a) does not require the Legislatures to eliminate every miniscule state-imposed cost associated with the practice of religion."[10] So much for protection from the tyranny of the majority. While the popular and common rhetoric is that we live in a secular state, the religious underpinnings of the so-called secular state, in the form of mainstream Christianity, frequently emerge when religious minorities such as Scientologists, Aboriginals or Wiccans seek to fit within the rights discourse of law. It is at this point that the discursive presence of mainstream Christianity is most strongly felt. Thus, religious freedom is bounded by notions of "normal" religion that map the beliefs, practices and organizational structure of "churches" and mainstream Christianity.

How does the identification of these two rights discourses help us to understand the *Trinity Western* case? I have presented the discourses as distinct packages, which of course they are not. They overlap, compete, shift, and both facilitate and limit the rights claims made by individuals or groups. "Sexual orientation" is an emerging "concept" in law that is counter-hegemonic. Religion has frequently been used as a means to the end of the preservation of that hegemony through the use of "moral" reasoning embedded in religion.[11] Religious freedom is defined by an intersection of legal and religious discourses that rely on notions of normal religion. Trinity Western University is sponsored by the Evangelical Fellowship of Canada and represents a group of Christians who are on the margins, but within the boundaries, of normal religion. They fall, by and large, within the hegemonic parameters of mainstream religion.

Bruce MacDougall argues that there is a long history of judicial protection of homophobia, especially when balancing the rights of gays, lesbians and bisexuals with religious expression. He attributes this to an underlying religious value system held by judges, or at least protected by them. MacDougall states: "Religious freedom should not prevail over freedom of sexual orientation just because religious freedom has been recognized for a longer time and religious ideas have infused the common law. Recognizing true equality for homosexuality does not impair religious freedom."[12] Based on MacDougall's work, it would seem that the decision in *Trinity Western* is not a particularly new or unique line of reasoning. What is perhaps most troubling about this is that the Charter of Rights and Freedoms seems to have had no effect on disturbing the status quo in cases in which religion and sexual orientation "compete." While Charter cases often involve multiple or competing rights claims, it is the manner with which they are assessed that is of particular interest in *Trinity.*

THE FACTS: TRINITY WESTERN

Trinity Western University, a small "private" evangelical university, applied to the British Columbia College of Teachers (BCCT) for permission to take on full responsibility for their teacher education program. At the time of the application, the teacher education program was offered at Trinity Western with the exception of the final year, which was offered at Simon Fraser University, a "public" secular university. The BCCT denied the application, citing the Community Standards Statement used by Trinity Western as potentially promoting discrimination by its graduates against gay and lesbian students in the public school system. The reasoning of the BCCT Tribunal is reflected in the following statement:

> Both the *Canadian Human Rights Act* and the *B.C. Human Rights Act* prohibit discrimination on the ground of sexual orientation. The Charter of Rights and the Human Rights Acts express the values which represent the public interest. Labelling homosexual behaviour as sinful has the effect of excluding persons whose sexual orientation is gay or lesbian. The Council believes and is supported by law in the belief that sexual orientation is no more separable from a person than colour. Persons of homosexual orientation, like persons of colour, are entitled to protection and freedom from discrimination under the law.[13]

On judicial review to the Supreme Court of British Columbia, the BCCT Tribunal was found to have overstepped its jurisdiction. In essence, the Tribunal turned to human rights legislation, including the

Charter and British Columbia human rights legislation, as an interpretive guide to the determination of what constitutes the "public interest." The Supreme Court of Canada upheld the finding of the BC Supreme Court.

The content of the "contract" that students, faculty and staff enter into with Trinity Western sets out "community standards," which apply both on and off campus and include a commitment to

> refrain from practices that are biblically condemned. These include but are not limited to drunkenness (Eph. 5:18); swearing or use of profane language (Eph. 4:29, 5:4; Jas. 3:1–12), harassment (Jn. 13:34–35; Rom. 12:9–21; Eph. 4:28), abortion (Ex. 20:13; Ps.139: 13–16), involvement in the occult (Acts 19:19; Gal. 5:19), and sexual sins including premarital sex, adultery, homosexual behaviour, and viewing of pornography (I Cor. 6:12–20; Eph. 4:17–24; I Thess. 4: 3–8; Rom. 2–26-27; Tim. 1:9–10). Furthermore married members of the community agree to maintain the sanctity of marriage and to take every positive step possible to avoid divorce.[14]

The Supreme Court of Canada held that this set of community standards was not evidence of any real risk of harm to gay and lesbian students in the public school system and that the BCCT Tribunal had been wrong to deny permission to Trinity Western to assume full responsibility for its teacher education program.

THE FRAMEWORK

Several years ago, I used Mary Jane Mossman's analytical framework as set out in "Feminism and Legal Method: The Difference it Makes" to think about the *Egan* case.[15] In that article, I argued that while sexual orientation had clearly been read into the Charter of Rights and Freedoms protections under section 15, the way in which the Court talked about sexual orientation — the manner in which it characterized the issues, used precedent and interpreted statutory law — left open the possibility of a narrow interpretation of that protection. The *Trinity Western* decision seems to support that position, and it seems appropriate to use Mossman's framework to articulate the manner in which gays and lesbians are still legally vulnerable. Mossman, like many other critical legal scholars, challenges the notion that law is objective and neutral, and explores a series of conceptual tools that can be employed to engage in a deconstruction of legal decision. Her framework continues to be a valuable contribution to the exploration of the ways in which legal method is used to maintain the status quo.

In essence, Mossman's argument is this: legal method, or, the structure of legal inquiry, presents itself as a neutral process by which the "truth," or at least the legal truth, is arrived at. This process is, in fact, value-laden and for the most part preserves the legal and cultural status quo. Mossman highlights the tendency of courts to accept uncritically the "ideas from the mainstream of intellectual life, as if they were factual rather than conceptual,"[16] a criticism that I apply to the *Trinity* case later in this chapter. Mossman identifies three principles of legal method: (1) the characterization of the issues; (2) the choice of legal precedents to decide the validity of the claims; and (3) the process of statutory interpretation, especially in determining the effect of statutes to alter common-law principles.[17] Each of these principles overlaps. For example, the manner in which an issue is characterized will impact on the ways in which precedent is used. In *Trinity*, precedent is distinguished based on the belief/practice dichotomy that is central to the reasoning of the majority decision.

Mossman's arguments were originally framed around this question: Is law impervious to feminism? Her conclusion, after a careful examination of several early decisions that were fundamental to women's legal equality (including the Person's Case and *French*),[18] is that law may be impervious to feminism. This careful conclusion allows for the possibility of resistance, struggle and, most importantly, the double-edged sword of choice: "choice as to which precedents are relevant and which approach to statutory interpretation is preferred; and choice as to whether the ideas of the mainstream or those of the margins are appropriate."[19] This is important if we are to avoid a monolithic, instrumentalist or functionalist view of law. Gays and lesbians *have* effected changes in the law as a result of strategic struggles. What remains to be explored are the parameters of the boundaries, perhaps using the framework provided by Mossman. But a second issue arises that requires a bit of an intellectual shift, and it is here that work on governance and risk, from its early articulation by Michel Foucault to more recent discussions by scholars like Joe Hermer and Alan Hunt is useful. By positing the issues presented in *Trinity* as being about regulation and governance, perhaps we can find our way out of the "competing rights" quagmire.

THE ANALYSIS

THE CHARACTERIZATION OF THE ISSUES

The entire legal process is about framing issues in particular ways. Lawyers look for unique ways to present their clients' interests and judges make decisions about which view of the issues is legally "correct." This process is represented as somehow being neutral and objective and as based on a set of legal rules that somehow precludes human decision-making about the ways in which particular narratives are presented in law. But the fallacy of this "objectivity" is revealed even within the parameters of the law. If we examine majority decisions and contrast them to dissenting judgements, we can see that the dissent often represents not only a different application of law but also a different manner of presenting the issues. The characterization of the issues is a critical component of including/excluding particular versions of the "facts," a word that in and of itself references a notion of objectivity and "the" truth. In *Trinity Western*, the characterization of the issues becomes a key to the pathway of the decision reached. But, as we will see, the ways in which the Court characterizes some of the issues assumes a particular position about evangelical Christians and their beliefs, as well as a taken-for-granted stance on the separability of the public and the private realms of life.

Belief and Practice

The manner in which the Court characterizes the easy separation of belief and practice is perhaps the most startling aspect of the *Trinity Western* case. Case law in the United States dealing with religion has dispensed with any division between these two aspects of faith. Admittedly, this is in relation to the protection of religious freedom; however, it seems that in the United States the separation of belief and practice has been recognized as a fruitless way to think about religious commitment. In other words, it is meaningless to talk about freedom of religion without incorporating both belief and practice within the parameters of that right. Indeed, this was certainly the early post-Charter position on religious freedom, at least as it was delineated in *Big M.* by Mr. Justice Dickson who stated: "The essence of the concept of freedom of religion is the right to entertain such religious beliefs as a person chooses, the right to declare religious beliefs openly and without fear of hindrance or reprisal, and the right to manifest religious belief by worship and practice or by teaching and dissemination."[20] The dichotomy between belief and practice flies in the face of this statement, and is especially profound in *Trinity* because it runs completely contrary to what evangelical Christians themselves believe.

The boundaries of beliefs and practices around those who make up the group "evangelical Christians" is somewhat complex. Like their fundamentalist counterparts, they are Bible-believing Christians who see the only way to salvation as being through belief in Jesus Christ. Faith is usually achieved through a conversion experience that provides a "before" and "after" narrative for adherents. For fundamentalists, the boundaries between the secular world and their world are clear; for evangelical Christians, the boundaries are more fluid and negotiable. Evangelicals are a diverse group, made up of people who espouse a wide variety of beliefs.[21]

A key marker of evangelical Christians is their integration of belief and practice. While it is important to avoid a monolithic interpretation of evangelical Christians,[22] theirs is a lived religion such that, to the greatest extent possible, belief is manifested in day-to-day practice. That evangelicals themselves want to emphasize their world-view approach and the separation between themselves and the rest of the world is illustrated by the following statement in the application for approval by Trinity Western University: "TWU's educational program, like those in public universities, is based on a particular worldview perspective. At TWU, that worldview is a Christian one."[23]

Given the predominance of the marketplace model that describes the religious practices of many Canadians, it is sometimes difficult to imagine that some groups of people are guided by religion as a prescriptive and an explanatory code. The marketplace model would have us believe that, in this so-called secular society (85 percent of Canadians still claim a mainstream religious affiliation), religious activity has been reduced to "C and E" (Christmas and Easter) Christianity. In this view, the extent of consumer choices related to religion include church attendance during Christmas and Easter and during selected rituals such as religious funerals, marriages and baptisms. But, even if this consumer typology is accurate, there are significant groups of religious believers for whom a world view rather than a marketplace is the better description of their spiritual approach.

What are the implications of this belief/practice merger in the context of the issues raised in *Trinity Western*? While evangelicals view "homosexuality" as biblically prohibited behaviour, they are also careful to point out that God calls on them to "love the sinner, hate the sin." While this is of scarce comfort to gays and lesbians, it does mean that the intertwining of belief and practice cannot be conceptualized simplistically. Also, part of the Community Standards Statement for students at Trinity is that they are to

> obey Jesus' commandment to his disciples ... echoed by the apostle Paul ... to love one another. In general this involves showing respect for all people regardless of race or gender and regard for human life at all stages. It includes making a habit of edifying others, showing compassion, demonstrating unselfishness, and displaying patience.[24]

So, what are we to make of the effects of beliefs that call for hating the "sin" of homosexuality and "edifying others"?

Research does not assist in this messy quagmire, as findings are mixed. In "Predicting Prejudice from Religious Fundamentalism and Right-Wing Authoritarianism," the authors attempt to sort through "religious fundamentalism" (RF), which they describe as a "subgroup within evangelicalism that accepts biblical authority, salvation through Christ, and a commitment to spreading the faith,"[25] and "right-wing authoritarian" (RWA) beliefs, described as incorporating three attitudinal clusters with sociopolitical roots that include "authoritarian submission, authoritarian aggression and conventionalism."[26] The results of the study are a bit confusing and, like the other literature they cite, mixed.

In summary, RF is a negative predictor of racism and a non-significant predictor of discrimination against gays and lesbians. However, RWA is a predictor of both racism and prejudice against gays and lesbians. The "catch" is that, as the authors point out, authoritarianism is often coupled with orthodox Christian belief. This must be contextualized in the varieties of interpretations employed by evangelical Christians in their approaches to homosexuality:

> Some Christians object to homosexuality on moral grounds, maintaining negative attitudes against gays and lesbians with respect to their

perceived unethical behaviour. Others may focus instead on Christian teachings of love, acceptance and tolerance as a basis for less negative attitudes about homosexuality. Many individuals attempt to combine both aspects into a unitary mandate to "hate the sin, but love the sinner."[27]

The nebulous terrain of evangelical beliefs and practices is illustrated by an interview I heard on CBC Radio shortly after the *Trinity* case was released. The host, Shelagh Rogers, interviewed two students from Trinity Western University, one of whom was gay.

> *Shelagh*: So in fact, Christian, what I think you're saying is that you signed it but you don't live by it.
>
> *Christian*: Uh … I don't want to get kicked out of here, but I struggle with certain portions. Also, I talk to teachers — not necessarily about me specifically — and they recognize that, you know, people make mistakes. As long as you're accountable to someone, friends and so forth, it shouldn't be a problem. It's not like the school has sex police running around, trying to catch people having sex or anything.
>
> *Shelagh*: But how comfortable are you, as a gay man on this campus?
>
> *Christian*: I guess it depends. With my fellow students in my program I was very comfortable. They basically all knew. Most of them, from what I could tell from what they told me, were very comfortable with it. They were actually … most of them thought it was morally fine, or neutral. There were some that didn't think it was morally fine, but they were very nice and caring. They didn't really make a big deal of it.[28]

This student later goes on to say that he had never felt harassed on campus: "I think most of the harassment or hate mongering that goes on is not typically, especially in Canada, done by evangelical Christians." The discussion illustrates the complexity of trying to anticipate behaviour from beliefs.

For evangelical Christians, the answer on homosexuality is found in biblical pronouncements like that found in Paul's letters to Timothy. Paul is equally (in)famous for his writings on women and their "proper" place. In *The Living Bible*, Timothy 1:11 reads: "Yes, these laws are made to identify as sinners all who are immoral and impure: homosexuals, kidnappers, liars and all who do things that contradict the glorious good news of our blessed God, whose messenger I am." The notes on this passage in *The Living Bible*, popular among evangelicals, reads:

> There are those who attempt to legitimize homosexuality as an acceptable alternative lifestyle. Even some Christians say people have a right to choose how they want to live. But the Bible specifically calls homosexual behavior sin (see Leviticus 18:22; Romans 1:18–32; 1 Corinthians 6:9–11). We must be careful, however, to condemn only the practice, not the people. People who commit homosexual acts are not to be feared, ridiculed, or hated. They can be forgiven and their lives can be transformed. The church should be a haven of forgiveness and healing for homosexuals without compromising its stance against homosexual behavior.[29]

The fact that there exists considerable exegesis[30] that contextualizes these statements and would undermine or eliminate any biblical support or justification for condemning homosexuality is of little consequence to many evangelicals. Such exegesis on the role of women has also met with limited acceptance. As John Corvino points out, there are many biblical passages that are restrictive. He notes that Leviticus 11:7–8 reads, "The pig ... is unclean for you. Of their flesh you shall not eat, and their carcasses you shall not touch; they are unclean for you." Upon which he remarks, "Taken literally, this passage not only prohibits eating pork, but also playing football, since footballs are made of pigskin."[31]

John Boswell has done extensive and carefully researched scholarship that includes both biblical interpretation and the contextualizing of biblical texts in their social and cultural milieu. He concludes that hostility towards homosexuality is linked to social and cultural events and is not condemned by Christian teachings.[32] In other words, the theology evolved to suit the times and does not connect to or follow Jesus' teachings. Despite the considerable evidence presented by scholars like Boswell, evangelical and fundamentalist Christians continue to insist that read properly (literally), the Bible condemns homosexuality. Ultimately, the Bible is read as the word of God that should not be, in the eyes of evangelicals, subjected to academic debate.

Whatever the results of the research, two points emerge in relation to the decision in *Trinity Western*. First, the Court is willfully blind to the teachings of evangelical Christianity — belief and practice are *not* easily separated. Secondly, while the results are mixed, social scientific research that explores the issue of the impact of religious beliefs on anti-gay and lesbian belief and practice should have been considered. Judicial instinct on this matter is not good enough, nor is the elevation of the belief/practice distinction to legal dogma an appropriate resolution for a group that experiences discrimination at the levels experienced by gays and lesbians.

Public/Private

One might argue, and in fact the Supreme Court decision implies, that the Community Standards Statement signed by students, staff and faculty at Trinity Western University is the private agreement between the student, the faculty staff member and the university, and as such has no implications for the treatment of GLBT persons. The translation of "private" beliefs into public practice begins with the assumption that there is some meaning in the dichotomy itself. However, it is difficult to see how one can separate the individual from her/his cultural and social setting, which is essentially the mental gymnastics required in order to separate the private realm from the public. How do evangelical Christians translate their beliefs into practice? In my research with evangelical women, I found that the call to evangelize, which is usually understood to be a strong call to spread the "word" and a central belief of evangelical Christianity, is often practised in less than obvious ways. Many women reported that they did not want to "shove their beliefs down people's throats," and so their evangelism consisted of modelling what they saw as a Christian life. Thus, their "private" beliefs are lived in "public" in particular ways. Religious practice takes a multiplicity of forms, and does not necessarily mean words, but can mean attitude or a statement about "what I stand for."

Such an interpretation begs the question, to some extent, and misses the point that the community-living contract has a symbolic value that extends beyond private relations and, indeed, that the declaration that one is an evangelical Christian carries with it a particular set of beliefs and values that are symbolically represented through the individual. This is one reason that reliance on the public/private dichotomy is problematic to the resolution of the issues presented in *Trinity*. The artificiality of the dichotomy is illustrated by the shifting ways in which "public" is used throughout the case.

The Court shapes an interesting rhetoric that situates anti-homo-sexual teachings clearly within mainstream Christianity by stating, "In this particular case, it can reasonably be inferred that the B.C. legis-lature did not consider that training with a Christian philosophy was in itself against the public interest since it passed five bills in favour of TWU between 1969 and 1985."[33] The Court juxtaposes the BCCT's consideration of public interest and classroom atmosphere with the legislature and the public interest. It transforms the "homosexuality as sin" position of one specific Christian institution into the position of all Christian philosophy, and thus elevates the homosexuality as sin approach to one that is consistent with the "public" interest. What is initially characterized as a "private" interest is reframed as being within the boundaries of the "public" good.

The Court uses the public/private distinction to construct a protec-tive cloak around Trinity Western University. In the first line of the majority decision, the university is described as a "private" institution, and yet TWU students are public citizens, if we wish to work within the confines of the public/private dichotomy. The implication of the "private" designation is set out later in the decision:

> It is important to note that this is a private institution that is exempt-ed, in part, from the British Columbia human rights legislation and to which the Charter does not apply. To state that the voluntary adop-tion of a code of conduct based on a person's own religious beliefs, in a private institution, is sufficient to engage s.15 would be inconsistent with freedom of conscience and religion, which co-exist with the right to equality.[34]

But what, in effect, does this mean? Should a lack of state sponsor-ship put boundaries around the degree to which citizens are exempt from human rights considerations? Further on, the Court states, "The per-ception of the public regarding the religious beliefs of TWU graduates and the inference that those beliefs will produce an unhealthy school environment have, in our view, very little to do, if anything, with the particular expertise of the members of the BCCT."[35] Yet the BCCT is called upon, by statute, to consider the public interest! Who better to consider the intersection of human rights and public education?[36]

STATUTORY INTERPRETATION

Like the characterization of the issues, the process of statutory interpretation reflects the notion that law is objective and neutral. The interpretation of statutes is presented as a legal science that can reach through the application of legally established principles. Yet the process of statutory interpretation is fraught with opportunities for subjectivity beyond the "plain meaning" of the statute, which is the legal equivalent of "common sense." At this point, the questions "Whose common sense?" and "In what context?" must be asked. The problem here lies not in the process, for once we acknowledge the illusive nature of objectivity, we must simultaneously admit the subjectivity of any legal decision. The difficulty is in the ostensible objectivity of this process. Techniques of statutory interpretation serve to reify the notion of a positivistic approach to legal interpretation that play on science, rationality and neutrality.

Interestingly, statutory interpretation in *Trinity* is less about the meaning of the wording of the statutes involved than about who has the right to interpret them. Carol Smart argues that law privileges itself above other discourses.[37] In *Trinity*, we see a refining of that point in that the Court makes it clear that certain issues are beyond the purview and ability of administrative tribunals, thus articulating the hierarchy of interpretive bodies. The contest in *Trinity* is over the interpretation and application of human rights legislation, specifically as it impacts on section 4 of the *Teaching Profession Act*, which calls the BCCT to "establish, having regard to the public interest, standards for the education, professional responsibility and competence of its members." After finding that section 4 gives the BCCT powers beyond the simple determination of skills and knowledge to include a consideration of discriminatory practices, the Court then states that the expertise of the BCCT "does not qualify it to interpret the scope of human rights nor to reconcile competing rights," and again "the Council is not particularly well equipped to determine the scope of freedom of religion and conscience and to weight those rights against the right to equality in the context of a pluralistic society."[38] The BCCT is charged with gatekeeping responsibilities in relation to the teaching profession in British Columbia. In this capacity, and in the process of making its decision, the BCCT considered the social and legal climate in which gays, lesbians and bisexuals live. It turned to human rights legislation, specifically to the BC Human Rights Code and the Charter of Rights and Freedoms, for guidance.

In the process of interpreting section 4 of the *Teaching Profession Act*, the Court engages in an interesting shift of focus. Rather than discussing the links between the public interest, the atmosphere in public schools and the potential impact of anti-GLBT teachings or beliefs among teacher-trainees and their educational milieux on the public school atmosphere, the Court spends considerable energy on an analysis of the Community Standards Statement and its impact on the living conditions of students at TWU as well as the impact on gay and lesbian students who might wish to attend TWU. This is clearly outside of the considerations of the Act and not the focus or concern of the BCCT.

THE USE OF PRECEDENT

Precedent as a legal decision-making tool is, superficially, a means by which legal continuity is facilitated. It also ensures that "higher" courts of appeal particularly have some stabilizing impact on lower-court decisions. A more critical interpretation would identify the hegemonic impetus of precedent. Precedent gives the court the legal justifications for maintaining a position that "this is how it has always been, and this is how it shall remain." But, precedent is not so binding as it is popularly perceived to be, and those who are familiar with legal decisions know that what can be justified using legal precedent can just as easily be distinguished. In *Trinity*, the Court must consider its previous decision in *Ross*. Through a series of interesting logical leaps, the Court is able to both cite *Ross* on the importance of the public school atmosphere and the special role of teachers while at the same time distinguishing the *Ross* case from the facts of *Trinity*.

The majority decision relies on a number of cases to support its decision that the Community Standards document is not evidence of potential harm or actual harm to public school students. The *Ross* decision, too, dealt with "competing rights" and the education system. The Court cites *Ross* in stating that "teachers are a medium for the transmission of values. It is obvious that the pluralistic nature of society and the extent of diversity in Canada are important elements that must be understood by future teachers because they are the fabric of the society within which teachers operate and the reason why there is a need to respect and promote minority rights."[39] However, while the Court accepts the special position of the teacher and the mission of schools to "develop civic virtue and responsible citizenship, to educate in an environment free of bias, prejudice and intolerance," it is careful to distinguish the facts in *Ross* from the facts in *Trinity*:

> We are not in a situation where the Council is dealing with discriminatory conduct by a teacher, as in *Ross*. The evidence in this case is speculative, involving consideration of the potential future beliefs and conduct of graduates from a teacher education program taught exclusively at TWU. By contrast, in *Ross* the actual conduct of the teacher had, on the evidence, poisoned the atmosphere of the school.[40]

It is difficult to understand the artificial juxtaposition in this case. Malcolm Ross's actions were statements of his beliefs about Jews in the form of published pamphlets. There was no evidence of any other "action" in that case. The *Ross* decision is a clear example of the Court (correctly) refusing to support beliefs that incite hatred or prejudice under the guise of the freedoms guaranteed in the Charter. The Court goes on to further distinguish *Ross* from *Trinity Western* by stating, "Perceptions were a concern in *Ross*, but they were founded on conduct, not simply beliefs."[41] The distinction here is puzzling, as the conduct in *Ross* is an articulation of beliefs.

The Supreme Court goes beyond the interpretation/distinction of legal precedent to come to its decision. It also invokes precedent of a different sort — the religious roots of public universities. In order to do this, the Court diverts attention from the central worry of the BCCT —— the impact of sending teachers who believe that homosexuality is a sin into the public school system. It recharacterizes the issue to discuss the impact of that teaching on admissions policy and then declares that "one must consider the *true nature* of the undertaking and the context in which this occurs."[42] The Court is then able to garner support for Trinity Western by stating, "Many Canadian universities, including St. Francis Xavier University, Queen's University, McGill University and Concordia University College of Alberta, have traditions of religious affiliations."[43] This is both an odd comparison and a peculiar justification, in that it implies that a history of discrimination would support its continuance.

Mossman argues that "legal method defines its own boundaries: questions that are inside the defined boundaries can be addressed, but those outside of the boundaries are not 'legal' issues, however important they may be for 'politics' or 'morals,' etc."[44] Thus, the majority can declare the obviousness of a belief/practice dichotomy and preclude/ignore the centrality of their integration to evangelical Christians. The contents of religious beliefs remain outside the scope of consideration, even as the Court's decision is based on notions that run in direct opposition to evangelical teachings. Similarly, "legal method defines 'relevance' and accordingly excludes some ideas while admitting others."[45] The determination of relevance works with the techniques of legal method — the characterization of the issues, statutory interpretation and the use of precedent — to frame legal claims within the confines of particular boundaries and to legitimize legal decisions on their own terms, using a circular logic that often supports the status quo.

AN ALTERNATIVE PERSPECTIVE

To illustrate the fluid nature of legal reasoning and the possibility of an alternative reading that characterizes the issues in *Trinity Western* in another way, I would like to compare briefly the dissenting judgement of Madam Justice L'Heureux-Dubé to that of the majority. That there is a profound difference between the two decisions is illustrated by the identification of the "essence" of the issues being decided. For the majority, "the issue at the heart of this appeal is how to reconcile the religious freedoms of individuals wishing to attend TWU with the equality concerns of students in B.C.'s public schools system, concerns that may be shared with their parents and society generally." On the other hand, Madam Justice L'Heureux-Dubé states: "At its core, this case is about providing the best possible educational environment for public school students in British Columbia."[46]

After setting out the importance of a positive environment in schools, Madam Justice L'Heureux-Dubé conducts a detailed administrative law analysis that supports the adoption of a "patently unreasonable" standard of review, allowing the BCCT the broadest possible leeway in its decision-making. She states: "The BCCT's equality based approach, focused on supportive atmospheres in public school classrooms, merits a standards of review of patent unreasonableness because it directly engages the specialization of the tribunal."[47] She pushes the characterization of the issue even further as an administrative one by stating that there are no conflicting rights here. The standard of review is a separate issue from the Charter analysis. Madam Justice L'Heureux-Dubé argues that the job of the BCCT was to consider the atmosphere in the classroom, which was, in her view, exactly what they did.

While the majority decision seems to accept the notion that one can "love the sinner and hate the sin," the dissenting judgement challenges this position, arguing that the pressure to change "a practice so central to the identity of a protected and vulnerable minority" is harmful and damaging. In her decision, Madam Justice L'Heureux-Dubé minimizes the distinction between "public" and "private," by stating that "actions in the private sphere can have effects in the public realm." She is unwilling to shelter the potential consequences of "hating the sin." The Community Standards Contract is a public expression of discrimination and is an embodiment of discriminatory practices. While Madam Justice L'Heureux-Dubé acknowledges that tolerance is part of the Community Standards values, in the case of schools, she argues, this may simply not be enough.

Perhaps Madam Justice L'Heureux-Dubé is able to appreciate the risk of harm because she actually examines it. Her judgement makes extensive use of outside sources — from sociological studies to statements by EGALE — about the position of GLBT persons in society. Unlike the majority decision, which dismisses the risk of harm by stating, "Any concerns should go to risk, not general perceptions," Madam Justice L'Heureux-Dubé considers the lives of GLBT persons in context, which is one of anxiety, stress, elevated rates of suicide and increased risk of physical harm from the homophobic majority. Her characterization of the issues shifts the focus from competing rights to the atmosphere in public schools. She sees the BCCT's decision as being squarely within their expertise and within the parameters of the statutory mandate. Her use of the *same* precedent as that cited by the majority — the *Ross* case — supports her decision, which emphasizes the special role and responsibility of public school teachers. In the end, she upholds the BCCT's decision. The distinctly different nature of the decisions indicates the fluid nature of legal method and the shifting nature of the "objective" terrain of law.

***

Perhaps the most perplexing and practical dilemma that remains from this case is the question of who should be allowed in public classrooms. Like any other group, evangelical Christians do not have a monolithic approach to gays and lesbians. Ideologically, the prohibition against homosexuality is matched with equally strong injunctions about how to treat fellow human beings. By the same token, evangelical Christians make no secret about the fact that they believe homosexuality is wrong, and this means that self-identification as an evangelical inevitably means at least a symbolic association with the person who self-professes a commitment to an evangelical Christian religion. The notion of governance may be of some assistance in helping us to make sense of the *Trinity Western* decision from a broader perspective. In the end, the distinction between belief and practice that is relied upon so heavily in the majority decision becomes much less relevant when the symbolic nature of a set of beliefs is considered as an aspect of the patrolling of the boundaries of "normal" and the process of governance.

Joe Hermer and Alan Hunt articulate the links between governance and risk reduction in their discussion of official graffiti. They explore everything from road signs to instructions for condom use as graffiti, which they argue is a form of regulation that marks, scars and defaces public spaces. The concept of governance, derived from the work of Michel Foucault, "concentrates attention on social action that controls, restrains, limits, directs, molds, facilitates and empowers." Hermer and Hunt stress that governance is practices and discursive tactics. In the case of official graffiti, regulation is tied up with governance "from a distance" that does not necessarily involve the state. They identify "risk society" as a central aspect of governance in their discussion. Integral to governance is also the assessment of risk.[48]

In *Trinity*, the Court bases its decision on the following propositions: Belief and practice are separate. There is no evidence that evangelical Christians act on their belief that homosexuals are at risk. In other words, there is no evidence of harm. Risk of harm assessments have become de rigeur in rights conflicts of late. Quasi-actuarial evidence is presented as determinative of rights issues. In *Trinity*, the fact that there is no measured harm becomes evidence that there is no actual harm, or no risk of harm. And yet, "we love you, but we hate what you do" is supposed to be a comfort to GLBT citizens. Such ideologies support a general atmosphere of, at the very least, disapproval. Is disapproval sufficient evidence of harm? There is plenty of evidence on harm if that is the direction the weighing of rights must take.

Elizabeth Kaminski explores the complex relationship between lesbians, a hostile environment and health. She has found that lesbians who lived in an environment hostile to homosexuality experienced significant health problems such as depression, anxiety, eating disorders and drug abuse.[49] The existence of work like Kaminski's raises the question of why this is not used as evidence of risk along with the vague construction of harm from denial of freedom of religion. Sharon Nichols reports that schools leave little room for the GLBT identity, and this is part of the overall atmosphere of intolerance and rejection faced by those individuals.[50]

Religious freedom is, indeed, a critical component of the rights and freedoms we are working to delineate as Canadians. Evangelical Christians are in a peculiar position in relation to that hegemony — they are on the margins of the mainstream in terms of their beliefs and practices, and have themselves at times been less than fully protected by rights discourse. However, the harms perpetuated by a denial of religious freedom are at least alluded to in *Trinity*, but the evidence of data on the harms experienced by gays and lesbians in a society that is undeniably homophobic are glossed over, returning us to questions about how issues are characterized in law.

Assessment of risk becomes part of the governance process, especially as it relates to the hegemonic reinforcement of "the normal." In the *Trinity Western* case, "normal" is constructed as heterosexual relations. Freedom of religion becomes the shield behind which homophobia hides. In this way, *Trinity Western* becomes part of the mechanism of governance of that normal. In this instance, the "signs" are less obvious than those examined by Hunt and Hermer. But, as a marker of a particular set of beliefs, evangelical Christians become symbolic signs of the heterosexual "normal," which incorporates a particular kind of homophobia — the characterization of the gay/lesbian/bisexual as a "sinner." This reinforces the anti-gay/lesbian/bisexual hegemonic impetus of the broader society in which we live.

NOTES

I would like to acknowledge the financial support of the Social Science and Humanities Research Council of Canada for this research. Thanks are owed to Chris Canning, Caroline Williams and Joy-Ann Smith for their valuable research assistance. I also wish to thank Heather McCuaig for her valuable insights and careful reading of an earlier draft of this chapter.

1. Neither the case nor the Trinity Western policy talks about bisexual or transgendered individuals. The policy talks about "homosexuality." The case discusses "homosexuals" in the majority decision and homosexuals, bisexuals, gays and lesbians in the dissent. In the interests of inclusivity, and in recognition that the protection of sexual orientation should be understood to encompass the widest possible range of persons who are denigrated or discriminated against on the basis of their sexuality, I will use GLBT throughout the chapter.

2. See, for example, Mary Jane Mossman, "Feminism and Legal Method: The Difference it Makes," *Australian Journal of Law and Society* 3 (1986), 30–52; Joe Hermer and Alan Hunt, "Official Graffiti of the Everyday," *Law and Society Review* 30 (1996), 455–480; Carol Smart, *Feminism and the Power of Law* (London: Routledge, 1989); Carol Smart, "Law's Power, the Sexed Body, and Feminist Discourse," *Journal of Law and Society* 17, no. 2 (1990), 194–210; and Michel Foucault, *Discipline and Punish: The Birth of the Prison* (New York: Vintage, 1977).

3. There have been some interesting developments on same-sex marriage in the past two years. The solemnization of marriage falls under the jurisdiction of the provinces under the constitutional division of powers. The Courts of Appeal in British Columbia, Ontario and Quebec have each held that bars to same-sex marriage are unconstitutional. See *Barbeau v. British Columbia (Attorney General)*, 2003 BCCA 251; *Catholic Civil Rights League v. Hendricks*, 2004-03-19; *Halpern v. Canada*, 2003-06-10. Nonetheless, the issue remains unresolved as the federal government has sent a reference to the Supreme Court of Canada on the constitutional question of same-sex marriage.

4. For a detailed discussion of this, see Kathleen A. Lahey, *Are We "Persons" Yet? Law and Sexuality in Canada* (Toronto: University of Toronto Press, 1999).

5. See Dianne Pothier, "M'Aider, Mayday: Section 15 of the *Charter* in Distress," *National Journal of Constitutional Law* 6 (1996), 295; and *Egan v. Canada* [1995] 2 S.C.R. 513.

6. Miram Smith, *Lesbian and Gay Rights in Canada: Social Movements and Equality-Seeking, 1971–1995* (Toronto: University of Toronto Press, 1999), 75.

7. Smart, *Feminism and the Power of Law*.

8. Lahey, *Are We "Persons" Yet?* 25.

9. *R. v. Big M. Drugmart Ltd.*, [1985] 1 S.C.R. 295.

10. *R. v. Edwards Books and Arts Ltd.*, [1986] 2 S.C.R. 713.

11. Bruce MacDougall, "Silence in the Classroom: Limits on Homosexual Expression and Visibility in Education and the Privileging of Homophobic Religious Ideology," *Saskatchewan Law Review* 61 (1998), 41–86.

12. Ibid., 83.

13. *Trinity Western University v. British Columbia College of Teachers*, [2000] 1 S.C.R. 772, 2001 SCC 31.

14. The university's contract cites from the *Living Bible*. In fuller detail, two of these key references read: "Those who live immoral lives, who are idol worshipers, adulterers or homosexuals — will have no share in his Kingdom" (I Cor. 6:9) "Yes, these laws are made to identify as sinners all who are immoral and impure: homosexuals, kidnappers, liars, and all others who do things that contradict the glorious Good News of our blessed God, whose messenger I am" (1 Tim. 1:10–11). Since the Supreme Court decision, Trinity Western has altered its Community Standards Statement somewhat to eliminate the reference to "homosexuality." It states that students will "refrain from practices that are contrary to biblical teaching. These include, but are not limited to, drunkenness (Eph. 5:18), swearing or use of profane language (Eph. 4:29, 5:4, Jas. 3:1–2), harassment (Jn. 13:34–35; Rom. 12:9–21; Eph. 4:31), all forms of dishonesty including cheating and stealing (Prov. 12:22; Col. 3:9, Eph. 4:28), abortion (Ex. 20:13; Ps. 139:13–16), involvement in the occult (Acts 19:19; Gal. 5:19), and viewing of pornography (1 Cor. 6:12-20; Eph. 4:17–24; 1Thess. 4:3–8; Rom. 2:26–27; 1Tim. 1:9–10). Observe biblical principles for marriage and sexual relationships. Members of the TWU community agree to respect the biblical teaching that sexual intimacy is to be practiced only within the context of marriage between a husband and a wife (Genesis 2:23–24) and to keep their sexual behaviour consistent with this teaching. Also, married members of the community agree to respect and maintain the sanctity of marriage and to take every positive step to resolve conflict and avoid divorce."

15. Lori Beaman, "Sexual Orientation and Legal Discourse: The *Egan* Case," *Canadian Journal of Law and Society* 14, no. 2 (1999), 173-201.

16. Mossman, "Feminism and Legal Method," 325.

17. Ibid., 327.

18. In re French 37 N.B.R. 359 (1905) Reference re Meaning of the Word "Persons" in S.24 of the B.N.A. Act, S.C.R. 276 [1928].

19. Mossman, "Feminism and Legal Method," 333.

20. *R. v. Big M. Drugmart Ltd.*, [1985] 1 S.C.R. 295.

21. See, for example, Lori Beaman, *Shared Beliefs, Different Lives: Women's Identities in Evangelical Context* (St. Louis, MI: Chalice Press, 1999); Lori Beaman,

"Collaborators or Resistors? Evangelical Women in Atlantic Canada," *Atlantis* 22 (1997), 9–18; Nancy Ammerman, *Bible Believers: Fundamentalists in the Modern World* (New Brunswick, NJ: Rutgers University Press, 1987); R. Stephen Warner, *New Wine in Old Wineskins: Evangelicals and Liberals in a Small-Town Church* (Berkeley: University of California Press, 1988).

22. For a discussion of a variety of approaches by congregations to issues of sexuality, see for example, Stephen Ellingson, Nelson Trebbe, Martha van Haitsma and Edward O. Laumann, "Religion and the Politics of Sexuality," *Journal of Contemporary Ethnography* 30 (2001), 3–55.

23. Trinity Western University application for approval statement, paragraph 3. The boundaries between "us" and "them" is also illustrated by the following statement: "You might not absolutely agree with the Standards. They might not be consistent with what you believe. However, when you decided to come to TWU, you agreed to accept these responsibilities. If you cannot support and abide by them, then perhaps you should look into UIG [University of Instant Gratification] or AGU [Anything Goes University]."

24. Trinity Western University Community Standards Statement, p. 16. The TWO Statement for staff can be found at ww.twu.ca/hr/documents/responsibilities-of-membership.aspx.

25. Brian Laythe, Deborah Finkel and Lee A. Kirkpatrick, "Predicting Prejudice from Religious Fundamentalism and Right-Wing Authoritarianism: A Multiple Regression Approach," *Journal for the Scientific Study of Religion* 40 (2001), 1–10, quoting Lyman Kelstedt and C. Smidt, "Measuring Fundamentalism: An Analysis of Different Operational Strategies," *Journal for the Scientific Study of Religion* 30 (1991), 259–278.

26. Laythe, Finkel and Kirkpatrick, "Predicting Prejudice from Religious Fundamentalism and Right-Wing Authoritarianism," 2.

27. Ibid., 8.

28. CBC Radio, *This Morning*, "The Trinity Western Affair," June 13, 2001.

29. Kenneth N. Taylor et al., *The Living Bible, Paraphrased* (Wheaton, IL: Tyndale House Publishers, 1971).

30. See, for example, Daniel A. Helminiak, *What the Bible Really Says about Homosexuality* (San Francisco: Alamo Square Press, 1994); L. William Countryman, *Dirt, Greed and Sex: Sexual Ethics in the New Testament and Their Implications for Today* (Philadelphia: Fortress Press, 1988); Robin Scroggs, *The New Testament and Homosexuality: Contextual Backgrounds for Contemporary Debate* (Philadelphia: Fortress Press, 1983); George R. Edwards, "A Critique of Creationist Homophobia," *Homosexuality and Religion* 18 (1989), 95–118; and Martin Samuel Cohen, "The Biblical Prohibition of Homosexual Intercourse," *Journal of Homosexuality* 19 (1990), 3–20.

31. John Corvino, "Why Shouldn't Tommy and Jim Have Sex? A Defense of Homosexuality," in John Corvino, ed., *Same Sex: Debating the Ethics, Science,*

and Culture of Homosexuality (New York: Rowman and Littlefield, 1999), 13.

32. See John Boswell, *Christianity, Social Tolerance, and Homosexuality: Gay People in Western Europe from the Beginning of the Christian Era to the Fourteenth Century* (Chicago: The University of Chicago Press, 1980); "Revolutions, Universals, and Sexual Categories," in Corvino, ed., *Same Sex*, 185–202; and "Concepts, Experience and Sexuality," in Gary David Comstock and Susan E. Henking, eds., *Que(e)rying Religion: A Critical Anthology* (New York: Continuum, 1997), 116–129.

33. *Trinity Western University v. British Columbia College of Teachers*, para. 34.

34. Ibid.

35. Ibid.

36. There are other aspects of the characterization of the issues that play an important role in the outcome of the case. One of the central legal issues is the question of the appropriate standard of review — whether a "correctness" standard should be used or a review for "patent unreasonableness." The majority decides that the former is the appropriate standard, while the dissenting judgement focuses on the latter as the appropriate choice. I have not dealt with this issue in any great detail here as there are other aspects of the case that provide more interesting analytical fodder.

37. Smart, *Feminism and the Power of Law*. See also Annie Bunting, "Feminism, Foucault and Law as Power/Knowledge," *Alberta Law Review* 30 (1992), 829–842.

38. *Trinity Western University v. British Columbia College of Teachers*, paras. 17 and 19, respectively.

39. *Ross v. New Brunswick School District No. 15*, [1996] 1 S.C.R. 825.

40. *Trinity Western University v. British Columbia College of Teachers*, para. 19.

41. Ibid.

42. Ibid., para. 34. Emphasis added.

43. Ibid.

44. Mossman, "Feminism and Legal Method," 332.

45. Ibid.

46. *Trinity Western University v. British Columbia College of Teachers*, para. 47.

47. Ibid., para. 60.

48. Hermer and Hunt, "Official Graffiti of the Everyday," 456, 458.

49. Elizabeth Kaminski, "Lesbian Health: Social Context, Sexual Identity, and Well-Being," *Journal of Lesbian Studies* 4 (2000), 87–101.

50. Sharon L. Nichols, "Gay, Lesbian and Bisexual Youth: Understanding Diversity

and Promoting Tolerance in Schools," *The Elementary School Journal* 99 (1999), 505–519. For a more extensive discussions of the "harm" suffered by GLBT youth, see Mary B. Harris, ed., *School Experiences of Gay and Lesbian Youth* (New York: Haworth Press, 1997).

PART II

ORGANIZATIONS IN ACTION

CHAPTER 5

LOCATING LANDMARKS: PRODUCING AN EDUCATIONAL VIDEO ON WOMEN AND THE LAW

Jan Kainer

That a woman could be put on Canada's highest court has opened a door that had never been opened before and now I would think it can't be shut again.

— Mary Eberts, Lawyer, Eberts, Symes, Street & Corbett

At the beginning of the twenty-first century we are well on our way to having a profession that is composed almost equally of males and females.

— Mary Jane Mossman, Professor of Law,
Osgoode Hall at York University

You need to engage the law as legal actors ... feminist litigation cannot proceed without the co-operation of grassroots women, women who are actually experiencing discrimination.

— Carissima Mathen, Former Director of Litigation,
Women's Legal Education Action Fund

In this chapter I reflect upon the process of developing a conceptual framework for an educational video on women and the law, which was supported by the Equity Initiatives Department at the Law Society of Upper Canada.[1] The aim of the project was twofold: to pay tribute to women's contributions to Canadian law with particular focus on women's journeys through the legal system of the twentieth century, and to highlight the many contributions women have made to gender equality law which have also addressed issues of gender bias within the legal profession. Anyone familiar with research on women and the law knows the enormity of this task. How do we realistically convey the sweep of women's contributions to Canadian law over the past century to students unfamiliar with legal matters? Deliberating on this question opened up a line of inquiry about how we conceptualize law and women's place within it. The following discussion outlines the theoretical concerns of understanding the relationship of law to society and the nature of legal decision making, issues which formed the basis for thinking about ways to frame the video project.

THE ISSUES

THE LAW–SOCIETY RELATION

Any broad investigation of the law must incorporate an analysis of law's relationship to society. There is significant debate as to whether the law operates as a mechanism to define and structure social relations. A recent contribution to this debate has been made by sociologist Elizabeth Comack. In her book entitled *Locating Law,* Comack attempts to *locate* the social impact of the law within a broader social context of race, class and gender relations. In this perspective, the law has the potential to substantially influence social relations and it asserts that the intersectionality of class, race and gender systems produce uneven social relations that subordinate disadvantaged groups.[2] Given this analysis, an understanding of women and the law should address how women from diverse social backgrounds, and living under varying social conditions, are affected by the legal system. Legal decisions affecting women's role in society, as well as women's participation in the legal system, are an obvious starting point in an analysis of women's participation in Canadian law. A further issue that arises in relation to legal decision making and its impact on social relations concerns the conceptualization of the judicial process.

CONCEPTUALIZING LAW

Further to the issue of placing law within a broader societal context is the problem of how to understand or theorize the nature of the judicial system. A traditional view assumes that the law operates in a technical manner in which legal method imposes a strict set of rules that are applied to determine the relevant facts of a case, that legal principles can be clearly interpreted and applied to determine fair legal outcomes and that judges arrive at the "truth" by remaining objective and impartial. This view of the law is widely contested and needs to be contrasted with a perspective that emphasizes the changing and indeterminate nature of legal logic. A more critical perspective interrogates well-established assumptions embedded in traditional views of the law, such as the problem of judicial neutrality as well as the paradoxical or changeable nature of legal decision making. Both of these themes need to be incorporated into a discussion of women and the law. The notion of judicial neutrality that often assumes judges exercise decision making without reference to social context raises serious questions for feminist legal theorists who argue that acknowledging social difference based on class, race and gender is crucial to advancing equality rights for women and other minorities in Canadian society. The paradoxical nature of law is evident in the unpredictable outcome of landmark legal decisions on women. For instance, female litigants who take all the risks of moving equality claims forward do not often benefit from their efforts; successful legal decisions may actually have contradictory effects and result in losses rather than gains for women; and legal decisions may result in a hollow victory when resources are not allocated to substantiate a rights claim. A significant barrier to women achieving their legal goals is connected to the masculine bias of the law.

GENDER BIAS IN THE LAW

Confronting masculinist bias within the law has been an intractable problem since the nineteenth century when the cultural and social definition of the good lawyer was to behave like a "gentleman" — a thoroughly white middle-class masculine construct.[3] This particular view of lawyers has pervaded the legal profession to the present day, and it has been extremely difficult for women in law school and in legal practice to confront the sexism that permeates the profession. Although women now comprise at least 50 percent of students at law schools, the culture of the profession is still defined by a male professional model. Women lawyers' experiences of gender bias have been the subject of much academic writing, and numerous task forces and reports have been written documenting the discriminatory barriers experienced by women in the profession. The process of exclusion is far reaching, involving all stages of a woman's career from law school, to articling, to achieving partnership. Women lawyers report a variety of barriers to advancement that include sexual harassment, blocked opportunities to leadership positions, limited access to articling positions, difficulties balancing family and work responsibilities and gender bias in the courtroom. The barriers experienced by racialized women, lesbians and women with disabilities are particularly severe. That women continue to experience exclusionary pressures in law is a sensitive issue within the profession, despite the vast amount of empirical evidence documenting its existence.[4]

The frustrations concerning gender bias within the profession came to a head in the early 1990s when the Canadian Bar Association (CBA) struck a task force to examine gender inequality and discrimination in the legal profession. In 1991 the task force began its research and consultations with the legal community and released its report, *Touchstones for Change: Equality, Diversity and Accountability* in 1993. Madam Justice Bertha Wilson, a former Supreme Court Judge, chaired the task force and took a leading role in its argumentation (hence the report is often referred to as the Wilson Report). It is an extremely important document and uncovers the systematic and systemic gender discrimination women lawyers of diverse backgrounds and experiences face on a daily basis from clients, colleagues and (male) judges. Significantly, the report is clearly informed by a gender perspective of equality: "Equality demands more than simply 'allowing' newcomers into the profession and forcing them to meet existing standards. It must include a reassessment of the standards themselves, and a recognition that they were created exclusively on the basis of male life experiences."[5]

This critique of the legal profession is at the core of the Wilson Report's analysis of the barriers to women's equal treatment in the profession. The report also questions "the extent to which an exclusively male perspective has conditioned the law, and in effect, suffused it with gender bias."[6] *Touchstones for Change* stands out as a major achievement within the legal profession in Canada, and it represents an important landmark for women in the law. However, to date, very few of the dozens of recommendations have been implemented or responded to by legal associations and law schools. As stated in the report, to fully address the "behaviours, attitudes, institutional policies and practices [in] the structure of the profession itself"[7] that condition gender bias is a huge challenge. It is important to point out that this challenge stems from women's engagement and participation in the law. Women from various walks of life have questioned the taken-for-granted masculinist assumptions that underpin the entire legal system. Today, women lawyers continue to press for changes around who is permitted access to the study and practice of law, about how law firms treat women and minorities and whether equity issues are being fully addressed and understood by lawyers within the profession. Women lawyers have also engaged in a litigation strategy based on a feminist approach to the law. This feminist strategy returns us to the theme of locating law within a historical and social context.

Feminist Legal Advocacy

Feminist legal advocates in Canada have broken new ground by insisting that equality claims be understood in their historical specificity. In 1985 the Women's Legal Education Action Fund (LEAF) was founded to advocate on behalf of women. Using Charter litigation, under the Canadian Charter of Rights and Freedoms, LEAF intervened in numerous gender equality cases, with the express purpose of presenting to the court the social and historical circumstances surrounding women's lives and relating these to specific legal issues.[8] The pivotal role of LEAF, and other advocacy groups such as the National Association of Women and the Law (NAWL), in developing new approaches to equality litigation is critical to understanding women's engagement in Canadian law. Applying feminism to the law entails challenging the gender bias inherent in legal reasoning. By calling attention to gender difference and other diversity issues, the feminist challenge acknowledges that class, gender, race and other differences matter in the social world and that it is not possible to ignore social distinctions if substantive equality is to be achieved. Advancing new approaches to equality litigation owes a great deal to LEAF and the feminist lawyers — sometimes referred to as the founding mothers — who have sustained a lasting Charter litigation strategy for women's equality. The foundation of LEAF stands as another important legal landmark for women.

THE PROJECT

These complex dimensions of the law — including the law–society relation, the mode of conceptualizing the law, gender bias in the law and feminist legal advocacy — provided the conceptual foundation for the video project. The video was co-produced with Diane Higgs who operates a video production firm specializing in educational videos. Higgs and I consulted with members of the Equity Initiatives Department at the Law Society of Upper Canada (LSUC), the regulatory body for lawyers in Ontario, as well as with the Feminist Legal Advisory Committee (FLAC) and other women lawyers at the LSUC who expressed interest in the project. As mentioned earlier, the initial project had a twofold objective. First, we wanted to introduce university undergraduate and high school students to the history of women's participation in the law, particularly as lawyers, and their efforts to gain recognition as equals with men in the legal profession. In making the video, we addressed gender bias within the legal profession through interviews with women lawyers and academics.[9] We asked them about their own law school experience and compared their stories with the struggles of Canada's first woman lawyer Clara Brett Martin, who fought to gain admittance to the legal profession in the nineteenth century. The purpose of the comparison was to stress the continuities from the late 1800s to that of the 1970s and into the present day concerning issues of sexism within the legal profession. Conversations with the interviewees about their law school experience produced colourful and amusing anecdotes of women's experiences of sexism in law school, as well as more serious observations about lawyering. For example, when Mary Eberts, an experienced and highly respected constitutional lawyer, was asked what advice she would offer to women graduating from law school, she remarked:

> Well, I repeat the advice [to new women lawyers] that is given apocryphally to almost everybody that goes into those large firms, [that] used to be given only to men but is [now] given to both men and women. Kiss your spouse and children goodbye because the life that one is expected to lead in a large firm, especially if one who is a beginner, is one of very rigorous dedication to the affairs of that firm and

its clients. The hours are very, very, long and the subjective requirements of loyalty and putting the firm and its clients above almost everything else are very strongly put.[10]

The second part of the objective was to educate students about women's struggles to achieve gender equality under the law. This objective was far more difficult to bring to a video screen. After pursuing discussions about the video with the Advisory Committee at the Law Society of Upper Canada, we decided that an effective way to present the wide-ranging issues in a video format was by focusing on legal landmarks, particularly Supreme Court decisions. We pinpointed legal cases that had a broad impact on the lives of women — specifically those which have affected the material and ideological conditions of women's social and economic position in Canada. Particular cases, which are discussed below, were seen to illuminate the gender-specific nature of legal decision making and to point to the importance of the law–society relation. We identified four broad categories of particular significance to women:

1. Citizenship or legal personhood that challenges liberal legal discourse and asserts the inclusion of women as equal citizens with men in a liberal democracy. Included in this category are cases pertaining to the right to equal participation with men in the public world, such as the inclusion of women justices on the bench.

2. Women's control of "the body." This category includes legal decisions that influence women's control over reproduction such as fertility and abortion, as well as violence against women and sexual harassment.

3. Women's right to own "property" and the right to "economic security" that incorporates access to the public world of work and the right to equal pay continue to be a struggle for women. Historically, the right to land ownership and possession of property was not a legal right for women.

4. "The family" and struggles around challenging patriarchal norms; legal battles concerning traditional family relations (marriage, child custody, definition of the family) are relevant here.[11]

With these four categories in mind, we identified the following landmark cases as being pertinent: the 1929 Person's Case regarding personhood; *Morgentaler v. The Queen* concerning women's struggles for control of their bodies and reproductive choices; *Murdoch v. Murdoch* on the division of family property; *M. v. H.* on the definitions of the family; and *R. v. Desmond* and *R.D.S. v. Her Majesty The Queen* on the importance of race and judicial neutrality. As discussed further below, some of these cases examine the activities of LEAF, which obtained intervenor status at the Supreme Court level; some highlight the historic and significant role of women litigants; and others emphasize the unique contribution of female judges in legal decision making.

In most instances, we deliberately chose cases whose legal claims benefit the general interests of women. But thinking about legal decisions in this way immediately raises a series of critical questions. At first glance, there may be pitfalls in emphasizing "landmarks" because we must consider the issue of "whose landmark?" As post-structuralists point out, when we talk about "women," we have to ask ourselves who do we really mean? Who is the category woman?[12] Which women have benefited from the legal process? Which women have been successful litigants, and which have been excluded? Who does the case represent? In framing the video, we were cognizant of the need to incorporate a diversity of women who are engaged in the legal process and who are working towards achieving gender equality. As previously discussed, we wanted to convey to our viewers that legal actions often result in different outcomes for women who are from different racial, class and cultural backgrounds.

BLINDFOLDED JUSTICE

That the legal process operates differently for women as compared with men, and treats people from dominant groups differently than those from minority groups, undermines the assumption that the law is gender or race neutral. As already noted, many legal theorists question whether the law operates in an impartial and objective manner. To help explain the complexities of the legal system, and to bring a more nuanced view of the law to the screen, we borrowed another theme from Comack's discussion about the meaning of law that is symbolized in the Justice imagery. By featuring the icon of Justice — the image of the blindfolded (white) woman wearing white robes and surrounded by attributes that include scales and a sword — we wished to convey to the viewer that commonly held assumptions about the meaning of the law, typically presented in popular discourse, are widely contested. In the icon of Justice, sometimes referred to as Justicia, we see the diverse ambiguities that are embedded in law.[13] First, the blindfold personifies many meanings surrounding the notion of judicial neutrality. In previous centuries, the blindfold implied that Justice must not be misled by powerful litigants who seek to intimidate nor must she be unrighteous to the weak and vulnerable. In the modern era, the blindfold has come to have a deeper and more problematic meaning as Comack explains: "That she is blindfolded suggests that she is not swayed or influenced by the characteristics of those who stand before her — she sees no class, no race, no gender distinctions."[14] This notion of judicial neutrality raises serious questions for feminist legal theorists. As I discuss below, the video took up the discussion concerning judicial method in two prominent Supreme Court decisions featuring female judges.

Second, in the Justice imagery lie other tensions inherent in the law, which are symbolized by the sword and scales. The scales represent a device connoting balance in decision making. In centuries past, the scales were viewed as personifying a balance in which punishment was neither too harsh nor too lenient; in another more recent interpretation, the scales hold principles of law on one side and facts on the other.[15] The latter meaning symbolizes the conventional understanding that "pure reason" and the rule of law combine to produce just outcomes; a problematic concept for many legal decision makers today. Still, another interpretation of the scales is the need to balance conflicting rights under constitutional guarantees, such as the Charter of Rights and Freedoms.[16]

Finally, the sword is a reminder that the law is a potent force that has substantial impact on the lives of citizens. The sword of Justice "cuts the knot of conflict" when other approaches to resolving disputes are ineffectual.[17] The image of blindfolded Justice offers a powerful symbol of how the law is constructed in our culture. In the video, we invoked this image because we want to urge viewers to question taken-for-granted assumptions about the purpose and role of law in society. The Justice imagery provides a symbolic device for understanding the complexity of the judicial process and can be used to interpret prominent legal decisions on gender equality.

THE LEGAL LANDMARKS

What follows is a brief summary of the legal cases featured in the video and an explanation of how we saw them fitting in with the project's legal themes. We titled the video *In the Face of Justice: Women's Challenge to Law in Canada* to reinforce the female image of blindfolded Justice.

Women Enter the Public Sphere:
Clara Brett Martin and the 1929 Person's Case

Clara Brett Martin, Canada's first woman lawyer, was admitted into the legal profession in Ontario in 1897. She came from an affluent and highly educated family whose connections to Ontario's progressive elite facilitated her admittance. Although Clara Brett Martin experienced hostility and alienation on account of her gender, particularly at law school, her class and race background secured for her a privileged position within the legal community.[18] Clara Brett Martin's struggle to enter law encouraged other Canadian women to fight for admittance to the profession. Mabel Penery French applied for enrollment to the Barristers' Society of New Brunswick in 1902, only to find she was not legally a "person" and therefore disentitled to practise law. French's efforts to enter law spurred legal action by five Alberta women who challenged the meaning of "person" under the *British North America Act*. The Person's Case was launched by a small group of white middle-class professional women,[19] known as the "famous five," who asked the government to appoint a woman to the Senate. The "famous five" were successful in bestowing citizenship rights in 1929 (although Emily Murphy who was the named appointee to the Senate was never made a senator), yet this important decision did not extend privileges of citizenship to all Canadian women. Status Indian women were not granted the right to vote until 1960,[20] and Aboriginal women, such as Jeanette Levell, did not engage in legal battles to gain recognition as "Indian persons" having the same rights as male Indians under the *Indian Act* until the mid-1980s.[21] The celebrated Person's Case is a clear example of a citizenship right that broadened rights for a particular group of women, but underscores the historical process of social exclusion for "other" women.

In the Person's Case, blindfolded Justice plays an ambiguous role in that gender is clearly in sight of the judiciary, indeed it lies at the heart of the problem, but by acknowledging gender difference the Canadian courts are unsure how women "fit" into the public world. Further, the "women" being acknowledged are of a specific race (and class). This dilemma of gender difference persisted throughout the twentieth century. In a sense, what the Person's Case accomplished was to take off the blindfold — or perhaps allow Justicia to peek through it — as she debated the status and treatment of her newly acknowledged citizens.

R. v. Desmond

Equality struggles for women in the early part of the twentieth century stretched beyond gender. In 1946, Viola Desmond, an African-Canadian middle-class woman living in Nova Scotia, led an impressive legal battle against racial segregation. When Desmond refused to sit in the balcony of a movie theatre, thereby opposing a racially segregated policy, she was physically and forcibly removed by the police and put into jail for the night. As Connie Backhouse explains, Desmond was charged with tax evasion under the *Theatres, Cinematographs and Amusements Act* of Nova Scotia because she was one cent short of paying the full price of a main floor ticket.[22] Although she lost the case based on technical grounds of criminal procedure, the publicity surrounding the litigation heightened awareness about the need for racial equality. The Black community of Nova Scotia went on to resist segregation in schools and churches and to promote greater access to occupations and residential neighbourhoods.

While the *Desmond* case may not be widely known as a legal landmark, its significance within Canadian equality law demands that it receive greater attention. It plainly illustrates the limitations of a race-blind legal system, an approach to law that denies the relevance of race in situations where racial inequality is self-evident. Rather than the case tackling racial segregation head on, the legal approach deflected attention away from the real issue of racial discrimination. As Backhouse comments, *R. v. Desmond* demonstrates "how Canadians hide their racist past through raceless measures."[23]

Murdoch v. Murdoch

As more women entered public life throughout the twentieth century, particularly in the post-war period of the 1960s and 1970s, their demands for equality became louder. The second wave of the women's movement advanced equality claims in a variety of arenas and individual women began to make greater demands for legal rights. A particularly important legal case that gained widespread support from the women's movement concerned division of family property upon divorce. In the early 1970s, Irene Murdoch sought a divorce and claimed one-half interest in the Alberta ranch she and her husband had farmed together for more than a decade. At issue in this divorce case was the fact that Mrs. Murdoch had been intimately involved in all aspects of running the ranch, including "haying, raking, swathing, moving, driving trucks and tractors, dehorning [cattle], vaccinating cattle and branding cattle."[24] While Irene Murdoch was ultimately unsuccessful at both the Supreme Court of Alberta and the Supreme Court of Canada, which dismissed her case in 1973, her legal action prompted public outcry leading to sweeping changes of family law reform acts across the country. It is a historic irony that Irene Murdoch lost her case because "applicable legal principles did not entitle a wife to share in property owned by her husband,"[25] yet it encouraged policy-makers to adopt the concept of equal partnership in marriage that was to benefit a great number of Canadian women. While *Murdoch* was path-breaking, especially in view of the attitudes of the day, it would take several decades before another legal landmark would impel major family law reform.

M. v. H.

In *M. v. H.*, the Supreme Court ruled on whether a woman in a lesbian relationship is obligated to pay spousal support to her former partner. In their decade-long relationship, M. and H. established an advertising agency in Toronto, although H. took primary responsibility of business concerns while M. took responsibility of domestic matters. M. sought support payments from H. when their relationship broke down in 1992. In 1999, the Court ruled that the Ontario *Family Law Act* applies to same-sex couples because a definition of common-law spouse that excludes same-sex couples discriminates on the basis of sexual orientation. As a result of this ruling, the Supreme Court required Ontario to amend the *Family Law Reform Act*. The Ontario government responded by introducing legislation that amended not only the *Family Law Reform Act* but other Ontario provincial statutes as well by adding the clause "same-sex partner."[26] In the eyes of M., the outcome of her legal action was a hollow victory, as she wished to affirm equality of gays and lesbians with married heterosexual couples. Instead, the amendments had the discriminatory effect of setting gays and lesbians apart from heterosexual "spouses" who have the legal right to marry and are recognized in the statutes separately from same-sex partners. M. filed an application at the Supreme Court to rehear her case, but it was turned down.[27]

M. v. H. not only raises questions over the definition of spouse in Ontario's family law, but it is also connected to a broader political debate over definitions of the family. For some people outside the lesbian and gay community, the extension of rights and obligations under family law to same-sex couples is an affront to the established patriarchal order.[28] For others within the lesbian and gay community, regulation of same-sex relationships under family law poses serious concerns about assimilation of gay men and lesbians into traditional heterosexual familial ideals. Not all members of the gay and lesbian community wish to have their relationships subject to state scrutiny and would prefer to be excluded from such a regime.[29] The case of *M. v. H.* tells us much about the politics of social inclusion/exclusion in the context of political struggle for legal reform. M. felt excluded and discriminated against on the basis of her minority status and sought equal entitlements with the dominant heterosexual majority. Meanwhile, others in the lesbian and gay community questioned the "strategy of seeking family status, pointing out that it is not necessarily a radical achievement to be equated with heterosexual people."[30] The struggle over legal strategy is significant in that it demonstrates how legal reform and legal decision-making produces inconsistent and even contradictory outcomes for those within equality-seeking groups.

Political action by individuals and advocacy groups play a crucial role in reforming law. Women who took legal action against gender discrimination — Emily Murphy, Viola Desmond, Jeanette Levell, M. and Irene Murdoch, for instance — were fundamental to the process of challenging legal thinking. These women took personal risks to press forward on legal rights that would improve their own lives as well as the lives of many other Canadian women. By featuring cases in which women initiated legal complaints, *In the Face of Justice* demonstrates that resistance often comes from "ordinary" women demanding social change. Yet it is the paradox of law, as Mary Jane Mossman points out,[31] that is also evident in these stories. In the example of Irene Murdoch, her loss of the division of family property triggered major family law reform that resulted in gains for women who filed for divorce after her case had been decided by the Supreme Court. In *M. v. H.*, M. was successful in obtaining support payments from her partner but was unsuccessful in convincing the court of her equality arguments concerning lesbian and gay rights under family law.

Morgentaler v. The Queen

Morgentaler is significant because, for the first time, a woman was present on the Supreme Court to influence legal decision making on a gender specific matter. In *Morgentaler v. The Queen*,[32] the Supreme Court struck down the law that made abortion a criminal offence, stating that the law violated women's rights to "life, liberty and security of the person" under section 7 of the Charter of Rights and Freedoms. As a result of this 1988 decision, free-standing abortion clinics that functioned without therapeutic abortion committees were legally permitted to continue abortion services. The women's movement had been lobbying and protesting for twenty years to ensure women's right to terminate a pregnancy. *Morgentaler* is a pivotal landmark in that it reflects intense political struggles by feminists to define the contours of debate on abortion — setting forth the view that women, who remain socially disadvantaged and subordinate to men in society, must have the right to freely decide to end a pregnancy. Although the question of whether women can legally access abortion services in private clinics was decided in *Morgentaler,* how those services are funded and how women can easily access free-standing clinics continue to be major issues. Women's "right" to reproductive choice is severely mitigated by the underfunding of Canada's medicare system.[33]

In spite of the serious issue of access and funding of abortion services, *Morgentaler* is still regarded by feminists as an enormous victory for women. It has special significance in that the decision was heavily influenced by the arguments of Justice Bertha Wilson, the only women Judge on the Supreme Court at the time. As lawyer Mary Eberts points out:

Madam Justice Wilson, in her reasons, recognized for the first time in a Supreme Court case, that I can recall, that women are independent moral agents and we act for ourselves, we are subjects, not objects, and we are fully entitled to make moral choices and will make them in an informed and responsible way.[34]

Justice Wilson's comments on the subjective meaning of abortion for women raise questions as to whether female representation on the bench impacts legal decision making. As many feminist legal theorists argue, women possess a distinct viewpoint on gender relations that is informed by their life experience of subordination to men. Although there is no unitary "women's point of view" in that women of diverse social backgrounds are situated differently in society and experience systemic gender discrimination in dissimilar ways, it is nonetheless recognized that what is common to women's life experiences is gendered subordination.[35] This "women's perspective" reflects socially constructed processes that operate in a systemic way to oppress women, offering insights that are absent from the male (or majority) point of view. The relevance of women's subject position, as Mary Eberts explains above, is especially apparent in Justice Wilson's remarks on abortion in *Morgentaler*:

It is probably impossible for a man to respond, even imaginatively, to such a dilemma [an unwanted pregnancy] not just because it is outside the realm of his personal experience (although, that is, of course, the case) but because he can relate to it only by objectifying it, thereby eliminating the subjective elements of the female psyche which are at the heart of the dilemma.[36]

The inclusion of female justices is sometimes justified on the grounds that without female representation women's experiences will simply not be understood or a crucial dimension of their social life will be ignored, thereby creating judicial bias.[37] This issue, present in the *Morgentaler* decision, portrays the complexity of legal decision making when acknowledgement of women's distinct social experiences are brought to the fore. To return to the theme of the icon of Justice, are the scales more properly balanced when female experience is represented on the court? And, is it possible to make sound legal judgements without the knowledge of women's social experiences? What about other types of social disadvantage such as racial discrimination?

R.D.S. v. Her Majesty The Queen

The issue of judicial bias is further highlighted in *R.D.S. v. Her Majesty The Queen*,[38] popularly known as the *Sparks* case since it involved an accusation of bias against Judge Corrine Sparks, the only Black female judge in Nova Scotia, who ruled in favour of a Black youth and against a white police officer. As in the *Morgentaler* case, Judge Sparks specifically referred to social difference but this time her comments spoke to the experience of racism. In 1994, Judge Sparks was required to determine whether a Black youth was telling the truth in relation to an altercation between himself and a white police officer that had taken place in Halifax. The police officer alleged that the youth had run into him with a bicycle, pushed him and yelled at him. The youth alleged that the police officer had threatened to arrest him and put him in a choke hold. Upon hearing the testimony Judge Sparks stated:

> The Crown says, well, why would the officer say that events occurred the way in which he has relayed them to the Court this morning. I'm not saying the Constable has misled the Court, although police officers have been known to do that in the past. And I'm not saying that the officer overreacted, but certainly police officers do overreact, particularly when they're dealing with non-white groups. That to me, indicates a state of mind right there that is questionable.
>
> I believe that probably the situation in this particular case is the case of a young police officer who overreacted. And I do accept the evidence of Mr. S. that he was told to shut up or he would be under arrest. That seems to be in keeping with the prevalent attitude of the day.[39]

By referring, albeit obliquely, to the local history of racial tensions between white police officers and the Black community in Nova Scotia, Judge Sparks incorporated a point of view into her legal decision making that raised serious concerns about judicial bias. This case eventually made its way to the Supreme Court where the majority decision, which included two female justices, ruled that a judge can take into account both personal experience and social context in legal decision making. While four Supreme Court Judges commented that attention to social context (such as race relations) provides background for the interpretation of law, the dissenting view argued that colour blindness is a better approach. The *Sparks* decision has been widely discussed because it explicitly addresses the "dilemma of difference" in connection to race. Although gender has been a focus of the courts since the passage of the Charter of Rights and Freedoms, the issue of race discrimination is much more recent and much more controversial. Indeed, while Justice Wilson made explicit reference to women's subjectivity in regard to reproductive choice and thereby acknowledged "women's difference," the comments by Judge Sparks on race relations were met with accusations of bias. As Sherene Razack remarks, the consequences of mentioning race are inherently political:

> ... what Judge Sparks did is notice race. She named it. She actually said, "white police officers," which is to immediately cause a reaction in the court because she's naming ... the predominant group as a race and that they may have an issue when they encounter Black youth. And although she was equivocal, and careful [by saying] "and maybe sometimes white police officers, not these ones, but maybe sometimes, others are known to overreact," it really didn't matter because her sin, if you like, a cardinal sin was to insist that Justice not be blind, that Justice notice [race], that this encounter that was before her was happening in Halifax.
>
> *R.D.S.* is a very powerful lesson. It is, I am convinced, intended to teach those of us who dare to be uppity by naming racism. It is intended to teach us what will happen to us. And, most of us have had a variation of this happen to us wherever we teach or work, if we're teachers in a classroom or if we give a speech, or if we sit on a board, or a committee. If we happen to be a judge or a lawyer there is very swift disciplinary action when one names racism.[40]

It would seem that social relations of gender can be more easily incorporated into legal decision making,[41] while mention of race relations and racist practices provoke a far more hostile response. Even more problematic, argues Razack, is the court's inability to comprehend the intersection between gender and racial oppression. According to her analysis, the courts have yet to grasp the specificity of racialized women's experiences in a white patriarchal society:

> We don't see many places where the realities of racism are named for women. When they are named, they're named with men in mind. So when I think about it, I think where, in what case, would we be able to find the court acknowledging that gendered racism exists? I can't think of a case where that exists ... where the court says racism exists. Cases have relied upon the situation of men, of Aboriginal men as in *Williams*, for example, or of Black men as in *Parks*.[42]

Returning to the issue of judicial representation, the case of *R.D.S.* not only raises issues about the problem of race blindness but also illustrates why a racially diversified bench is desirable in balancing the "scales of justice." Knowledge of a racialized perspective of social relations, including gendered racialization, will enhance the capacity of judges to make informed and just decisions. The fact that Judge Corinne Sparks is the only Black female judge in Nova Scotia (and the first in Canada) is significant; she is vulnerable not only on account of her race but also on account of her gender. The argument in favour of a bench that is diversified along race and gender lines is a controversial claim that is certainly not shared by all legal thinkers; however, as the producers of the video, we would argue it is a legitimate perspective of law that should be presented for discussion and debate in the university or college classroom.

GENDER AS A FORCE OF CHANGE

That gender operates "as a force" within the legal system is a conceptual thread running throughout analyses of women and the law. *In the Face of Justice* demonstrates how gender operates on several levels. Women have participated in the legal system not only as lawyers and judges but also as litigants. In each instance, women have engaged in law at different levels, confronting various facets of the legal process. Feminist legal advocates have challenged traditional masculinist assumptions of the law and fashioned a new litigation strategy; female litigants have bravely pursued their equality claims despite substantial barriers; and female judges like Madam Justice Bertha Wilson have pioneered new approaches to judicial decision making. In all of this activity, women have brought a gendered perspective of justice to their political and legal actions. A gender analysis of the law forms the basis for a feminist response to equality jurisprudence and it upholds a critique of the legal profession itself. The overarching message is that the law is neither neutral nor objective and static. Law is influenced by social ideas and ongoing political and social struggles and is constantly undergoing change in response to those forces.

***

As this review of case law indicates, the issues surrounding women's struggle for equality are very complex. Many of the issues concerning the meaning and operation of the law — the influence of social structures on women's struggle for equality rights, the problem of gender and race bias in the law and feminist legal response to that bias, as well as women's judicial representation — are exemplified in these specific cases. For instance, *Morgentaler* demonstrates the significance of having women on the bench, Eberts and Mathen comment on the important role of LEAF in challenging masculinist assumptions embedded in legal liberalism, while the use of judicial imagery drew out some of the contradictions of a blindfolded Justice, as noted by Razack and Backhouse with respect to race. Lastly, discussions with women lawyers about gender bias in the legal profession illustrate the everyday encounters of discrimination female law students and lawyers face.

One of the greatest difficulties in devising a video project on women's participation in the law is to capture the complexities of the legal process while structuring a narrative that can be understood by students unacquainted with the legal system. The interviews with lawyers and academics who commented on the legal cases resulted in many hours of interviews and dozens of pages of transcript from which we had to build a logical narrative. It was extremely difficult to choose a small number of cases to represent key aspects of legal reform on gender equality, and we had to omit many path-breaking cases. Much to our regret, only passing reference was made to disability and to violence against women (e.g., *Lavallee*). A further limitation was having to translate complex legal argument into a visual presentation. Legal cases are fraught with intricate references to legal principles or legal procedure and often involve relating a detailed story about a particular life experience or life event. The abstract nature of legal reasoning, in conjunction with presenting the complicated and tangled facts of a case, does not easily lend itself to a visual account.[43] The strength of a video, however, is that it can reach a wide audience. Today's students, who are accustomed to the visual mediums of television and the Internet, will readily connect with a visual presentation over the written text.

A great deal of thought went into developing the narrative script and in selecting the case law. It is hoped viewers will conclude that women's legal actions, pursued individually and collectively through organizations such as LEAF and NAWL, have sensitized the legal system to social relations of gender and to other social inequalities. We also hope that *In the Face of Justice* demonstrates how women's presence in the law has made a difference to the legal system, particularly in relation to the practice and method of law, and how women's legal contributions have improved women's political and economic status within Canadian society.

NOTES

1. The 40-minute video, entitled *In the Face of Justice: Women's Challenge to Law in Canada*, was co-produced with Diane Higgs of Outlook Communications. It was sponsored by the Law Society of Upper Canada and General Motors Corporation. The video is available from the Law Society of Upper Canada, Equity Initiatives Department, 130 Queen St. W., Toronto, Ontario.

2. Elizabeth Comack, *Locating Law: Race/Class/Gender Connections* (Halifax: Fernwood Publishing, 1999).

3. Lani Guinier, Michelle Fine and Jane Balin, *Becoming Gentlemen: Women, Law School, and Institutional Change* (Boston: Beacon Press, 1997), 29, 85, argue gentlemanly behaviour implies a masculinist ideal in which lawyers are expected to behave in a courteous but detached and dispassionate manner — an ideal informed by race and class assumptions. Also see Cecelia Morgan, "Women, Gender and the Legal Profession at Osgoode Hall," *Canadian Journal of Law and Society* 11, no. 2 (1996), 19–61, and Abby Bushby, "The Early Years: Sources of an Enduring Tradition. The Women's Law Association of Ontario 1919–1950," paper prepared for the 80th Anniversary Celebration of the Women's Law Association of Ontario, Toronto, Ontario, January 14, 2000.

4. See, for example, F. Kay, N. Dautovich and C. Marlor, "Barriers and Opportunities Within Law: Women in a Changing Legal Profession, A Longitudinal Survey of Ontario Lawyers 1990–1996," presented to the Law Society of Upper Canada, November 1996; Sheilah Martin, "The Dynamics of Exclusion: Women in the Legal Profession," paper presented at the Canadian Bar Association Conference: Gender Equality — A Challenge for the Profession, Toronto, Ontario, October 1992; and the Appendix "Women of Colour in the Legal Profession," in The Canadian Bar Association, *Touchstones for Change: Equality, Diversity and Accountability: The Report on Gender Equality in the Legal Profession* (Ottawa: The Canadian Bar Association, 1993).

5. The Canadian Bar Association, *Touchstones for Change*, 10–11.

6. The taskforce specifically requested input from sections of the Canadian Bar Association concerning gender bias within substantive areas of law and reviewed their responses in the report. See *Touchstones for Change*, 257.

7. Ibid., 271.

8. This approach to equality jurisprudence was argued by the Legal Education Action Fund in *Andrews v. The Law Society of British Columbia and the Attorney General of British Columbia (1986)*.

9. The interviewees included Richard Devlin, Dalhousie Law School; Mary Jane Mossman, Osgoode Hall Law School, York University; Sharene Razack, the Ontario Institute for Studies in Education/University of Toronto; Constance Backhouse, Faculty of Law, University of Ottawa; Mary Eberts of Eberts, Symes, Street & Corbett law firm; Carissima Mathen, former director of litigation, LEAF National; and Madam Justice Rosalie Abella, appointed to the Supreme Court of Canada in October 2004.

10. Mary Eberts, Interview, Toronto, June 13, 2000.

11. See Constance Backhouse, *Petticoats & Prejudices: Women and Law in Nineteenth-Century Canada* (Toronto: Women's Press, 1991), 4–5.

12. For a post-structuralist discussion of the category women, see Monique Wittig, "One Is Not Born a Woman," in Linda Nicholson, ed., *The Second Wave: A Reader in Feminist Theory* (Routledge: New York, 1977).

13. For a detailed historical discussion of legal imagery, see Dennis E. Curtis and Judith Resnik, "Images of Justice," *Yale Law Journal* 96 (1986–87), 1727–1772.

14. Comack, *Locating Law*, 21–22.

15. Richard Devlin, Interview, Toronto, April 25, 2000.

16. As Carisimma Mathen explains, "Charter litigation is ultimately about balance; it's balancing the state's right to make decisions about policy and translating that into law against individual- and group-based rights guaranteed in the Charter." Interview, Toronto, June 27, 2000.

17. Eberts, interview.

18. See Constance Backhouse, "Lawyering: Clara Brett Martin, Canada's First Woman Lawyer," in Backhouse, *Petticoats & Prejudice*, 293–326.

19. Emily Murphy was named as the appointee to the Senate. The other four women were Nellie McClung, Louise McKinney, Irene Parlby and Henrietta Muir Edwards. The case was heard before the Supreme Court of Canada in 1928 where it was decided that women were not persons. It was subsequently appealed to the Judicial Committee of the Privy Council in London, England, in 1929 where it was ruled that women were persons.

20. See Lisa Young, "Fulfilling the Mandate of Difference: Women in the Canadian House of Commons," in Jane Arscott and Linda Trimble, eds., *In the Presence of Women: Representation in Canadian Governments* (Toronto: Harcourt Brace, 1997), 82. The Inuit were granted the federal vote in 1950, while Chinese and East Indian Canadians in 1947 and Japanese Canadians in 1948. Women in Quebec were not allowed to vote in provincial elections until 1940, many years after the Dominion of Canada granted women suffrage in 1918. See also

Michael Whittington and Glen Williams, eds., *Canadian Politics in the Twenty-first Century*, 6th ed. (Toronto: Nelson Publishers, 2004), 378–379.

21. For a discussion of the struggle by Aboriginal women to gain recognition under the *Indian Act*, see Elizabeth Acheson, Mary Eberts, Beth Symes and Jennifer Stoddart, *Women and Legal Action: Precedents, Resources and Strategies for the Future* (Ottawa: Canadian Advisory Council on the Status of Women, 1984). On the subject of extending citizenship rights to racialized groups in Canada, see Jennifer Arnott, "Re-Emerging Indigenous Structures and the Reassertion of the Integral Role of Women," in Arscott and Trimble, eds., *In the Presence of Women: Representation in Canadian Governments*, 64–81.

22. Constance Backhouse, "'Bitterly Disappointed' at the Spread of 'Colour Bar Tactics': Viola Desmond's Challenge to Racial Segregation, Nova Scotia, 1946," in Constance Backhouse, *Colour-Coded: A Legal History of Racism in Canada, 1900–1950* (Toronto: University of Toronto Press, 1999), 226–271.

23. Constance Backhouse, Interview, Toronto, June 27, 2000.

24. *Murdoch v. Murdoch* [1973] at pp. 367–377.

25. Mary Jane Mossman, "The Paradox of Feminist Engagement with Law," in Nancy Mandell, ed., *Feminist Issues: Race, Class and Sexuality* (Toronto: Prentice Hall, Allyn and Bacon, 1988), 187.

26. Amendments applied to sixty-seven provincial statutes that refer to common-law spouses.

27. See Kirk Makin, "Lesbian Wants Court to Rehear Historic Case," *The Globe and Mail*, 8 April 2000, A8.

28. See Caroline Mallen, "Same-Sex Couples Granted New Rights," *The Toronto Star*, 28 October 1999, A7.

29. For a review of the debates on gay and lesbian response to family law reform, see Susan B. Boyd, "Expanding the Family in Family Law: Recent Ontario Proposals On Same-Sex Relationships," *Canadian Journal of Women and the Law* 7, no. 2 (1994), 545–563; Brenda Cossman, "Same-Sex Couples and the Politics of Family Status," in Janine Brodie, ed., *Women and Canadian Public Policy* (Toronto: Harcourt Brace,1996), 232–244. See also Martha McCarthy and Joanna Radbord, "*M. v. H.*: The Case for Gay and Lesbian Equality in Marriage and Family Law" in this volume.

30. Boyd, "Expanding the Family in Family Law ," 548.

31. Mossman, "The Paradox of Feminist Engagment with Law."

32. *Morgentaler v. The Queen* (1988) 92 N.R. 1.

33. The Canadian Abortion Rights Action League (CARAL) announced in a press release that the number of hospitals providing abortion services has declined: "In 1990, clinics accounted for 22 percent of abortions. By 1995, this number had grown to 33 percent of abortions." As explained in the release, women who can

afford private clinics can obtain access to abortion services while poor women are denied this service. CARAL Press Release, 8 March 2000.

34. Eberts interview.

35. For a detailed discussion of this point, see Deborah Rhode, "The Women's Point of View," in Frances E. Olsen, ed., *Feminist Legal Theory II: Positioning Feminist Theory Within the Law* (New York: New York University Press, 1995), 39–68.

36. Cited in T. Brettel Dawson, ed., *Relating to Law: A Chronology of Women and Law in Canada*, 2d ed. (Toronto: Captus Press, 1998), 65.

37. On the issue of gender representation in the judiciary, see Maryka Omatsu, "The Fiction of Judicial Impartiality," in this volume; and "On Judicial Appointments: Does Gender Make a Difference?" in Joseph Fletcher, ed., *Ideas in Action: Essays on Politics & Law in Honour of Peter Russell* (Toronto: University of Toronto Press, 1999), 176-187.

38. For an in-depth analysis of this case, see Sherene Razack, "*R.D.S. v. Her Majesty The Queen:* A Case About Home" in this volume.

39. Cited in Richard Devlin, "We Can't Go On Together With Suspicious Minds: Judicial Bias and Racialized Perspective in *R. v. R.D.S.,*" *Dalhousie Law Journal* 18, no. 2 (1995), 411. This article presents a thorough discussion of the case in relation to the rulings in Nova Scotia courts regarding judicial bias.

40. Sherene Razack, Interview, Toronto, June 13, 2000.

41. For example, Madam Justice Claire L'Heureux-Dubé traces the significance of gender on equality jurisprudence in Canada over a fifty-year period in "Stepping Forward, Stepping Back: Women's Equality at Century's End," paper presented at the Massey College Symposium, Toronto, March 3, 2000.

42. Razack, interview. Also see Sherene Razack, *Looking White People in the Eye: Gender, Race, and Culture in Classrooms and Court Rooms* (Toronto: University of Toronto Press, 1999).

43. For example, we had wanted to include a discussion of the "reasonable person" test that was revised from the "reasonable man" (the man on the omnibus) hypothesis in reference to *Lavallee* but found it too involved to adapt to a video format.

CHAPTER 6

International Women's Rights and Evidence-Based Advocacy

Marilou McPhedran

"Rights"... is still deliciously empowering to say. It is the magic wand of visibility and invisibility, of inclusion and exclusion, of power, and no power. The concept of rights, both positive and negative is also the marker of our citizenship, our relation to others.

— Patricia J. Williams, *The Alchemy of Race and Rights*

I originally wrote this, less in my capacity as the volunteer national chair of LEAF — the Women's Legal Education and Action Fund — and more as an international women's rights activist. But the phrase "Evidence-Based Advocacy" in the title is my term, derived from assessing how high impact litigation strategies of LEAF have catalyzed systemic change through strategic legal interventions in cases interpreting the domestic laws and policies affecting women and girls in Canada. Twenty plus years ago, I was a spokeswoman and a legal counsel to the historic Ad Hoc Committee of Canadian Women and the Constitution, which sprang up in 1981 to lead unprecedented grassroots political action by women to secure a "made-in-Canada ERA" (the Equal Rights Amendments to the Canadian Constitution through sections 15 and 28 of the Canadian Charter of Rights and Freedoms). On April 17, 1985, the first possible day for using the new Charter to litigate on equality issues, LEAF was launched by filing — and winning — three sex-discrimination cases in three regions of Canada. LEAF had a number of very good and rather heady years where it seemed that what we undertook resulted in success, measured in groundshifting decisions from our courts that advanced gender equality in Canada, often generating significant and substantial benefits in the daily lives of many Canadian women.[1]

It was the famed Canadian feminist journalist, Michele Landsberg, who first pointed out to me when LEAF was barely a decade old, that a pattern was emerging in the cases — a pattern that revealed how male sexual privilege was embedded in the legal system and how the sexual subjugation of women's bodies would be the battleground of our lifetime. LEAF interventions lend support to Michele's analysis. A few of these examples include *Seaboyer*, the 1991 "rape shield" case that LEAF "lost" in court but paved the way for subsequent pro-victim legal amendments by Parliament; the 1995 *O'Connor* case, in which LEAF challenged the privilege of the Catholic priest who sexually assaulted Aboriginal women under his authority in a residential school setting, leading to a new law (Bill C-46) rebalancing the Supreme Court's myopic view of the right to a fair trial by including privacy and equality rights; and the 1999 *Ewanchuk* case, which generated the "no means no" principle on sexual assault, as a result of how an Alberta appeal court judge (ironically, the late grandson of twentieth-century suffragette Nellie McClung) was overruled by a brilliantly stinging opinion penned by now retired Madam Justice Claire L'Heureux-Dubé.[2] When examining the Supreme Court decisions in such cases of the past two decades, we reach the LEAF intervention arguments in *Darrach*[3] — the most recent challenge to the "rape shield" provisions in the Criminal Code. On closer examination, we can see that these are all criminal cases related to sexual assault in which LEAF arguments on constitutional equality rights figured prominently and where the bilateral dynamic between legislation and adjudication was in full swing. The various "sides" have different perceptions of fundamental rights in the Charter, but all sides have passionately engaged the criminal legal system in these cases. It has been an exhilarating and exhausting period of steps forward and steps back, but more often than not, LEAF evidence-based advocacy has had influence on broadening the Supreme Court's perspectives on just whose "rights and freedoms" are at stake in sexual assault cases.

Christopher Manfredi, known as a critic of judicial activism, described LEAF in his 2004 book *Feminist Activism in the Supreme*

Court as "the most active and visible feminist litigating organization in Canada," concluding that "LEAF's activity has contributed to reversing litigation defeats of the 1970s, to protecting important legislative victories, and to expanding women's rights in areas such as reproductive freedom and family law."[4] Furthermore, women's rights activists in other countries began to notice that Canadian feminists were "winning" on key equality issues.

But when LEAF ran into a number of negative rulings in the late 1990s, many of us started to ask whether we were using an optimal portfolio of arguments, whether we had indeed assembled the full tool kit we needed to reframe women's rights in the Canadian context. I was only one of the early leaders in LEAF — with others such as Mary Eberts, Lucie Lamarche, Catharine MacKinnon and Shelagh Day — who had started to look at the impact of international covenants (in particular, the United Nations covenants) and international multilateral institutions, wondering what application they might have in a Canadian context. It was not until 1997 that I was given the opportunity to found a new project at York University in Toronto called the International Women's Rights Project (IWRP). Our mandate was to work with organizations and individuals within the academic community and to connect with and foster the efforts of NGOs in Canada and in other parts of the world in a partnership that focused on international laws and programs to support the global quest for women's rights — a somewhat unusual endeavour for an academic setting, because community/academic joint ventures are not theoretical in nature and not easily "written up" to boost an academic's profile. As a result of my work with the IWRP, I found myself in regular daily contact with women in many different countries, and it changed my perspective on how we do legal literacy and advocacy in Canada. One of the first initiatives of the IWRP, funded primarily by the Canadian International Development Agency (CIDA) and the Ford Foundation, was an impact analysis of the major UN human rights treaty for women, CEDAW, the Convention on the Elimination of all forms of Discrimination Against Women,[5] using qualitative research to assess whether and how CEDAW was affecting women's rights in Canada and internationally.[6]

THE COMMISSION ON THE STATUS OF WOMEN
AND CEDAW OF THE UN

When the acronym CEDAW is used, most Canadians hear it as "CIDA." I suspect this misinterpretation occurs because until recently, we have paid very little attention to international human rights treaties as they apply to Canadians, perhaps believing that the country which has often been rated Number One by the UN on the Human Development Index (HDI) may be above international standards. However, Canada has not only slumped on the HDI. Researchers like Gwen Brodsky and Shelagh Day have documented the erosion of women's economic and social rights over the past decade and have argued persuasively for the relevance of international standards.[7] But before an erroneous impression that the UN is the source of Canadian women's equality is made, it may be helpful to look at some of the gender inclusion issues that were foreshadowed when the *Universal Declaration of Human Rights* was being negotiated as part of the founding of the United Nations in San Francisco sixty years ago.[8]

American lawyer Felice Gaer has described how, at that founding meeting, Eleanor Roosevelt initially opposed other women delegates who lobbied hard for the establishment of a separate body on women's rights. The resulting "Subcommission on the Status of Women" was made subordinate to Roosevelt's Commission on Human Rights. A veteran of contemporary UN gender battles, Gaer notes how the appointment of three men, in addition to the seven women on the Subcommission to "ensure" it "was not composed of women only," demonstrated that concerns over gender balance were highly selective. "Ironically the Commission on Human Rights also began with seven members, with its chairperson, Eleanor Roosevelt, being the only female, yet no one insisted on gender balance in that or any U.N. body other then the Subcommission on the Status of Women."[9] Gaer shares the heartening news that the cogent, tenacious lobbying by other UN women delegates eventually shifted Mrs. Roosevelt from her initial opposition to supporting two crucial changes: (1) upgrading the Subcommission on the Status of Women to full commission status under the Economic and Social Council (ECOSOC) of the UN, and (2) convincing drafters of the Universal *Declaration of Human Rights* to replace "All men" in article 1, with "All human beings are born free and equal in dignity and rights," but they did not convince the drafters to change the credo in article 1 that these human beings "should act towards one another in a spirit of brotherhood."[10]

In fact, Canadian lawyer John P. Humphrey, was the principal drafter of the *Universal Declaration of Human Rights*, which was described in its Preamble as the UN's "common standard of achievement for all peoples and all nations." Gaer recounts how Humphrey — after whom the prestigious annual international human rights award, presented by the Canadian NGO Rights and Democracy, has been named — "worried that, left to itself, the new Commission on the Status of Women (CSW) would establish different rights and different standards for women."[11]

Few of us appreciate that these structural changes resulted only after intense, at times very difficult, struggles went on often in the hallways, because many of the women's rights advocates in attendance were there as representatives of NGOs and not, like Mrs. Roosevelt, as official delegates. These women had to make their case in the hallways because they could not enter the closed meeting room where decisions were being made — providing a classic example of the concept of lobbying, which persists in the halls of the UN to this day. According to Gaer, women from several countries lobbied Eleanor Roosevelt to support changes that openly acknowledged women's unequal status and to address the need for a women-focused mechanism within the United Nations machinery in order to acknowledge and redress the fact that women in the world lived their daily reality at a huge disadvantage.

Members of the CSW pressed constantly for equal rights, but it was not until 1967 — after two decades of documenting disparity between men and women — that the CSW shepherded the precursor to CEDAW through the UN General Assembly, resulting in adoption of the policy embodied in the *Declaration on the Elimination of Discrimination Against Women.*[12] Finally, the policy in the *Declaration* morphed into law in the form of *The Convention on the Elimination of All forms of Discrimination Against Women*, with official adoption of this "women's convention" or CEDAW, by the UN General Assembly in 1979.[13]

There are six UN human rights treaties that are considered to be the major means of addressing discrimination and oppression. Each treaty has a committee of independent experts that monitors the performance of obligations of UN member states, as outlined under that specific treaty. Common to all treaties is a state's obligation to report regularly on the steps it has taken to put the treaties into effect. Although it did not have the force of law at the time of its passage in 1948, the Universal *Declaration of Human Rights* was described by the UN as "the first step in the formulation of an international bill of human rights." But this composite bill of rights could not have the force of law until "the entry into force of three significant instruments: *The International Covenant on Economic, Social and Cultural Rights* [ICESCR], *The International Covenant on Civil and Political Rights* [ICCPR] and the *Optional Protocol* to the latter covenant [ICCPR] ... allowing individuals as well as States to present complaints of rights violations" to the Human Rights Committee members appointed by states that had ratified the *Optional Protocol* as of March 1976.[14]

The first of these treaties with a reporting procedure was the *International Convention on the Elimination of All Forms of Racial Discrimination* (CERD), which entered into force in 1969, before ICCPR, ICESCR and CEDAW were activated. Much of the advocacy that International NGOs — or "INGOs" — practise is based on experience under one or more of these treaties, which is not limited to their reporting procedures but includes the development of jurisprudence under each treaty in the form of "general comments" or "general recommendations," as well as decisions under individual complaints or inquiry procedures attached to the treaties. Yet very few Canadian advocacy groups are paying attention to this jurisprudence. In Toronto, the African Canadian Legal Clinic paid particular attention to CERD, and legal staff at ACLC adopted an internationalization strategy through advocacy on systemic change and more specific initiatives such as a checklist for their cases in order to determine whether any of the international treaties were relevant and potentially useful in developing the arguments. The ACLC played a national leadership role in the preparations for the UN World Conference Against Racism held in Durban, South Africa, in 2001. Sadly, the Clinic became embroiled in administrative controversy, which cut short its leadership on international aspects of legal aid.

CERD has influenced some important political initiatives. For example, in the 1980s, the City of Cincinnati in Ohio adopted the entire Convention as a bylaw, incorporating its principles as the base level of the city's domestic law. The Cincinnati initiative is an exception, however, and has not been reflected at the national level. As the world's superpower, the U.S. does not welcome external scrutiny and while it may sign the major UN human rights treaties, it does not ratify most of them. It's fascinating to attend delegates-only sessions at UN meetings in New York to witness the active role the American delegates sometimes play in blocking human rights initiatives in the committee process. Did you know that only two member states — Somalia and the U.S. — have *not* signed the UN Convention on the Rights of the Child? American reticence regarding international law has been noted. Addressing the UN General Assembly, Secretary-General Kofi Annan said, "I believe that every government that is committed to the Rule of Law at home must be committed to the Rule of Law abroad. All states have a clear interest as well as a clear responsibility to uphold international law and maintain international order."[15]

Lest you think Canada is without reproach, it is noteworthy that our country failed to file its promised reports to the CERD monitoring committee from 1988 right up to the World Conference Against Racism (WCAR) in 2001. One would have thought that this situation would have improved following the conference, but it did not. Canada still lags in its reporting timeline for this treaty obligation, which leaves us with the question: Why would the UN human rights treaty on racial discrimination appear to rank so low on Canada's list of priorities in fulfilling its international obligations as a state member of the United Nations?

CEDAW and CERD are both examples of when assumptions are made that "everybody" benefits from gender and racial "neutrality" in treaties. This assumption, however, dismisses the natural differences that operate so strongly in a multicultural context like the UN — differences around race, culture, age, physical ability and sexual orientation. Each time there is a meeting related to women's rights and the United Nations, these differences come into play and are addressed in varying degrees. For example, sessions of the Commission on the Status of Women (CSW) — which meets at UN headquarters in New York every spring and which is as the "mothership" from which women's rights initiatives emanate — are frequently led by women from South America, Latin America, Africa and other international communities. Over the years, women's rights leadership has grown to reflect global racial diversity at the CSW and CEDAW sessions — a key factor in reframing women's rights within the international legal context.

The CSW meetings that are best known to us are the World Conferences on Women, of which there have been four, one held every five years between 1975 and 1995. In June 2000, there was a special session of the UN General Assembly in New York that followed up on the 1995 Beijing Declaration strategies adopted by various governments. This special session and its related meetings have came to be known as "Beijing +5," followed by "Beijing +10" in 2005. Although Beijing +5 was a special session of the UN member states, it was not similar to the world conference of women with an NGO forum in the manner of Beijing. Nevertheless, an estimated ten thousand people — mostly women from all over the world who were highly diverse in their characteristics but quite singleminded in their collective activist efforts — came to New York to influence their government delegates to hold onto women's human rights as they were articulated at the Beijing world conference. The Political Declaration and Outcome Document in 2000 was seen as a stalemate: no great gains but no great losses. Clearly, the "pushback" from the likes of the Vatican had hit and the bland language in the Beijing +5 Outcome Document has become the "code" for more lobbying battles at Beijing +10. There were some advances, at least in the language of the Outcome Document, naming certain issues more specifically than in 1995, such as women's access to peacemaking and peacekeeping decisions; the impact of armed conflict on women; and the crucial role women play in the fight against HIV/AIDS, not only because they make up the majority of those newly infected but also because of "their crucial role in fighting the pandemic" of the global HIV/AIDS crisis.[16]

To understand how we got to this point in international women's rights activism at the UN, we need to understand how women's NGOs have reframed traditional notions of human rights. A turning point occurred at the World Conference on Human Rights in 1993 in Vienna, which grew out of the fifteen years of Human Rights Committee deliberations. Although not specific to women's rights or to CEDAW, the Vienna conference and its follow up generated significant changes in the jurisprudence of CEDAW and other UN human rights treaties. Perhaps the most significant event was the shift, prompted by women's unsanctioned activism, in the interpretation of "human rights" to include specific reference to "violence against women" that acknowledged, for the first time, that rape is a war crime. Let me give just one example — the "Vienna Tribunal," brilliantly effective advocacy where, once again, leadership was taken up by women from numerous countries in the South, with North American women initially contributing resources such as policy papers, advocacy training and materials.

The Vienna Tribunal was not an "official" UN meeting, but it exemplified the alchemy of shared leadership across differences that has fuelled the successes of the international women's rights movement. The UN World Conference on Human Rights was held in Vienna in June 1993, attended by delegates representing 171 member states. Only member states had delegate status to the world conference, but almost a thousand representatives of women's NGOs made their way to Vienna determined to influence the agenda of the conference and, in turn, the UN Human Rights Committee. Women's rights activists filmed their own version of a human rights tribunal, made possible by years of networking and advocacy, resulting in shocking testimony of their personal experiences by violated women and girls from twenty-five countries being presented to the Vienna Tribunal. Following the day-long Tribunal, the chair of the General Assembly of the formal conference recognized the work of the internationally respected human rights experts who had volunteered to act as Tribunal judges, including Canada's Ed Broadbent. The following recommendations were submitted to the General Assembly of the Conference "for urgent action," each one resulting in significant degrees of implementation:

1. Recognize widespread violations of women's human rights occur within what is considered the "private sphere" of women's lives and that these rights must also be respected.

2. Confirm that Domestic Violence in its many forms is also a violation of women's human rights, through adoption by the Conference of a UN *Declaration on the Elimination of Violence Against Women*. NOTE: The definition adopted by the Conference in the *Vienna*

Declaration represented a major shift and victory: "Any act of gender-based violence that results in, or is likely to result in, physical, sexual or psychological harm or suffering to women, including threats of such acts, coercion or arbitrary deprivation of liberty, whether occurring *in public or private life*."[17]

3. Enact standards that prohibit violence against women, including the following measures: (a) the establishment of the position of a Special Rapporteur on Violence Against Women (currently Ms.Yakin Ertürk of Turkey is Special Rapporteur, United Nations Commission on Human Rights on violence against women, its causes and consequences), and (b) the creation of an International Criminal Court capable of addressing women's rights to protect and enforce women's rights. *The Statute of the International Criminal Court* (ICC) was adopted by the Rome Convention in July 1998. The Court's jurisdiction is limited to crimes against humanity, war crimes and crimes of genocide. The ICC operates independently of all political powers, and its power to investigate is not subordinated to any agreement by any States. It will only intervene when national courts are unwilling or unable to prosecute their own citizens. Seven of the eighteen elected judges are women, compared to only one woman on the International Court of Justice.

4. Enforce the existing rights articulated in the UN human rights treaty for women, CEDAW (*Convention on the Elimination of All forms of Discrimination Against Women*), General Recommendation 19 in particular, which establishes the links between violence and discrimination: "Violence against women is both a consequence of systematic discrimination against women in public and private life, and a means by which constraints on women's rights are reinforced. Women are vulnerable because of disabilities imposed on them in economic, social, cultural, civil and political life and violence impairs the extent to which they are able to exercise *de jure* rights."[18]

Ironically, the term "violence against women" is not even mentioned in a single clause of CEDAW. In fact, it did not become a topic for UN attention until fifteen years ago. One of the key leaders who shifted the debate at the Vienna Conference was Susana Chiarotti, a Latin American women's rights activist. Her perspective is recounted in *Activists Beyond Borders*:

We began to make the connection between violence and human rights when a "companera" brought us the article by Charlotte Bunch on "women's rights as human rights" which she got at a meeting in California. I was the only one in my group who read English, and when I read it, I said to myself: "Hmmm, a new approach to human rights. This we have not seen before. And a new approach to violence as well." So I told the other women in my group, "It seems to me that this would be the key to end our isolation" ... I am an activist but this theoretical piece made a great difference in our work. Later, we learned about the petition campaign calling for UN recognition of women's rights as human rights. We thought the petition was a useful tool because it was so well crafted. Its language is irrefutable; you would have to cover yourself with shame if you didn't accept it. This began a new conceptualization of the violence theme, and we started to bother people from human rights organizations to broaden their vision.[19]

BROADENING THE VISION THROUGH IMPACT ANALYSIS

By and large, the first fifty years of the United Nations has been dedicated to what is often called "armchair diplomacy," or what I describe as "drafting, expensive meal, drafting, expensive meal, drafting." Much of the energy, and virtually all of the resources, have gone into this process so that we have an impressive volume and variety of text in the UN international covenants and treaties. Canada, unlike the United States, has ratified all of the major human rights treaties of the United Nations, including the Optional Protocol to CEDAW, which is relatively new.[20] And yet, when we try to assess what positive difference has actually been made in the day-to-day lives of women, we find, as has been well argued by Ann Bayefsky, that there are few records, little research and an extremely limited organizational ethos around measuring or comparing implementation of the human rights treaties.[21] International alliances to further women's rights are varied in their capacity to communicate and co-operate, but they have grown quite steadily, against great odds. These alliances, forged by international women's INGO leaders such as Shanthi Dairiam of Malaysia, are largely responsible for bringing attention to the gap that exists between rights expressed on paper and the actual implementation of remedies through mechanisms such as the CEDAW committee. Their considerable sophistication in diplomatic dealings has increased the need and desire for research that is customized to support activists' evidence-based advocacy.[22]

More effective enforcement of human rights standards does make a difference when it comes to surviving times of crises, and can certainly influence the quality of women's lives and their communities. Such implementation cannot occur without complementary, innovative research. As they say in the movies, "Show me the money," and the money spent at the UN flows heavily towards the armchair diplomacy of delegates in meeting after meeting.

Thus, it is no surprise that, as the UN celebrated the fiftieth anniversaries of its founding (1945) and of the Universal Declaration on Human Rights (1948), women delegates began to shift the paradigm away from the *drafting* of international standards to their *implementation* "at home" so that they benefit real people in their daily domestic lives. Strategies for implementation are built on effective advocacy, but these strategies must be grounded by what I call "evidence-based advocacy," created at the nexus of research and activism. As part of gathering the evidence needed to design effective advocacy, it becomes imperative to find a way to assess the impact of fifty years of "drafting, drafting, drafting" — if only to strengthen the argument that there should be less of it.

In order to do that, there are a number of approaches that have been taken over the last few years. As mentioned earlier, I directed the first CEDAW impact study which attempted to capture data, both qualitative and quantitative, through a network of researchers and academics in ten countries. To be selected, the national correspondents in the study had to have connections with women's NGOs in their countries: Canada, Germany, Japan, Nepal, the Netherlands, Panama, South Africa, South Korea, Turkey and Ukraine. Through this network, we began to build a base of information that would inform decisionmakers within each country and at the UN. Our research shed light on what was and wasn't working in these countries, especially when it came to awareness and application of CEDAW.[23]

Women's involvement was enhanced through NGO affiliated national correspondents in all ten countries because data were gathered directly from women active on the issues. The evidence gathered through comparative analysis of the impact of CEDAW locally can advance women's NGOs in the UN processes, as well as increase the level of knowledge and skill among women activists in their own countries and when they come together at the UN. Qualitative rights research like this gives us a clearer picture of the effectiveness, or the lack thereof, of international law in women's day-to-day lives, hopefully accelerating the shift away from armchair diplomacy towards the allocation of resources dedicated to the implementation of women's human rights. Thus, the flow of evaluative information into the UN processes helps assess how the resources are really being applied and strengthens the platform for action. For example, the 1999 country report done by the national correspondent for Nepal (one of the better papers in the CEDAW Impact Study, in my opinion) provided a baseline for subsequent specialized analysis of women's inheritance rights.[24]

THE LAST CITIZENS OF THE WORLD

Over the past twenty-five years, we have seen a tremendous growth in the concept of women as full citizens of the world, where personhood as a citizen equals safe womanhood, and safe womanhood equals implementation of women's human rights. In shifting the emphasis, we are seeing where NGO advocacy has been critical in achieving concrete steps towards implementation of human rights standards, rather than constraints imposed in the name of safety. For example, under the Optional Protocol to the CEDAW Convention, adopted by the UN in 1999 and ratified in Canada in 2002, women can take their human rights grievance to the CEDAW Committee at the UN, once they have exhausted the internal recourses available within their country.[25]

Women's NGOs fought for the Optional Protocol because they were convinced that creating another avenue for appeal and for more public exposure of alleged violations would result in greater justice. Some readers may recall the 1970s march of Aboriginal women from the Tobique Reserve in New Brunswick, when Sandra Lovelace and her supporters called attention to the injustice of the *Indian Act*, which stipulated that Aboriginal women who married non-Aboriginal men were disallowed from passing on their Aboriginal personhood to their children, whereas Aboriginal men who married non-Aboriginal women were able to do so.[26] When she was national speaker of the Native Women's Association of Canada (NWAC), Gail Stacey-Moore noted how Aboriginal women's equality advocates have often experienced significant resistance from influential leaders within a number of important bodies, such as governments, academia and the media: "Aboriginal women have been legally, politically and socially subordinated by the federal government and by Aboriginal governments."[27] In the 1970s, Ms. Lovelace only had the option of appealing to the UN Human Rights Committee, which monitored the application of the *International Covenant on Civil and Political Rights* (ICCPR).[28] The UN Human Rights Committee found the Canadian government to be in violation of its obligations under Article 27 of the ICCPR and the *Indian Act* was amended (although not broadly enough to encompass ensuing generations) as a result.[29] Now that the CEDAW Optional Protocol is activated, Canadian women may be able to choose to take their grievances to outside Canada in pursuit of justice.

As tempting as it may be, this chapter should not be closed without exploring some of the tensions embedded within the intersectionality of gender, race, rights and culture, as part of balancing aspects of Aboriginal sovereignty. Canadian legal scholar Douglas Sanders, soon after the Canadian Charter of Rights and Freedoms was activated in the early 1980s, reasoned, "If Canadians are serious about cultural autonomy for aboriginal collectivities, then sexual discrimination should be acceptable so long as it authentically reflects the continuing traditions of the communities."[30] By contrast, some twenty years later on March 8, 2004, Phil Fontaine, National Chief of the Assembly of First Nations, issued the following statement for International Women's Day: "Being a woman should not make a First Nations person less under the *Indian Act* or any other legislation ... Our rights are vital to our growth and prosperity. We view constitutionally guaranteed and inherent Aboriginal rights, gender equality rights and human rights issues as being part of the whole: ensuring equality and protection for all Canadians. As First Nations citizens we know directly the dangers of limiting or reneging on recognized rights and the importance of protecting and upholding rights."[31]

Yet the question must be put: Is it worth spending so much time in the basement of the UN in New York — where the CSW and CEDAW sessions are headquartered? What we are really seeking to do there is to create checks and balances that provide some sort of framework for the implementation of women's rights. National governments can no longer govern the global corporate structures that now have such influence over people's daily lives, and inevitably, in country after country we see that it is women — Aboriginal women, women of colour, poor or old, disabled or illiterate women — who bear the brunt of inadequate (if existent) human rights checks and balances in their countries. In countries like Afghanistan, war is internalized, women and children are the casualties in more ways than one. Highlighting Afghanistan and South Africa, Penelope Andrews has explored the tensions caused by universalizing legal norms in CEDAW as part of aggressive reforms, noting reservations regarding campaigns "which appeared tinged by a certain evangelism, embracing the narrative of rescue: women in non-Western societies needed to be rescued from barbaric and oppressive cultural practices."[32]

Restructuring in the name of "reform" in some countries is, in effect, warfare — economic warfare against civilians. Destructive government cutbacks to health and education triggered by government responses to the internal agendas and external forces (such as the International Monetary Fund and the World Bank) are destroying generations of social capital, including here in Canada. By gathering data at the local level from the perspective of women, valuable information from the frontlines helps us analyze how this economic warfare is devastating the lives of women and children at both national and international levels.

We have built border-crossing quasi-governmental bodies to act as international legal systems: the United Nations, the Council of Europe, the European Union, the Organization of American States and the Organization of African States. Although they are not fully operational, we look to these international bodies to provide some countervailing influence. As well, we have to look at how we can push the agenda to have them fulfill what is largely unrealized potential: to change these systems so that they meet the interests of the majority of the world's population, and to treat women as full citizens in their respective countries. To make these changes, we require more relevant uptake of information — and evidence-based advocacy.

CEDAW impact analysis revealed some positive outcomes that promote the citizenship and well-being of women in the countries involved. For example:

- In Canada, unprecedented references to CEDAW and to the 1994 UN Declaration on the Elimination of Violence Against Women were used as interpretive aids to weighing the equality rights of women under the Canadian Charter in sexual assault cases, as part of the Supreme Court of Canada decision in *Ewanchuk*. Madam Justice L'HeureuxDubé, Mr. Justice Gonthier, concurring, in 1999, wrote: "The Convention in article 1 defines discrimination against women. The definition of discrimination includes gender based violence, that is, violence that is directed against a woman because she is a woman or that affects women disproportionately." It is interesting to note that although LEAF was an intervenor in *Ewanchuk*; LEAF counsel concentrated on domestic laws and did not make the international arguments relied upon by two of the Supreme Court Justices.[33]

- In Nepal, CEDAW has the status of national law because it is included in the Constitution. Women advocates have been using the legal standards in CEDAW to illuminate the need for reforms to inheritance laws and to stimulate public discourse on women's rights.[34]

- CEDAW is a also a part of the Constitution in Costa Rica, and has been used as an interpretive tool in several cases. One judicial ruling found that the requirement of a husband's consent before a women could undergo sterilization contravened the anti-discrimination clause and equality in marriage and family matters covered by CEDAW.[35]

- When faced with a case that highlighted the equality principles in CEDAW that had been ratified by the Government of Tanzania, compared to clear discrimination on the basis of sex in the customary inheritance law, the High Court of Tanzania declared the customary law to be in contravention of international and constitutional equality standards.[36]

***

Evidence is mounting that international laws can be helpful additions to our advocacy kit for equality. While it is true that these legal instruments do not come with enforcement mechanisms, women's rights advocates "have creatively carved out an international conversation that has challenged national and global leaders to confront national and international policies, practices and laws that continue to subordinate and disadvantage women."[37] We need to continue building this practice through evidence-based advocacy by increasing effective application skills and ongoing education among lawyers and among the population of people most affected.

Women's constitutional rights in Canada have been hard won and have proven to be crucial in a significant number of diverse cases over the past two decades since section 15 Charter equality rights were activated in 1985. However, the status of women's rights is declining in Canada, especially for multiply disadvantaged women. International women's rights advocates are quick to remind us that when standards for Canadian women are lowered, it reduces the "art of the possible" for women and girls in many parts of the world. It is imperative, therefore, that we engage in the process of securing human rights for women in Canada by exploring if and how international instruments can strengthen our domestic foundation. By doing so, we bolster our efforts and those of our international colleagues to achieve improvements for women locally and globally. Some significant change in positive use of the international treaties will expand the common ground for human rights advocates in the years ahead. By openly bringing powerful differences such as gender and race to the challenge of seeking equality, we improve our chances of gathering more effective evidence on which to build our strategies for achieving equal benefit and protection of the law for all women making their human rights, lived rights.

NOTES

The author wishes to express appreciation for research collaboration with wonderful women since 1997, when the International Women's Rights Project (IWRP at www.iwrp.org) was founded. My co-director of the IWRP, Susan Bazilli, and our research assistant at the University of Victoria Centre for Global Studies, Laurel Sherret, have been particularly helpful, along with Valerie Markides and Angela Mcleod, who helped me prepare the Law Society of Upper Canada lecture in 2000, from which this essay evolved.

1. Canadian Charter of Rights and Freedoms, Part I of the *Constitution Act 1982*, being Schedule B of the *Canada Act 1982* (UK), c.1. LEAF grew out of women's constitutional activism focused on sections 15 and 28. Tarnopolsky and Beaudoin described the relationship between section 15 and section 28 of the Charter: "Section 28 has also to be viewed in the light of the 'limitations' clause in s. 1 of the Charter and the 'non abstante' clause in s. 33. Based upon past experience, there was fear either that the legislatures through s. 33 might, on the one hand, exempt a law discriminating against women from the ambit of the Charter, or, on the other hand, that the courts might, through the 'limitations' clause in s. 1, so construe a law which discriminates against women as to consider it such a reasonable limit 'as can be demonstrably justified in a free and democratic society'. Therefore, the purpose of s. 28 is clear." *The Canadian Charter of Rights and Freedoms: Commentary* (Toronto: Carswell, 1982), 436. LEAF's purpose is to promote equality for women by intervening in carefully selected cases, usually before the Supreme Court of Canada, by making its research, analysis and expertise available in the process of law reform, by taking part in public inquiries and by providing public education on sex equality and multiple forms of discrimination experienced by women and girls in Canada. See LEAF online at www.leaf.ca. See also Christopher P. Manfredi, *Feminist Activism in the Supreme Court: Legal Mobilization and the Women's Legal Education and Action Fund* (Vancouver: University of British Columbia Press, 2004).

2. See *R. v. Seaboyer*, [1991] 2 S.C.R.577; *R. v. O'Connor*, [1995] 4 S.C.R. 411; and *R. v. Ewanchuk*, [1999] 1 S.C.R. 330. Nellie McClung was one of the "Famous Five" Canadian feminists, represented before the Judicial Committee of the Privy Council in England by renowned Canadian lawyer (and later judge) Newton Rowell, in their challenge of the Canadian courts through the *Reference as to the Meaning of the Word "Persons" in Section 24 of the British North America Act, 1967*, [1928] S.C.R. 276, rev'd *Edwards v. Canada (A.G.)*, [1930] A.C. 124 (P.C) This judgement has become known generally as the "Person's Case" and on October 18, 1929, the Law Lords of the British Privy Council released their positive response to Mr. Rowell's arguments. For different perspectives on this historic case, see D. Bright, "The Other Woman: Lizzie Cyr and the Origins of the 'Person's Case,'" *Canadian Journal of Law and Society* 13, no. 2 (1998); and K. Lahey, "Legal 'Persons' and the Charter of Rights: Gender, Race and Sexuality in Canada," *Canadian Bar Review* 77, no. 3 (1998).

3. *R. v. Darrach* [2000] 2 S.C.R. 443.

4. Manfredi, *Feminist Activism in the Supreme Court*, xiv.

5. *The Convention on the Elimination of Discrimination Against Women*, G.A. Res. 34/180, U.N. GAOR, 34th Session, Supp. No. 46, at 193, U.N. Doc. A/RES/34/180 (1980) (hereinafter CEDAW). Note: Canada acceded to CEDAW in 1981, just as the ad hoc domestic battle, discussed at the beginning of this paper, over women's rights in the new constitution, was being waged. CEDAW influenced the wording of changes demanded by Canadian women, due to its positive, proactive stance in Article 2 — obligating state parties to "embody the principle of the equality of men and women in their national constitutions ...

and to ensure, through law and other appropriate means, the practical realization of this principle."

6. Marilou McPhedran, Susan Bazilli, Moana Erickson and Andrew Byrnes, *The First CEDAW Impact Study: Final Report* (Toronto: York University Centre for Feminist Research and International Women's Rights Project, 2000).

7. Gwen Brodsky and Shelagh Day, "Beyond the Social and Economic Rights Debate: Substantive Equality Speaks to Poverty," *Canadian Journal of Women and the Law* (2002).

8. The *Universal Declaration of Human Rights* was adopted and proclaimed by General Assembly Resolution 217 A (III) of December 10, 1948. December 10 is now recognized annually as International Human Rights Day.

9. Felice D. Gaer, "And Never the Twain Shall Meet? The Struggle to Establish Women's Rights as International Human Rights," in C.E. Lockwood, D.B. Magraw, M.F. Spring and S.I. Strong, eds., *The International Human Rights of Women: Instruments of Change* (New York: American Bar Association, 1998), 5–7.

10. Ibid.

11. John P. Humphrey, "The Memoirs of John P. Humphrey: The First Director of the United Nations Division of Human Rights," *Human Rights Quarterly* 5 (1983), 405–406, cited in Gaer, "And Never the Twain Shall Meet?"

12. *Declaration on the Elimination of Discrimination Against Women, G.A. Resolution 2263, U.N. GAOR, 22nd Session., Supp. No.16, at 35, U.N. Doc. A/6716 (1967).

13. *The Convention on the Elimination of All Forms of Discrimination Against Women* (CEDAW), see note 5 above.

14. UN Office of Public Information, *The International Bill of Human Rights 1948–1978* (Reprinted by Human Rights Program, Department of Secretary of State, 1978); *The International Covenant on Civil and Political Rights, G.A. Res.2200 A (XXI) of 16 December, 1966. Entry into force: 23 March 1976, in accordance with Article 49.

15. UN Secretary-General Kofi Annan, Address to the UN General Assembly, September 12, 2002 (New York: UN Department of Public Information, 2002). Available online at www.un. org.

16. Kofi Annan, "Beyond Beijing: Realizing Gender Equality in the Twenty-first Century," in *Beijing Declaration and Platform for Action with the Beijing + 5 Political Declaration and Outcome Document* (New York: UN Department of Public Information, 2001), 181–182. Available online at www.un.org. In Canada, organizing for the follow-up to Beijing led to the formation of the Feminist Alliance for International Action (FAIFA), which co-ordinated the Beijing +5 follow-up process and is now preparing for NGO contributions to Beijing +10. See www.fafia.ca.

17. CEDAW, G.A. Res.48/104. Emphasis added.

18. *Report of the World Conference on Human Rights, Vienna, 14–25 June 1993 (A/ CONF.157/24 (Part I))*, chap. III. Available online at www.un.org/womenwatch. General Recommendation 19, see U.N. CEDAW, 11ᵗʰ Sess., Agenda Item 7 at 3, U.N. DOC. CEDAW/C/1992/L.1/Add.15 (1992)

19. Susana Chiarotti, "Transnational Networks on Violence Against Women," in Margaret Keck and Kathryn Sikkink, *Activists Beyond Borders: Advocacy Networks in International Politics* (Ithaca, NY: Cornell University Press, 1998), 172. Note: Charlotte Bunch, mentioned in the quotation, is the founder of the Center for Global Leadership at Rutgers University and was a chief organizer of the "Vienna Tribunal."

20. *The Optional Protocol: Text and Materials* (New York: UN Division for the Advancement of Women, May 2000), Resolution 34/180, annex. For a list of countries that have signed and ratified the Optional Protocol to CEDAW, visit www.womenwatch.org.

21. Anne Bayefsky, "CEDAW: Threat to, or Enhancement of, Human Rights?" *American Society of International Law Proceedings* 94 (2000), 197–199.

22. Maria Green, "What We Talk about When We Talk about Indicators: Current Approaches to Human Rights Measurement," *Human Rights Quarterly* 23 (2001), 1062–1097; and Nancy A. Naples and Manisha Desaijeds, eds., *Women's Activism and Globalization: Linking Local Struggles and Transnational Politics* (New York: Routledge, 2002). To quote Shanthi Dairiam: "The CEDAW Committee sets standards for women's human rights using the framework of the CEDAW Convention with its emphasis on substantive equality. This is a critical function as it is the only United Nations body mandated to do so and as you know this is done through the treaty reporting process. Through this process the individual governments are held directly responsible through the constructive dialogue between the Committee and the governments with NGOs playing an informal role. In all the many years I have observed this process, it is my opinion that the effectiveness of the dialogue is influenced by how effective the participation of NGOs is. The Convention demands the elimination of discrimination (direct and in-direct) and hence this brings a much needed gender perspective to the analysis and to the solutions; squarely addressing male domination and female subordination as manifested in law, policy and practice. This is indeed a feminist agenda." Personal communication on the occasion of her appointment to the CEDAW Committee, e-mail, January 6, 2005.

23. Andrew Byrnes and Jane Connors, Introduction, in McPhedran et al., *The First CEDAW Impact Study: Final Report*, 11–16.

24. Sapana Pradhan Malla, "Using CEDAW to Fight for Women's Inheritance Rights," in Cynthia Meillon, ed., *Holding on to the Promise: Women's Human Rights and the Beijing +5 Review* (New Brunswick, NJ: Center for Women's Global Leadership, 2001).

25. *The Optional Protocol*, see note 20 above.

26. Audrey Huntley and Fay Blaney for the Aboriginal Women's Action Network, *Bill C-31: Its Impact, Implications and Recommendations for Change in British Columbia. Final Report* (Vancouver: AWAN, 1999); Royal Commission on Aboriginal Peoples, *Report of the Royal Commission on Aboriginal Peoples*, vol. 4 (Ottawa: Minister of Supply and Services Canada, 1996), chap. 2, "Women's Perspectives"; Sally Weaver, "First Nations Women and Government Policy, 1970–92," in Sandra Burt et al., eds., *Changing Patterns: Women in Canada*, 2d ed. (Toronto: McClelland and Stewart, 1993).

27. National Speaker of NWAC, Gail Stacey-Moore, "Aboriginal Women, Self Government, The Canadian Charter of Rights and Freedoms, and the 1991 Canada Package on the Constitution," an Address to the Canadian Labour Congress, Ottawa, December 3,1991.

28. *The International Covenant on Civil and Political Rights*, see note 14 above.

29. Communication No. 24/1977 (1)-(2), decided July 30, 1981, U.N. Doc. CCPR/C/OP/2 at 224 (1990). Anne Bayefsky, "The Human Rights Committee and the Case of Sandra Lovelace," *Canadian Yearbook of International Law* (1982). See also Beverley Jacobs in this volume for a detailed discussion of these amendments to the *Indian Act*.

30. Douglas Sanders, "The Renewal of Indian Special Status," in Anne Bayefsky and Mary Eberts, eds., *Equality Rights and the Canadian Charter of Rights and Freedoms* (Toronto: Carswell, 1985), 561-562. However, it is interesting to note that Sanders wrote this article after the American Supreme Court decision in *Santa Clara Pueblo v. Martinez*, where the membership ordinance was enacted only two years before Ms. Martinez brought her suit against her tribe, but he did not comment on the case. *Quare* whether the Pueblo prohibition against Pueblo women or the current application of patrilineal rues under the *Indian Act* would qualify as "acceptable so long as it authentically reflects the continuing traditions of the communities." *Santa Clara Pueblo v. Martinez*, U.S.S.C. 436 U.S. 49 (1978).

31. Phil Fontaine, National Chief of the Assembly of First Nations, Statement for International Women's Day, March 8, 2004. Retrieved from www.afn.ca, December 2004.

32. Penelope Andrews, "Women's Human Rights and the Conversation across Cultures," *Albany Law Review* 67 (2003), 609–617. "Transitional Perspectives in Women's Rights" *Interights Bulletin* 14, no. 4 (2004), 143–147.

33. *R. v. Ewanchuk*, [1999] 1 S.C.R. 330.

34. The. *Dhungana v. Nepal* inheritance case is discussed in Ilana Landsberg-Lewis, ed., *Bringing Equality Home: Implementing the Convention on the Elimination of All forms of Discrimination Against Women* (New York: UNIFEM, 1998), 22.

35. Ibid., 24–25.

36. In the Tanzanian case of *Ephrohim v. Pastory*, the customary inheritance laws were found to be unconstitutional and in contravention of CEDAW. Ibid., 21.

37. Andrews, "Transitional Perspectives in Women's Rights."

38. Marilou McPhedran, "The Positive and Negative of International Women's Rights," in Canadian Research Institute for the Advancement of Women, *Organize!* (Ottawa: CRIAW, forthcoming 2005). There are two kinds of international human rights obligations: negative ones that prohibit government action violating specified rights, and positive obligations that require governments to take proactive steps, exemplified by legislation passed by a government on, for example, pay equity or equal property rights, with the purpose of ensuring and protecting basic human rights. Note: CEDAW figures in the current Canadian debate over privatization of family law by allowing arbitrations based on particular interpretations of religious regimes, such as "shari'a" Muslim law, in that article 2(f) imposes a negative obligation on CEDAW and states parties are to "abolish ... customs and practices" and article 5(a) requires them to "modify ... social and cultural" practices that have an unjust impact on women.

CHAPTER 7

AN ATTEMPT TO SAVE EMPLOYMENT EQUITY: COMMUNITY ADVOCACY VERSUS THE ONTARIO GOVERNMENT

Daina Green

When the Harris government of Ontario came into power in 1995, the dismantling of social justice programs began. One of the government's first targets was the dismantling of the employment equity legislation, which had just been brought in under the NDP administration of Bob Rae the previous year. The legislation guaranteed that employers and employees would identify and remove barriers to employment opportunities for certain groups facing historic disadvantage, namely, women, people of colour, Aboriginal peoples and persons with disabilities. The struggle to maintain a piece of social legislation that had come under attack may have been a reactive form of advocacy, but it did provide an opportunity to *propose* a model of social relations. That is, in the process of expressing opposition to the dismantling of employment equity, the opportunity arose to promote the benefits of the new measures. The Alliance for Employment Equity, an advocacy organization in Toronto, made such a proposal. We proposed a society in which it is normal and expected for workplace partners to "root out" any unintended obstacles to the employment of such groups. Such measures foster respectful workplaces where all employees are valued not just for "fitting in" to existing workplace culture but also for the diversity of their contributions. At the same time, we saw a chance for a public platform to counter negative myths about employment equity. For example, the media harped on the concept of "job quotas," reinforcing an untrue belief that the law would lead to hiring members of the designated groups simply to meet numerical goals whether or not they were qualified for the jobs. This chapter is a personal reflection on these actions and in my writing I take a non-legalistic approach to analyzing how judicial instruments were used to achieve social programs, in this case, legislated programs to guarantee employment equity in the workplace.

I focus here on the particular way that the Alliance for Employment Equity attempted to resist the dismantling of the recently enacted employment equity legislation. I do not look at how the lawyers might have resisted this dismantling. Instead, I address our organization's response to its repeal, our four-year legal and political struggle to keep the issue of social equity in the workplace alive and our attempts to maintain some unity among equity-seeking communities, as well as our forward-looking perspectives during this struggle. Throughout this process I was the chair and vice-chair of the Alliance.

THE ALLIANCE FOR EMPLOYMENT EQUITY

The Alliance for Employment Equity, which was formed in 1987 and disbanded in October 2003, was a community and labour coalition that brought together nearly a hundred groups and hundreds of individuals, mainly in Ontario. We had an open membership that varied from year to year, with a number of core supporters that remained close to the issue throughout the Alliance's existence.

From the outset we were concerned about the state of employment conditions and the need for programs to eliminate systemic discrimination, and always took great pride in two things:

1. We were a point of intersection among equity-seeking groups. Our members, both individual and organizational, came from many groups in Ontario society. We historically provided a forum for these many groups — which experienced discrimination in distinct ways — as a way to learn about one another's issues and approaches and to learn how to support one another in advocating for change on matters of social justice, employment equity and so on.

2. We always defined equity-seeking groups very broadly. While various pieces of employment equity legislation have been limited to one,

two, four or five designated groups, we took a wider view. For that reason, we always had significant input from groups representing gays, lesbians, bisexuals and transgendered persons as well as from people who had suffered discrimination in the workplace because of their accent or appearance.

Our fight for employment equity legislation went through many stages. As an organization composed of multiple equity-seeking groups, our first task was to sensitize one another to the kind of discrimination each group faced and how attitudes and practices affecting each group were manifested in the workplace. This was an ongoing process, advanced through formal and informal seminars, in discussions around the boardroom table and at other gatherings sponsored by the Alliance. It became increasingly clear that white-skin privilege did not prevent a person from experiencing discrimination based on a disability or on sexual orientation. By the same token, our members learned that a thorough understanding of racialization and the lived experience of race-based discrimination did not automatically lead to a gender analysis or a sensitivity to someone's mental or physical disability. Teaching each other about our respective issues was an intentional activity that sometimes led to misunderstandings and conflicts within the organization. A belief in one another's goodwill and a common, external focus helped us to get through some tough moments. In the end, the arguments we practised internally helped us in our lobbying efforts. As well, our process strengthened the collective resolve of the groups belonging to the Alliance in achieving a piece of legislation that addressed and redressed as many forms of discrimination as possible. We also vowed not to allow ourselves to be divided in this struggle and not to agree to a hierarchy of oppression in which one group's issues could be effectively excluded from the remedies we sought.

When we were formed in 1987, there were no laws in Canada requiring employers, let alone employers and their workers, to make plans to identify and eliminate discriminatory employment practices. By 1993, we had achieved a legislative framework for employment equity in Ontario, namely, the *Employment Equity Act*, which was brought into law under the Rae government. However, the new law was short lived. In 1995, this Act, as well as equity-related sections of the *Police Services Act* and the *Education Act* were repealed by the new Ontario

government of Mike Harris. At the moment of repeal, we asked ourselves, What recourse do people have when a government arbitrarily
removes equity-promoting legislation? In other words, what could we
do about it?

PREPARING LEGAL RESISTANCE

Our first response was certainly not a legal one. It was political. We
canvassed key groups and their leaders around the province to determine our political strength and mobilization capacity. We found our
momentum was low; by the late fall of 1995 there had already been
blows to the structure and laws concerning welfare, social housing,
women's shelters and labour relations. Many more ominous announce-
ments were in the wings. Our main allies in the social justice movement were scrambling to defend themselves from the body blows that
threatened the survival of their organizations, clients and members of
their groups. In talking to our affiliates and contacts, we constantly
heard that activists were too involved with survival issues to focus any
energy on employment equity, although the issue was clearly seen as a
bellwether.

As a small organization, the Alliance had taken a major hit as well
— we lost every penny of provincial project funding and knew we
would not be able to recover it. Fortunately, we still had some project funding from other sources that allowed us to continue our work.
Internally, our all-volunteer board decided that we would need to re-
focus the work of the organization. Our main objective was to be in a
position to challenge the backlash against "designated groups" in the
media and other public forums, and to defend the legitimacy of equity-promoting initiatives. The term "designated groups," expunged by
the Harris Tories in their first months in office, is a short-hand way of
referring to Aboriginal peoples, persons with disabilities, racial minorities and women. The Alliance's own view of which groups historically
faced discrimination in employment extended significantly beyond
these four groups.

The Tories moved quickly to introduce Bill 8, *An Act to Repeal Job
Quotas and to Restore Merit-based Employment Practices in Ontario*, in
the fall of 1995. The doublespeak in the title alone was infuriating.
The title led to a proliferation of the derogatory reference to "quota
law" in the print and electronic media, a term widely used to discredit

the employment equity legislation before it had been enacted. "Quota law" created an imaginary identification between affirmative action law in the United States and the model proposed for Ontario. In this characterization, American affirmative action programs were seen as a failure because of their supposed focus on "filling quotas" rather than on increasing recruitment of qualified candidates from among equity-seeking groups. While the facts were never evinced to support this vilification, many media unquestioningly parroted the supposed weakness in Ontario employment equity mechanisms, both before they were adopted and after the bill was passed. The characterization was the more unfortunate because the new Ontario statute did not require the setting of quotas, but only called on employers themselves to establish attainable numerical goals that would guarantee progress towards full representation of designated groups within the workplace.

Bill 8 was offensive in other ways as well. Two of its principal characteristics lay the groundwork for the legislative attack: (1) the bill repealed three pieces of legislation, extending beyond the *Employment Equity Act, 1993*, to halt mandated processes in several sectors; and (2) it required the destruction of demographic survey data, erecting obstacles to parallel employment equity initiatives, including voluntary programs, beyond those required by law. Within the public sector, all employers were required to destroy recently collected information on the representation and under-representation of equity-seeking groups within their workforces at all levels. This made it very hard to proceed with voluntary programs.

In December 1995, the government moved its bill through second and third reading. On the eve of the final vote, the Alliance was approached by a lawyer who was willing to fight the bill, Chile Eboe-Osuji who had been referred to us by the Ontario Federation of Labour. Our first legal move was quite urgent, and the Alliance quickly assembled a group of applicants willing to lend their names to an interlocutory injunction, along with a few experts willing to speak to the damage the bill was inflicting. The motion, filed in December 1995, focused on the urgency of blocking the destruction of data, which we argued impinged sections 1 and 15 of the Charter.

After our motion was heard a few months later, the Alliance took a moment to catch our collective breath. Did we want to begin a major legal battle? Would the fight help us do our central work or distract us from it? Where would we find the resources? A corollary concern was our sudden whole-hearted defence of a piece of legislation of which we had been so publicly critical only a few years earlier. We also found ourselves questioning the use of the Charter to protect equality rights, and wondering how this instrument would serve us during this period of government dismantling of protections and initiatives.

During the early months of 1996, our community and labour-based board of directors discussed the matter with our staff. We reviewed our organizational goals and weighed them in the light of our perceived obligations: the need to act and our desire not to let the government's anti-democratic actions go unchallenged. It cannot be denied that a key factor in our ultimate decision was the fact that as activists, we warmed to the chance to fight. Our conclusion was that if our major work during this period was to keep the issue alive, in front of the public and in the media, a legal strategy would be complementary rather than diversionary.

We did not make this decision based on our belief that we could or would be able to win the case. Eboe-Osuji advised us that he thought it unlikely that a lower court would find in our favour on such a controversial topic. He told us that we might find ourselves at the Supreme Court of Canada some day or perhaps before an international tribunal. We learned how little jurisprudence was available on the repeal of statutes generally and about government attacks on equity legislation in particular. At that stage, concern about unfavourable precedents did not loom very large.

As we informed other groups in the wider community about our interest in taking the case forward as a challenge under the Charter, we found a great deal of support. We formalized our stewardship of the case, bringing on a second lawyer, Mark Hart, who had extensive experience in human rights law and expertise on the specifics of employment equity. Eboe-Osuji and Hart agreed to take on the case, despite our inability to guarantee any payment for their work. We discovered a great willingness among leading practitioners, advocates and academics from each of the designated groups to provide expert testimony, mainly on a pro bono basis. It was at this point that the Alliance established a legal advisory committee, made up of a range of lawyers who came from these designated groups, to vet our developing legal arguments. Law students came to us offering to help with research. All of these individuals invested time and reflection in the development of our factum and Brandeis brief (a compendium of learned articles and sworn expert testimony intended to provide the judge with background on the issues), representing a tremendous amount of volunteer hours. In addition, the Ontario Legal Aid Plan agreed to give us a small amount of assistance with legal costs; major unions provided in-kind contributions to offset disbursements; and a third lawyer joined the legal team, Barbara Bedont. In this phase, there was significant community interest in our case. Members of both the board and legal team accepted numerous speaking invitations, participated in community forums and communicated with the Alliance's members.

The legal arguments we took forward in this case mobilized public opinion. They can be summarized briefly as follows:

- Our primary position was that the bill, which affected the repeal of the *Employment Equity Act, 1993*, as well as the employment-equity provisions of the *Police Services Act* and the *Education Act*, did constitute government action subject to review under the Charter.

- We maintained that the repeal violated section 15 of the Charter by removing a government-legislated remedy to address continuing, systemic and intractable employment discrimination experienced by members of the four designated groups. The requirement to destroy the workforce composition information collected under the *Employment Equity Act, 1993* was a further Charter violation, impinging on section 15. Destroying such data thwarted employers who wished to implement or continue with voluntary employment equity programs. The Government of Ontario, by falsely claiming that the *Employment Equity Act* imposed job quotas, created reverse discrimination and ran counter to the so-called merit principle, actually exacerbated employment discrimination experienced by the four designated groups. We held this to be yet another violation of section 15.

- We furthermore believed that the government was in violation of section 1 of the Charter in that it never justified nor was it able to justify the repeal of the employment equity legislation.

- An alternative position put forward at the Court of Appeal was that section 15 of the Charter created a positive duty on a government to enact employment equity legislation to address demonstrated employment disadvantage experienced by the four designated groups.

PREPARING FOR COURT

In 1996, the Alliance's focus was trained on the upcoming hearing dates scheduled for the Ontario General Division Court (which would become the Superior Court of Justice in 1999). A sophisticated media strategy netted our organization a great deal of positive comment and discussion on the principles of employment equity in the weeks prior to the hearing. We were quick off the mark in establishing a Web site to update our technologically privileged supporters on the progress of the case. In court, we had a large turnout of community members packing the tiny hearing room and robust media attention during the four days of the hearing. We would later revive this media strategy on several occasions: when we announced the negative decision of the lower court and made our decision to appeal; to announce the upcoming dates of our hearing at the Court of Appeal; to make public our opinion about the hearing we had been given at the appeal; to announce the negative decision of the Court of Appeal; and, finally, to publicize our decision to seek leave to appeal to the Supreme Court of Canada.

Throughout, we were not unduly "invested" in the outcome of the court challenge. Since we never believed we could rely on the Charter to further equality rights, our main concern was to stay in the game, riding on the publicity that was so key to the continued visibility of our issue. We fulfilled our objective of challenging the government publicly, annoyingly and tenaciously. By doing so, we successfully kept employment equity on the "front burner," galvanizing community energies in the process. As well, from the perspective of our position in the broader community, we reinforced our role as a "convenor" and collective spokesperson on issues relating to workplace equity. Through the case, we strengthened our links to academics, community expert practitioners, lawyers and sympathetic government officials across Canada and beyond. In many cases, we helped these parties strengthen links among themselves by providing a focus and a forum.

Not insignificantly, we were able to cheer up one another in very dire times. No words can express the feelings of solidarity and vindication felt by the many observers who filled the court room during our hearing by the Court of Appeal in April of 1998. The government's presentation was a disgrace: factually ignorant, full of arrogance and showing a marked disdain for groups which have experienced historic discrimination. The Alliance's case was coherent, audacious, grounded in social justice and well constructed. For the many advocates in attendance, it was an opportunity to break out of the isolation into which many of us had been thrown, to feel proud of our collective and individual commitment to furthering equity, and even to reaffirm that commitment.

The three intervenor groups, LEAF (also representing the DisAbled Women's Network, DAWN), the Ontario Federation of Labour and the African Canadian Legal Clinic (also representing the Congress of Black Women) worked in co-ordination with the Alliance to make maximum use of our "day in court," including the media strategy we crafted. The overwhelming show of support from major actors on the social justice front and the high-quality legal power the combined groups brought to the Court of Appeal heartened us further, showing that the issue of employment equity was far from dead. Of course, we had moments of concern and alarm about setting unfavourable precedents, particularly while awaiting the decision of the Court of Appeal. As anticipated, we did not win a favourable judgement, so we decided to apply for leave to the Supreme Court of Canada.

In developing our application for leave to the Supreme Court, we had many moments of collective soul-searching. We consulted as widely as we could given the timing of the appeal and the financial constraints, through meetings with our legal committee, community groups and the three intervenor groups, as well as discussing the issues with legal counsel in meetings of the board of directors. We were very aware of the alarm among some groups at the idea that we might drop our challenge at this late date. The Alliance decided to go forward with the application for leave, despite fears that doing so could lead to less favourable application of the Charter in similar matters. For example, a ruling that a government may repeal human rights-type legislation with impunity could lead to other governments following suit on issues such as pay equity and accommodation of minority group rights.

We submitted our application in 1990. In the response, the Attorney General of Ontario, Charles Harnick, issued a press release attacking the Alliance for advocating discrimination — so-called reverse discrimination, naturally. Interestingly, there was no take-up from the media on this salvo, perhaps showing the government that the anti-equity animus it counted on in its first campaign had lost its punch.

It wasn't until December 1999 that the Supreme Court notified us that it had denied our application for leave. This marked the end of our battle in the courts. The Alliance received many expressions of support from organizations around the country following that announcement. The general tone of the notes was one of encouragement and gratitude for our perseverance, for having brought many communities together to fight the good fight and for our success in raising the profile on an issue that was clearly coming into its own, with or without the support of the Ontario government. During this period, the federal government brought in a much-improved *Employment Equity Act*, which closely mirrored the repealed Ontario statute. Put into force in1996, the federal law, which has had a rather low profile, escaped the high level of irrational attacks its provincial counterpart faced. This Act, in conjunction with the Federal Contractors Program, calls for measures to be put into place to overcome workplace barriers and to monitor these measures for effectiveness in making workplaces more representative of the communities in which they are located. Nearly one million workers in Ontario could stand to be involved in and benefit from programs that identify workplace barriers.

***

Despite the fact that we did not win our case, there was a clear message to all governments in our fight: they would not be able to revoke equity measures without consequence. Legally, we had hoped to establish that subsequent governments must, at the very least, pause and justify their actions if they were going to consider repeal. Although we were unable to establish this obligation through the courts, we felt we had established it politically and that our message to the Harris government had been an extremely clear one. By doing so, we moved the defence of equity rights onto a firmer footing. In addition, by having mounted an effective fight, governments came to know that we would not accept such actions silently. If we could raise so much dust over fledgling employment laws, they need only to imagine the fight we could mobilize if the government ever took steps to weaken the Ontario Human Rights Code.

In closing, I offer a few reflections on this battle. At the outset we asked, How can we stop the government from taking away our hard-won advances? Today, we can ask, Where would we be today if we had not embarked on this intense tussle with the government through the courts? We might have succumbed to a long hibernation which would force us to rebuild our movement, and our organization, from scratch. From an organizational perspective, the case was a major factor in the ability of the Alliance to survive the Tories' entire first term of office, a period in which we might have perished. Instead, we moved the debate forward, maintained its profile, increased its credibility and outlasted our opponents. Although the Alliance ultimately closed its doors in 2003, there continues to be interest in the issue and supporters believe that proactive legislation that removes workplace barriers for groups still facing discrimination in employment will once again be implemented in Ontario. Unfortunately, the federal Act and the Federal Contractors Program, under which large companies and universities were to implement equity programs based on the Ontario model, have suffered from indifferent enforcement and have had too low a profile to spark significant change. At the end of 2004, most activist groups focusing on social legislation at the federal level are lobbying on behalf of pay equity programs, which made some gains in Ontario in the 1990s.

NOTE

This chapter is based on a paper presented to the Law Society of Upper Canada on International Women's Day, March 13, 2000. Since then it has undergone several revisions.

PART III

LAW IN ACTION

CHAPTER 8

GENDER DISCRIMINATION UNDER THE INDIAN ACT: BILL C-31 AND FIRST NATIONS WOMEN

Beverley Jacobs

The amendments to the *Indian Act* over the past fifty years have done very little to assist First Nations women and their children in their fight to reclaim their identity and their connections to their ancestry. The Act, originally enacted in 1876, was amended in 1985 when the federal government removed discrimination in all of its legislation, following the enactment of the Charter of Rights and Freedoms in 1982. These amendments, commonly referred to as Bill C-31, have resulted in many heated and disturbing conflicts between First Nations people,[1] including First Nations women who have been directly affected by the sexually discriminating sections of the Act. This chapter provides a historical overview of the Act, its origins and its inherent racist and sexist policies. As well it discusses those amendments affecting First Nations women, specifically the registration and membership provisions.

HISTORICAL OVERVIEW

PRE-CONFEDERATION

The early history of the tripartite relationships between Indian nations and the Crown in British North America during the stage of displacement can be described in terms of three phases in which first protection, then civilization, and finally assimilation were the transcendent policy goals. Although they may appear distinct from each other, in fact, these policy goals merge easily. They evolved slowly and almost imperceptibly from each other through the nineteenth century when the philosophical foundations of the *Indian Act* were being laid.[2]

The *Indian Act* originated in the British policies of the 1850s, before the enactment of the *Indian Act* and prior to the *British North America Act* of 1867. The definitions of membership to an Indian band in 1850 did not discriminate based on gender. For example, the definition of an "Indian" in the Act for the Better Protection of the Lands and Property of the Indians in Lower Canada of this period read:

V. And for the purpose of determining any right of property, possession or occupation in or to any lands belonging or appropriated to any Tribe or Body of Indians in Lower Canada, Be it declared and enacted: That the following classes of persons are and shall be considered as Indians belonging to the Tribe or Body of Indians interested in such lands:

First — All persons of Indian blood, reputed to belong to the particular Body of Tribe of Indians interested in such lands, and their descendants.

Secondly — All persons intermarried with any such Indians and residing amongst them, and the descendants of such persons.

Thirdly — All persons residing among such Indians, whose parents on either side were or are Indians of such Body or Tribe, or entitled to be considered as such.

And

Fourthly — All persons adopted in infancy by any such Indians, and residing in the Village or upon the lands of such Tribe or Body of Indians, and their descendants.[3]

It is interesting to note that the purpose of this particular Act was to determine who held the rights of property and who had the right to possess or occupy any lands belonging to the Tribes or Indians in Lower Canada. The legislation did not distinguish between male and female registrants.

Gender discrimination began in 1857 with the British Parliament's creation of its civilization and enfranchisement policies through the Gradual Civilization Act.[4] Under this Act, the definition of Indian status came to be defined through the male head of the household. The

Act contained many references to "any such Indian of the male sex" in section 3 and "any male Indian" in section 4. In its preamble, it defined the meaning of enfranchisement as "desirable to encourage the progress of Civilization among the Indian Tribes ... and the gradual removal of all legal distinctions between them and Her Majesty's other Canadian Subjects, and to facilitate the acquisition of property and of the rights accompanying it."

For example, an Indian man who could be legally registered as an Indian was automatically enfranchised if he "was not under twenty-one years of age, [was] able to speak, read and write either the English or the French language readily and well, and [was] sufficiently advanced in the elementary branches of education and [was] of good moral character and free from debt." Enfranchisement happened automatically under these circumstances, which meant that not only was the Indian man enfranchised but so were his wife and children. At that point, they were no longer considered Indian persons. This Act also provided that widows or female lineal descendants of enfranchised men could marry a non-enfranchised Indian man and become a member of his tribe. This meant that the woman, although entering the marriage as an enfranchised individual, would no longer be enfranchised once married. Her status as an Indian would be defined through her husband.

During the pre-Confederation period and the initial period of these British policies, changes to the traditional roles of First Nations women changed and their connections to their traditional territories became non-existent once they were forced to identify their status through First Nations men. If a woman married a First Nations man and he decided to become enfranchised, she and her children were forced to become enfranchised. If a woman married a non-First Nations man, she lost her status and was considered to be non-First Nations and was forced to leave her home community.

In the *Corbiere* case, the Supreme Court of Canada made an excellent comment on this pre-Confederation period and the patriarchal notions that were embedded in the legislation during this period:

> In the pre-Confederation period, concepts were introduced that were foreign to Aboriginal communities and that, wittingly or unwittingly, undermined Aboriginal cultural values. In many cases, the legislation displaced the natural, community-based and self-identification approach to determining membership — which included descent, marriage,

residency, adoption and simple voluntary association with a particular group — and thus disrupted complex and interrelated social, economic and kinship structures. Patrilineal descent of the type embodied in the *Gradual Civilization Act,* for example, was the least common principle of descent in Aboriginal societies, but through these laws, it became predominant. From this perspective, the *Gradual Civilization Act* was an exercise in government control in deciding who was and who was not an Indian.[5]

POST-CONFEDERATION

In 1867, the passing of the *British North America Act* gave the federal government the authority to govern "Indians and lands reserved for Indians" under section 91(24). Two years later, in 1869, an Act for the *Gradual Enfranchisement of Indians*[6] was passed and provided that any Indian woman marrying any other than an Indian man as well as the children of such a marriage would no longer be considered Indians. It also provided that an Indian woman who married an Indian man from another band would no longer be registered under her own band but under her husband's band. The children of this marriage would belong to their father's band. As a result of the patriarchal notions of this legislation, many First Nations peoples who were once matriarchal (for example, the Haudenosaunee and Mik'maq) and followed the lineal descent of the women were forced into following a foreign process in order to determine their identity with and their connections to traditional territories.

The first *Indian Act* of 1876 was a compilation of existing legislation and British policies regarding Indians. The foundations of gender discrimination and enfranchisement within the *Indian Act* were laid through the earlier British Indian policies of patriarchy, civilization and assimilation, as noted above. With the 1876 Act, the notion that the status of an Indian was determined through Indian men was reinforced. It is important to note the definitions of a non-treaty Indian, an enfranchised Indian, a status Indian and a "person" according to this Act in order to understand the membership provisions. A "non-treaty" Indian meant any person of Indian blood who belonged to an "irregular band" or who followed the Indian mode of life, "even though such person be only a temporary resident in Canada." An "enfranchised Indian" meant any Indian, his wife or unmarried child, or any unmarried man, who received letters patent granting him in fee any portion of reserve land. A "status Indian" meant "any male person of Indian blood belonging to a particular band, his children and any woman who is or was lawfully married to him." The term "person" meant an individual other than an Indian. In this context then, Indians were not considered persons. These notions of identity, combined with enfranchisement, would have profound influences on First Nations peoples, especially women.

An Indian man could pass his status on to any woman, whether she was a First Nations woman or a non-First Nations woman. It also meant that even if the man and woman divorced, these women — Indian or non-Indian — would maintain their Indian status. Furthermore, if an Indian woman married a non-status man, she and her children would no longer be considered Indian. This occurred even if she married a First Nations man who lived in the United States, because Native Americans were considered to be non-status. These rules had deleterious effects on the Haudenosaunee and other Nations who had members living on both sides of the border. Illegitimate children were excluded from the membership of the band unless the band consented to the distribution of band monies to the families for more than two years.

The Act also provided that a female "half-breed" was not entitled to be registered as a status Indian unless she was the widow of an Indian or the widow of a half-breed who was already admitted into a treaty. In most cases, unless under very special circumstances, the superintendent general or his agent had the power to determine whether or not a "half-breed head of a family" be counted as an Indian or be admitted into any Indian treaty.

Through the Act of 1876, many First Nations peoples lost control over their own identities, specifically First Nations women and their children because they were forced to completely disenfranchise themselves and disassociate themselves from their home communities. Despite the fact that there were minor amendments made to the *Indian Act* in 1951 and 1970 (as noted in the sections below), gender discrimination against First Nations has women continued. Even the 1985 Amendments, which were designed to eliminate gender discrimination in the Act, have not done so. In fact, the Amendments have caused a tremendous amount of conflict and continue to maintain control over who is and who is not a "status Indian."

1951 & 1970 AMENDMENTS

Amendments regarding membership were not made to the *Indian Act* until 1951, which further entrenched the definitions of enfranchisement and membership and gave greater controls over First Nations identity to the federal government. For example, an Indian man (whether single or married) could have voluntarily applied for enfranchisement. He would no longer be considered an Indian under the law. If a married Indian man applied and if it was the opinion of the minister of Indian Affairs that he was twenty-one years old, was capable of assuming the duties and responsibilities of citizenship and capable of supporting himself and his dependents, then "the Indian and his wife and minor unmarried children" were enfranchised. If the husband and wife were separated and living apart when the husband applied for enfranchisement, the wife and children were not included in the enfranchisement. However, if the governor in council was satisfied that the wife was back together with her husband, she and her children were enfranchised. A woman who married a person who was not an Indian was automatically enfranchised as of the date of marriage. The point of this assimilationist policy is well expressed by the Supreme Court in *Corbiere:*

> The enfranchisement provisions of the *Indian Act* were designed to encourage Aboriginal people to renounce their heritage and identity and to force them to do so if they wished to take a full part in Canadian society. In order to vote or hold Canadian citizenship, status Indians had to "voluntarily" enfranchise. They were then given a portion of the former reserve in fee simple, and they lost their Indian status. At various times in history, status Indians who received higher education, or became doctors, lawyers or ministers were automatically enfranchised. Those who wanted to be soldiers in the military during the two World Wars were required to enfranchise themselves and their whole families, and those who left the country for more than five years without permission also lost Indian status.[7]

Patriarchal notions were also re-entrenched in the 1951 amendments. This fact was pointed out in the 1999 report of the Aboriginal Women's Action Network of Vancouver, which argued that sexual discrimination against Native women existed in section 11 of the amendments. The section "dictated that if Native women had children with non-status or non-Native fathers they would not be eligible for status, yet Native men were not restricted in this way and their children could be registered at their request." Furthermore, the amendments had introduced the "double-mother" clause which meant that "if a child's mother and paternal grandmother were non-status or non-Indian, the child lost status at the age of 21."[8]

Twenty years later, the sexual discrimination provision reappeared in the 1970 amendments to the *Indian Act*, but this time they were disputed in *Lavell and Bedard* at the Supreme Court of Canada.[9] The case was brought forward by Jeanette Corbiere-Lavell and Yvonne Bedard, who were both registered Indians and band members of their respective communities. As a result of their marriages to non-Indian men, they were no longer considered members of their communities, were deleted from the Indian registry and were exiled from their homes. Both argued that section 12(1)(b) of the 1970 *Indian Act* should be rendered inoperative by section 1(b) of the Canadian Bill of Rights because it denied them equality before the law by reason of sex.[10] As Kathleen Jamieson explains it: "Their argument was eloquent in its simplicity: that the *Indian Act* discriminated against them on the basis of race and sex and that ... the Bill of Rights prohibiting such discrimination should override the sections of the *Indian Act* which discriminated against them as Indian women."[11]

In his decision in *Lavell and Bedard*, Mr. Justice Ritchie of the Supreme Court of Canada held

(1) that the Bill of Rights is not effective to render inoperative legislation such as s. 12(1)(b) of the *Indian Act*;

(2) that the Bill of Rights does not require federal legislation to be declared inoperative unless it offends against one of the rights specifically guaranteed by s. 1, but where legislation is found to be discriminatory, this affords an added reason for rendering it ineffective;

(3) that equality before the law under the Bill of Rights means equality of treatment in the enforcement and application of the laws of Canada before the law enforcement authorities and the ordinary Courts of the land, and no such inequality is necessarily entailed in the construction and application of s. 12(1)(b).[12]

The majority of the Supreme Court of Canada thus ruled that Indian women were not being discriminated against. Despite this heartbreaking decision for First Nations women, Jeanette Corbiere-Lavell persisted and worked even harder to make this small change in the *Indian Act*. She stated that "women have to take the lead going into the new millennium. They should rely on their traditions, their role models and their teachings. It is important to persist, not to be deterred from the goal of protecting the children, their future and the community."[13]

As noted by Patricia Monture-Angus, the decision in this case was very hard to understand and did not make sense. In her response to the decision, Monture-Angus provides this evaluation:

> The best I can do at explaining what the Chief Justice said was to direct you to look at who is being discriminated against. Look at all Indians. All Indians are not being discriminated against. The men are not being discriminated against. Therefore, there is no discrimination based on race. Look at women ... All women are not being discriminated against because this does not happen to all White women. Therefore there is no gender discrimination. The court could not understand that this pile of discrimination (race) and that pile of discrimination (gender), amount to more than nothing. The court could not understand the idea of double discrimination. Double discrimination is not an acceptable category of equality. Grounds of discrimination are listed as separate entities.[14]

In following Monture-Angus's line of argument, I believe that the Supreme Court of Canada was not willing to take the leap at that time to support First Nations women, and I agree with the obvious: that these women were being discriminated against based on their race and gender. As a result of this decision, Indian women who had lost their status upon marrying non-Indian men had no further recourse to the courts in Canada.

This is why Sandra Lovelace took her case to the United Nations Human Rights Committee in 1977.[15] A Maliseet woman from the Tobique First Nation in New Brunswick, Lovelace had lost her Indian status when she married a non-Indian man, in accordance with section 12(1)(b) of the *Indian Act*. As a result, she and her son were denied access to education, health and housing benefits. In protest, Lovelace

> moved back to her reserve and pitched a tent on band land because she had no other place to stay. Because of the controversy around her fight, her tent was burned to the ground. The struggle for public support led her to occupation of the band office, which was also later burned down.

Leaders were not supportive: they told her to go back to where she came from and asked her what she was trying to prove.[16]

At the United Nations, Sandra Lovelace argued that the discriminatory section of the *Indian Act* violated four articles of the International Covenant on Civil and Political Rights, namely:

Article 23(1), which provides for the protection of the family;
Article 23(4), which requires the equality of spouses in marriage;
Article 26, which provides for the right to be equal before the law and to equal protection of the law, and protection against discrimination, and;
Article 27, which provides for the right of individuals belonging to minorities to enjoy their culture, practice their religion, and use their language in community with others of their group.[17]

The Committee made its decision on July 30, 1981, focusing on whether Article 27 had been violated. In doing so, it agreed that "Sandra Lovelace, because she is denied the legal right to reside on the Tobique Reserve, has by that fact been denied the right guaranteed by Article 27 to persons belonging to minorities, to enjoy their own culture and to use their language in community with other members of their group."[18]

The Committee understood "persons belonging to the minority" as meaning "those persons who are born and brought up on a reserve, who have kept ties with their community and wish to maintain those ties."[19] Although the Committee noted that Article 27 did not guarantee the right to live on a reserve, it was of the opinion that "the right of Sandra Lovelace to [have] access to her native culture and language 'in community with the other members' of her group, has in fact been and continues to be interfered with, because there is no place outside of the Tobique Reserve where such a community exists."[20] The Committee therefore found that Canada's *Indian Act* did violate Article 27 of the Covenant on Civil and Political Rights.

Despite this finding and despite the arguments made by Yvonne Bedard and Jeanette Corbiere-Lavell and by the Native women's lobby groups that emerged after these cases were decided, Canada's Parliament made no attempt to amend the *Indian Act*. As Monture-Angus states:

The legal advancement of the position of all women in Canada has been based on the struggle by Indian women for Indian women. The result of the struggle advanced by Indian women is the betterment of the legal position for all women. Indian women, however, walked away with nothing tangible, Indian women still had section 12(1)(b).[21]

THE 1985 AMENDMENTS

Amendments to the *Indian Act* were made in 1985 to bring the Act "into accord with the Canadian Charter of Rights and Freedoms to ensure equality of treatment to Indian men and women."[22] Equality rights are defined in section 15(1) of the Charter. These amendments are commonly known as Bill C-31. According to the Department of Indian Affairs, there were three fundamental principles to the amendments: (1) to eliminate discrimination from the *Indian Act*; (2) to restore Indian status to individuals who may have voluntarily or involuntarily lost their status; and (3) to give First Nations control of their membership.[23]

Despite these amendments, there is still a requirement under the *Indian Act* to define who is and who is not entitled to be registered as a status Indian. The registrar at the Department of Indian Affairs makes the final determination of this entitlement. The only difference now is that First Nations communities have the chance to control their membership by creating their own membership codes, which has become a contentious issue. I now turn my attention to the issues of registration and membership and how they affect First Nations women.

REGISTRATION

The Native Women's Association of Canada has succinctly summarized the relevant sections of Bill C-31 that pertain to registration: Those who are entitled to be registered or entitled to Indian status are now registered under section 6(1) or 6(2) of the *Indian Act*. This basically means that all registered Indians are "Bill C-31" Indians, not just those who have been reinstated as status Indians.[24]

The amendments themselves are not so clear cut, but instead have created confusing subcategories of status. For example, there are six subsections under section 6(1): 6(1)(a), (b), (c), (d),(e) and (f). As a bit of background, I will briefly describe each of these.

Section 6(1)(a) applies to those who were already registered under the previous provision of registration of the *Indian Act* (that is, section

11). Section 6(1)(b) applies to those individuals who are members of bands newly created by government. Section 6(1)(c) refers to the reinstatement of status for those who lost status through sections 12(1)(a) and (b), 12(1)(b) and 109 of the previous *Indian Act*. Section 6(1)(c)(iii) refers to the reinstatement of status to those Indian women who were involuntarily enfranchised as a result of marrying a non-Indian man, as well as any or all of her children from a former union who were involuntarily enfranchised due to that marriage. Section 6(1)(d) refers to the reinstatement of status to those men as well as their wives and unmarried children who were "voluntarily" enfranchised. Section 6(1)(e) applies to those persons who were enfranchised as a result of living outside of Canada for more than five years without the consent of the Indian Agent as well as those who became enfranchised as a result of becoming a lawyer, doctor, clergyman or upon receiving any degree from a university. Section 6(1)(f) refers to the reinstatement of children whose parents are entitled to be registered under any subsection of section 6, whether or not their parents are alive. In addition, section 6(2) refers to the reinstatement of status of children, only one of whose parents is entitled to be registered under subsection 6(1)(a) to (f).

Furthermore, section 7 provides two categories of persons who are not entitled to be registered as status Indians: non-Indian women who gained status through marriage under the old section 11(1)(f), and non-Indian women who lost this status for any reason and children of these women whose fathers are non-Indian. There were exceptions added to this section, which guaranteed that the Act would protect women and children who were entitled to status at birth.

When Bill C-31 was first introduced, many First Nations women and their families were quite excited about the possibility of reclaiming their status. However, when they encountered the bureaucratic process of the Department of Indian Affairs (DIA), it became quite apparent that registering would be very difficult. For example, in order to determine eligibility for reinstatement, applicants had to produce various types of documentation to "prove" who they were and who their ancestors were. Sometimes, it was difficult to find proof of ancestry, either because the records never existed or because church records had been lost or destroyed in fires.

In many instances, it took two to three years to go through this process. For example, one woman interviewed for the report prepared by Aboriginal Women's Action Network (AWAN) reported that she submitted an application with all of the required documentation for registration on July 10, 1986. DIA received it on July 18, 1986, but she did not hear from them until August 14, 1989 — three years later![25] It was noted by another interviewee that DIA did not automatically cross-reference applications from members of the same extended family, even if they all registered at the same time. Each individual person was required to submit her own information. In some cases, the time span in responding to each individual from the same extended family also varied.[26] First Nations women also felt that there was no process to assist them with the application and registration process. Another AWAN interviewee commented:

> I don't think that there was any group anywhere that represented the needs of the First Nations People who lost their status. They more or less floundered. And there is nowhere for them to go to. My mother lost her status, she is illiterate. How would she know where she could go to get the help? Because at every turn that she ever had, she had a hard time dealing with government agencies. If it wasn't for my sister helping my mother get her status back, then the rest of us, quite likely, would not even have it. She had problems with her birth certificate and her marriage certificate. It was a big problem.[27]

UNSTATED PATERNITY

A difficulty facing single mothers who wish to register is the fact that they are required to submit proof of First Nations paternity of their children in order for their children to be registered as status Indians. If they refuse to submit this proof, their children will not have status. If the father is not identified, DIA automatically assumes that he is non-status. This could lead to the children not having status despite the fact that their father might have status. This requirement is causing grave invasions of privacy as well as creating difficult and risky situations that First Nations women are having to put themselves into, for example, being forced to disclose the names of the men who fathered their children even if the women have been raped by these men or if they are living in terrible situations of domestic violence with these men. As noted by AWAN:

> The mother may not wish to disclose the identity of the father, in particular, in cases of sexualized violence. Not only dehumanizing, but to put

a woman into the position of having to ask her rapist for the confirmation of his deed is more than absurd. Irregardless of the circumstances, women are placed at the mercy of the father's consent. Understandably, women who find themselves faced with this dilemma express frustration and a sense of helplessness.[28]

As a result of this enforced paternalistic law, single First Nations women and their children are targets of "institutionalized sexism."[29]

REGISTRAR'S CONTROL

Another issue that affects both male and female reinstated members under Bill C-31 is the process of the registrar's decision when determining the status of a particular member. Many members who are entitled to be status Indians are appealing the registrar's decisions by arguing that they should be registered under specific subsections of section 6 of the 1985 *Indian Act*. In some cases, the registrar makes decisions arbitrarily. For example, a case that clearly illustrates how this has occurred appeared before the British Columbia Court of Appeal in 2000.[30] The registrar had removed Christine Joyce Marchand, a woman of First Nations ancestry, from the register. Her registration history began in 1972, when she married a member of the Okanagan First Nation and registered as a member of that Nation; she registered under what was then section 11(1)(f) of the 1970 *Indian Act*. In 1984, she divorced and married a non-member, immediately notifying the department of her remarriage. In 1994, she divorced again and married a man from a different band. Her name remained on the band list until 1996, when she was advised by the registrar that it had been removed.

Marchand's name was on the register immediately prior to April 17, 1985, thereby conferring her status under section 6(1)(a). The Crown, however, was arguing that the word "validly" should be included in the section, but the court said there was no basis for this. The court held that if Parliament had intended to restrict registration then it would have done so in Bill C-31 and it would have made it clear in the legislation. The court was unwilling to allow the registrar to start a roving commission to determine whether someone had Indian status. It would lead to too much uncertainty and would give rise to concerns of discriminatory and arbitrary treatment. The court found that Marchand's name should remain on the Indian registry.

In September 2000 Sharon McIvor, a lawyer and activist from the Lower Nicola Band in BC, brought a case before the BC Supreme Court, which is still before the Court.[31] She argued that the 1985 Amendments discriminated against her and her children on the basis of sex. McIvor was entitled to reinstatement of her status under section 6(2); however, her children were not considered by the registrar to be entitled unless both parents were registered Indians.

With respect to the discrimination against herself she argued that if she were a man, she would be entitled to be registered as an Indian, as would her spouse, prior to 1985. Her children would therefore be entitled to be registered, as both their parents would be registered Indians. Because she was a woman, however, McIvor's spouse was not entitled to be registered and therefore neither were her children. With respect to the discrimination against herself and her children, she argued that if she were a man and was registered as an Indian, she would have been entitled to pass her status on to her male child but not her female children.

The Act further discriminated against her because if her grandfather, rather than her grandmother, had been entitled to be registered as an Indian then her mother would have been entitled to be registered as the child of a male band member, and she would then be entitled to be registered under section 6(1)(a) and entitled to pass her status to her children under section 6(2).

She also claimed that the 1985 Act violated sections 15 and 28 of the Charter and breached international human rights law, including the *International Covenant on Civil and Political Rights* (1967), the *International Convention on the Elimination of All Forms of Racial Discrimination* (1966), the *International Convention on the Elimination of All Forms of Discrimination Against Women* (1981) and the *Convention Against Torture and other Civil Inhuman or Degrading Treatment or Punishment* (1984).

SECOND GENERATION "CUT-OFF" RULE

It is also important at this point to review the second generation "cut-off" rule of the 1985 *Indian Act* amendments, which imposes a new rule for all second-generation descendants, that is, section 6(2) Indians. Those persons and their children (the first generation) who lost their status through the old enfranchisement provisions of the *Indian Act* are to be reinstated. In order for the second generation to have status, both parents have to have status under section 6(1) or 6(2) or at least one parent has to have status under section 6(1). For example: If only one parent has status under section 6(1), the first generation child will have status under section 6(2). If that child marries another status Indian, their children (second generation) will have status under section 6(1)(f). On the other hand, if the first generation child has a non-Indian spouse, their children will not be registered.[32]

An example of this issue was brought to the Federal Court as a class-action law suit by Connie Perron and her son Michael Perron.[33] Connie Perron lost her status when she married a non-Indian man, and her sons were not granted status because of this. When her sons were grown, they married non-Indian women and as a consequence her grandchildren did not have Indian status. Perron regained her status under section 6(1)(c) of the 1985 *Indian Act*, and her sons regained their status under section 6(2). However, her grandchildren, despite being raised on the Tyendinaga reserve and learning the Mohawk culture and language, were not granted status.

Meanwhile, Connie Perron's brother married a non-Indian woman and both became registered status Indians under section 6(1)(a) of the 1985 *Indian Act*, as did their children. Even though her brother's children married non-Indian partners, the grandchildren retain their status under section 6(2).

The consequence of the second generation cut-off rule is that, unlike Connie's brother, "Connie and Michael cannot transmit Indian status to their descendants. Rather than removing the sex-based discrimination in the *Indian Act*, Bill C-31 merely added to the discriminatory consequences of section 12(1)(b) of the 1951 Act by also discriminating against her children and grandchildren."[34] Michael's children will not be able to live in the community once they become independent of their father. If their parents separate or divorce and Michael's wife has custody of them, the children will not be permitted to live on the reserve. Connie's grandchildren will never be able to inherit the family's on-reserve property.[35]

The second generation cut-off rule has been termed the Abocide Bill[36] as well as generational genocide.[37] What this means is that the status Indian could eventually die off if the parents who are status Indians do not keep track of who their children marry and if the parents do not advise the children who they need to marry in order to maintain their status.

MEMBERSHIP

As noted earlier, one of the principles of Bill-C31 was to give First Nations bands the choice of controlling their own membership. This meant that membership into a particular First Nation became separate from being registered as a status Indian. It did not necessarily mean that a status Indian was a member of her or his particular band nor did it infer that being a member of a particular First Nation granted status. "If a band's rules do not match Federal rules regarding status, an individual accepted as a member of a band may not be accepted by the Government as a status Indian. Similarly, loss of band membership does not mean loss of status."[38]

Following the introduction of the 1985 amendments, all bands had until June 29, 1987 to decide whether or not they were taking control of their membership. According to section 10 of the 1985 amendments, those bands that did choose to control their own membership, a process had been set in place for this to happen. According to section 13.1, if bands chose not to control membership, the federal status rules would continue to apply as long as a majority of electors consented that control of the band list would be left with the Department of Indian Affairs and that the decision to do so was provided to them in writing. This decision did not prevent a band from assuming control of its band list in the future (section 13.1(3)). Furthermore, a band could initially choose to control its own membership but then decide to return control to the Department of Indian Affairs. If a band did decide on this process, it became the responsibility of the department to maintain the band list. The government's rules rather than the band's would then apply.

The Native Women's Association of Canada pointed out an important fact about the membership rule:

> It is important to note that a band that takes control of membership can either include or exclude all those "conditionally" entitled. Again, though, it is important to keep in mind when the band assumes control. If this is before June 28, 1987, the band can validly exclude all the conditionally entitled. After June 28, 1987, the band may not exclude anyone

who, immediately before that date was entitled to band membership.[39]

Those who were "conditionally entitled" were mostly the women and their children who were applying for reinstatement of their status. June 28, 1987 was an important date to those who had to register as a conditional member. Bands who took control of their membership prior to this could validly exclude those people. As noted by Mary Eberts:

> Bands are permitted to shape their own membership codes, and there is no requirement for these codes not to discriminate against Bill C-31 reinstates. There is essentially no oversight mechanism for these codes, and it is very difficult to access them. In addition to these flaws, the separation of status and Band membership penalizes those Bands which do wish to be inclusive: the federal government allocations to Bands cover only status Indians, so that a Band which includes in its membership the non-status spouses and children of reinstates must care for them out of the funds provided for those Band members who are status Indians.[40]

This creates further divisions between families and explains the source of some of the conflict. Parliament may have believed it deleted those sections of the *Indian Act* that discriminated against women, but instead it added even more sections that are discriminatory.

One of the most controversial issues with respect to the membership sections of Bill C-31 is that First Nations women are bringing cases forward and asserting that their right to determine their own membership is not being upheld by the bands. This has happened because once they are reinstated, they are denied membership by their respective bands that have developed their own membership codes that exclude "reinstated women."[41]

One prominent example of this is the Sawridge Band in Treaty Eight Alberta. The Sawridge Band has been involved in litigation related to aspects of Bill C-31 since 1987.[42] Initially, representatives from the Sawridge Band, Ermineskin Band and the Sarcee Band challenged Bill C-31 due to the belief that only First Nations have the right to determine their own citizenship. The bands felt that once a First Nations woman married a First Nations man from another community, then she must move to her husband's reserve. They believed that "the woman must follow the man." As a result of this tradition, women and their children could not access what was rightfully theirs. The Federal Court found against the bands for a multitude of reasons, suggesting that First

Nations had lost the right to determine their citizenship as result of the *Indian Act*. The Federal Court of Appeal overruled this decision based on the bias of a Federal Court trial judge and sent the case back to trial. It has taken a number of years, but the Sawridge Band has now refiled the case, which will be heard in 2005 at the Federal Court.

Since the initial case was rejected, the Sawridge Band has tried other tactics to deny membership to reinstate women. It devised an extremely lengthy application form, which asked many unrelated questions about membership. During this time, the band only reinstated members of the Twinn family,[43] while other women were denied membership. Ultimately, these women brought a case to the Federal Court challenging the application form and requesting their reinstatement. Many of these women were elderly and one woman died while waiting to be reinstated. In December 2003, Justice Hugessen, of the Federal Court Trial Division, ordered that the Sawridge Band reinstate the eleven "acquired rights" women until the Sawridge Band's initial case is heard.[44]

Another struggle that is facing First Nations women and their children who are reinstated to band membership and Indian status is the distribution of per capita shares of the bands to which they belong. For example, in 1987, the Garden River Band of the Ojibways received a land-claim settlement and distributed a portion of the settlement to its members on a per capita basis (i.e., the average per person).[45] When the shares were distributed to band members, the band leadership deducted from the shares belonging to "reinstated women" the amount of money that the band had given to these women when they were enfranchised and forced to leave their communities. When the women were reinstated, the band was entitled to recover this money if the payment had exceeded $1,000. However, none of the women had been paid an amount over $1,000. So, as a result, the women did not receive a fair share of the per capita payments because they would have been penalized for monies that they never received.

Therefore, in 1992, a group of women and their children brought a class-action law suit representing members of their class (that is, all of the women reinstated to and entitled to membership and all of their respective children). They argued that they were denied an equal per capita distributive share of the land-claim settlement monies. They also argued against the band's decision that their children were ineligible to receive a portion of the per capita shares. Administrative backlogs with the DIA in the processing of their applications meant that the children had not yet been reinstated when the per capita shares from the land-claim settlement were distributed. Even though the children would be reinstated eventually, the band determined they were not eligible. Thus the delays in reinstatement interfered with the children's entitlement to their shares. To add insult to injury, the band made a distinction between these women's children and those children born to unmarried Indian women who had never been enfranchised and had never lost their status or band membership. These children did receive their shares of the land-claim settlement.

The trial court dismissed the claims made by the women and their children; they in turn appealed this decision to the Court of Appeal for Ontario. At issue was whether the band had breached its duty as a trustee to act impartially by deducting the enfranchisement payments from the women and their children's portion of the land-claim settlement. However, the Court of Appeal found that the band had established an express trust through which to make per capita payments and, that as a trustee, the band was obligated to treat all beneficiaries impartially. By deducting amounts received by the women on enfranchisement and not deducting from other members who owed money to the band, the band was discriminating against the women. Full shares should have been advanced to them. The band also knew that the children would have been reinstated eventually. The court concluded that all of the women and their children were entitled to a payment of an equal distributive share without any deduction of any kind. This was a very successful "win" for the women and their children, yet it was a disappointment that they had to take their case to court for what was rightfully theirs in the first place.

What is most difficult in these cases is the fact that although bands are given "control" over membership, some bands are still discriminating against a group of band members: those women and their children who have been reinstated under Bill C-31. The real issue at hand in First Nations communities is about identity and how members of a certain community can determine their identity. Traditionally and culturally, membership was always determined by First Nations women. In order to be true when returning to cultural ways and customs, each

First Nations must ensure that the women are included in the decisions to determine membership.

***

Clearly, there are a number of injustices facing First Nations women under Bill C-31. The Native Women's Association of Canada (NWAC) and the Aboriginal Women's Action Network (AWAN) have provided concrete recommendations to address these issues and to lobby for much-needed changes to the amendments. These recommendations include a legal review of the discrimination that still exists in Bill C-31 that would include the full participation of First Nations women in the decision-making process of legal reform and policy change. Both NWAC and AWAN recommend that both the second generation cut-off rule and the proof of paternity required by single mothers be abolished, and that advocacy and education on all issues affecting Bill C-31 be carried out. Finally, they strongly argue on behalf of launching a challenge at the international level to argue that the effects of section 6(2) are nothing less than human rights violations.[46]

Another strong advocate for change on behalf of First Nations women comes from Pam Paul of the Atlantic Policy Congress of First Nations Chiefs. In considering how traditional approaches used to determine band membership can be detrimental to women, she has recommended that "the Micmac and Maliseet First Nations should examine thoroughly the traditional methods of identity determination and incorporate these methods into a modern system of registration."[47] These traditional methods of identity determination also exist within the Haudenosaunee peoples as well as the Gitxsan Nation in British Columbia.

When Parliament enacted Bill C-31, its intention was to eliminate sexual discrimination in the *Indian Act*. First Nations women, their children and their grandchildren are, however, are still being discriminated against because of their gender. In some cases, First Nations women have "lesser" status than men. In other cases, they are being denied membership or are being denied services on-reserve because they are "Bill C-31 women." As noted by AWAN,

> … the most pervasive long-term effect [of Bill C-31] appears to be the division of community … The community has been divided along

gender lines with women receiving the brunt of discrimination; with respect to identity by degrees of "Indianness" which have produced stigmatization and racism; with respect to allocation of resources, which has created competition and nepotism; and finally, with respect to the exclusion of future generations from their birthright.[48]

There are many cases being brought before the courts challenging Bill C-31. It is interesting that many reinstated women and bands are challenging the validity of the bill because it contravenes the equality section (section 15) of the Charter, the very piece of legislation that enabled the amendments to the *Indian Act* in the first place. Many First Nations women are demanding that the courts recognize just how section 6 of the *Indian Act* continues to discriminate on the basis of gender and that such gender discrimination be read out of the Act. As a result of this continued gender discrimination, many First Nations women, their children and their grandchildren are still fighting for what is rightfully theirs — a home and a community.

NOTES

I am very thankful to my husband Sheldon Cardinal and to Katherine Hensel (a practising lawyer in Toronto) for their excellent research skills and case summaries that assisted in the writing of this chapter. The original version of this chapter was commissioned by the Aboriginal Legal Services of Toronto for its national roundtable discussions on Bill C-31.

1. As noted in the *Constitution Act of 1982,* an Aboriginal person is defined as a First Nations, Inuit and Metis. This chapter's focus is on the people that are most affected by the *Indian Act,* mostly First Nations women. The *Indian Act* defined First Nations peoples as "Indians"; however, many First Nations peoples refer to themselves as being members or citizens of their specific First Nation (Mohawk, Cree, Ojibway, Maliseet, Mik'maq and so on). The term First Nations will be used interchangeably with "Indian" when making specific reference to the *Indian Act.*

2. The Royal Commission on Aboriginal Peoples, *Report of the Royal Commission on Aboriginal Peoples,* vol. 1, *Looking Forward, Looking Back* (Ottawa: Ministry of Supply and Services Canada, 1996), 263.

3. *Act for the Better Protection of the Lands and Property of the Indians in Lower Canada,* 13 & 14 Vict., c. 42, 1850.

4. *An Act to Encourage the Gradual Civilization of the Indian Tribes in this Province,* 20 Vict., c. 26, 1857.

5. *Corbiere v. Canada* (Minister of Indian and Northern Affairs), [1999] 2 S.C.R. 203 at para. 86.

6. *An Act for the Gradual Enfranchisement of Indians and the Better Management of Indian Affairs,* 32-33 Vict. C. 6, 1869.

7. *Corbiere v. Canada* at para. 88. Source omitted.

8. Audrey Huntley and Fay Blaney, "Bill C-31: Its Impact, Implications and Recommendations for Change in British Columbia — Final Report" (Vancouver: Aboriginal Women's Action Network, 1999), 7. Hereinafter referred to as the AWAN Report.

9. *A.G. Can. v. Lavell: Issac et al. v. Bedard* (1973), 38 D.L.R. (3d) 481.

10. It is necessary at this point to consider s. 12(1)(b) in the context of Sections 11 and 12 as follows:

   S. 11 (1) Subject to section 12, a person is entitled to be registered if that person is

   (a) on the 26th day of May, 1874…considered to be entitled to hold, use or enjoy the lands and other immovable property belonging to or appropriated to the use of the various tribes, bands or bodies of Indians in Canada;

   (b) is a member of a band

   …

   (c) is a male person who is a direct descendent in the male line of a male person described in paragraph (a) or (b);

   (d) is the legitimate child of
   i) a male person described in (a) or (b), or
   ii) a person described in paragraph (e);

   (e) is the illegitimate child of a female person described in paragraph (a) (b) or (d); or

   (f) is the wife or widow of a person who is entitled to be registered by virtue of paragraph (a), (b), (c), (d) or (e).

   (2) Paragraph 1(e) applies to persons born after the 13th day of August, 1956.

   S. 12 (1) The following persons are not entitled to be registered, namely,
   (a) a person who
   i) has received or has been allotted half-breed lands or money scrip,

ii) is a descendant of a person described in paragraph (i),

iii) is enfranchised, or

iv) is a person born of a marriage entered into after the 4th day of September, 1951 and has attained the age of 21 years, whose mother and whose father's mother are not persons described in paragraph 11 (1)(a), (b) or (d) or entitled to be registered by virtue of paragraph 11(1)(c), unless, being a woman, that person is the wife or widow of a person described in section 11, and

(b) a woman who married a person who is not an Indian, unless that woman is subsequently the wife or widow of a person described in section 11.

11. Kathleen Jamieson, *Indian Women and the Law in Canada: Citizens Minus* (Ottawa: Advisory Council on the Status of Women, 1978), 86.

12. *A.G. Can. v. Lavell: Issac et al. v. Bedard* (1973), 38 D.L.R. (3d) 481.

13. Presentation by Jeanette Corbiere-Lavell at the "Equality for All in the Twenty-first Century: Second National Conference on Bill C-31 Report," Edmonton, Alberta, May 14–16, 1999.

14. Patricia Monture-Angus, *Thunder in My Soul: A Mohawk Woman Speaks* (Halifax: Fernwood Publishing, 1995), 136.

15. *Lovelace v. Canada,* [1981] 2 H.R.L.J. 158 (U.N.H.R.C.).

16. Presentation by Sandra Lovelace at the "Equality for All in the Twenty-first Century: Second National Conference on Bill C-31 Report," Edmonton, Alberta, May 14–16, 1999.

17. Anne F. Bayefsky, "The Human Rights Committee and the Case of Sandra Lovelace," *The Canadian Yearbook of International Law* (1982), 245.

18. *Lovelace v. Canada,* para. 13.2.

19. Bayefsky, "The Human Rights Committee and the Case of Sandra Lovelace," 251.

20. *Lovelace v. Canada,* para. 15.

21. Monture-Angus, *Thunder in My Soul,* 137.

22. Thomas Isaac, *Aboriginal Law: Cases, Materials and Commentary* (Saskatoon: Purich, 1999), 570.

23. See www.inac.gc.ca.

24. Native Women's Association of Canada, *Guide to Bill C-31: An Explanation of the 1985 Amendments to the Indian Act* (Toronto: NWAC, 1986), 1.

25. AWAN Report, 21.

26. Ibid., 22.

27. Ibid., 23.

28. Ibid., 24–25.

29. Ibid., 25.

30. *Marchand v. Canada* (Registrar, Indian and Northern Affairs), [2001] 2 C.N.L.R. 106 (B.C. Court of Appeal).

31. *Sharon Donna McIvor et al. v. The Registrar, Indian and Northern Affairs Canada*, Statement of Claim, September 20, 2000, filed in the British Columbia Supreme Court.

32. Ibid., 9.

33. *Connie Perron et al. v. Attorney General of Canada*, Statement of Claim under Class Proceedings Act, 1992.

34. Ibid., para. 65.

35. AWAN Report, 48.

36. Chief Harry Daniels, "Abocide Bill," paper presented at the Native Women's Association Conference on Bill C-31, Ottawa, Ontario, May 14–16, 1999.

37. Jack Wilson, "A Sociological Analysis of Bill C-31 Legislation" (MA thesis, University of Sasktchewan, 1998).

38. Native Women's Association of Canada, *Guide to Bill C-31*, 27.

39. Ibid., 17.

40. Mary Eberts, "Aboriginal Women's Rights are Human Rights," *Canadian Human Rights Act Review*, www.chrareview.org/pubs/ebertse.html. Ms. Eberts is a litigation lawyer who focuses on equality rights and Charter litigation. She is currently counsel for the Native Women's Association of Canada, which has intervener status in the *Twinn* case.

41. See, for example, *Noade v. The Blood Tribe Chief and Council* (October 24, 1995), Federal Court of Canada, Trial Division, Notice of Motion, File No. T-2243-95; *Elizabeth Courtoreille v. Walter Twinn et al.* (July 25, 1996), Federal Court of Canada, Trial Division, Statement of Claim, File No. T-1763-96; *Krahenbil et al. v. The Queen et al.* (January 24, 1996), Federal Court of Canada, Trial Division, Statement of Claim, File No. T-131-97; *Poitras v. Walter Twinn, The Council of Sawridge Band, The Sawridge Band and Canada* (Indian Affairs), Federal Court of Canada, Trial Division, Court Number T-2665-89 (September 4, 1998); *Gilbert Anderson et al. v. The Attorney General of Canada*, General Notice of Motion, October 9, 1996, T-2224-96; *Huzar et al. v. The Queen and the Sawridge Band*, Federal Court Trial Division, July 20, 1995, T-1529-95; *Prince et al v. The Queen, the Province of Alberta and the Sucker Creek Band*, Federal Court of Canada, Trial Division, T-2642-91, October 17, 1991.

42. *Sawridge v. Canada* [1995] 4 C.N.L.R. 121 (F.C.T.D.).

43. The late Walter Twinn was the chief of the Sawridge Band at the time of the initial case in 1987. He stayed in power until his death in October 1997. During this period, the late chief only reinstated his sisters, who had regained their status under Bill C-31.

44. *Sawridge Band v. Canada* (T.D.) 2003 FCT 347.

45. *Barry v. Garden River Band of Ojibways* (1997), 33 O.R. (3d) 782.

46. AWAN Report, 75.

47. Pam Paul, "The Politics of Legislated Identity. The effect of Section 6(2) of the *Indian Act* in the Atlantic Provinces." A report prepared for the Atlantic Policy Congress of First Nations Chiefs, Amherst, NS, September 28, 1999.

48. AWAN Report, 49.

CHAPTER 9

R.D.S. v. HER MAJESTY THE QUEEN: A CASE ABOUT HOME

Sherene Razack

A white police officer arrested a black 15-year-old who had allegedly interfered with the arrest of another youth. The accused was charged with unlawfully assaulting a police officer, unlawfully assaulting a police officer with the intention of preventing an arrest, and unlawfully resisting a police officer in the lawful execution of his duty. The police officer and the accused were the only witnesses and their accounts differed widely. The Judge weighed the evidence and determined that the accused should be acquitted. While delivering her oral reasons, the Judge remarked, in response to a rhetorical question by the Crown, that police officers had been known to mislead the court in the past, that they had been known to overreact particularly with non-white groups, and that such behaviour would indicate a questionable state of mind. She also stated that her comments were not tied to the police officer testifying before the court. The Crown challenged these comments as raising a reasonable apprehension of bias. After the reasons had been given, and after an appeal to the Nova Scotia Supreme Court (Trial Division) had been filed by the Crown, the Judge issued supplementary reasons which outlined in greater detail her impressions of the credibility of both witnesses and the context in which her comments were made. The Crown's appeal was allowed and a new trial ordered on the basis that the Judge's remarks gave rise to a reasonable apprehension of bias. This judgment was upheld by a majority of the Nova Scotia Court of Appeal. At issue here is whether the Judge's comments in her reasons gave rise to a reasonable apprehension of bias.

INTRODUCTION

Recently, meeting for the first time a white woman well acquainted with my family, I was drawn into a conversation about racism in the university. This young woman wanted to know about my experiences of racism, but this will to know, as it so often happens, was accompanied by anxiety. Her question, "Is there really racism in your work life?" seemed to me to be underpinned by another question: "There couldn't possibly be racism in your work life by people from my race, gender, and class, could there? What would you think of me, then?" In the face of this will not to know, I felt that I had only two choices; either one would cost me dearly. If I asserted with passion that there was indeed racism, I would most certainly spoil the pleasantness of the mood and the holiday setting in which the conversation occurred. I would be asked for proof and, as the proof would entail describing personal encounters with white people like herself, she would soon begin to feel implicated, if not accused. Few interracial encounters seem to bear the weight of the naming of racism. On the other hand, if I brushed off the question or even uttered a vague disclaimer, I would undermine my own sense of security that my social environment was a safe one, one, that is, where the realities of my life could be named and acknowledged. There is of course a gendered dimension to this story. As women we are schooled to keep the peace, to smooth feathers, to make things nice. There is also a race dimension. People of colour know from experience that there is usually a price to pay for making white people feel accused. And, there is also class. Well-mannered, middle-class girls learn quickly not to be rude by bringing up unpleasant things.

In white society, racism is a story that cannot be told without consequences. It cannot be told with ease in a hot tub on a holiday, in a classroom, or in a courtroom. The legal case that I discuss in this chapter, *R.D.S. v. Her Majesty The Queen*, illustrates this simple point in the context of the law. The courtroom is, of course, different from a hot tub, and the words of judges have different consequences than do the words of friends, family and acquaintances. While the will not to know is the same in each setting, in the courtroom, it cannot go unchallenged, as it might in interpersonal relations. Courtrooms are places where stories become official accounts of who we are as Canadians. They are places where the work of symbolic reproduction goes on. If the courts say there is no racism, it becomes exceptionally difficult to fight racist practices.

A trial is a moment of public education, a lesson in lines to be crossed and not crossed. Describing the O.J. Simpson trial as one such moment, Toni Morrison comments that such trials construct a national narrative, an agreed upon public truth. In the case of O.J., the official story, Morrison contends, is one of racial culpability. The trial teaches us about Blackness as deviance. Mr. Simpson is thrown into the role of standing in for the entire Black race.

> The official story has thrown Mr. Simpson into that representative role. He is not an individual who underwent and was acquitted from a murder trial. He has become the whole race needing correction, incarceration, censoring, silencing; the race that needs its civil rights disassembled: the race that is sign and symbol of domestic violence; the race that has made trial by jury a luxury rather than a right and placed affirmative action legislation in even greater jeopardy. This is the consequence and function of official stories: to impose the will of a dominant culture.[1]

I propose to read *R.D.S. v. Her Majesty The Queen* as a similar moment of public education in Canada, when an official story, an agreed-upon public truth, is told. This public truth is also about race. It is the story that race does not matter except under highly specific and limited circumstances. The heroes of this story are innocent, white subjects.

The power of official stories should not be underestimated, as Morrison also contends. She observes that after the O.J. trial,

> [M]any African Americans found themselves intimidated in the workplace, unwilling to voice even minor aspects of a counter-narrative lest they be accused of ... what? showing race preference? It was easier to say nothing or agree.
>
> Women were especially intimidated — because to question the story amounted to approving of or dismissing domestic violence.[2]

April Burie, representing the Congress of Black women, an intervenor in *R.D.S.,* made a similar point about the impact of R.D.S. on people of colour. If the official story is that there is no racism in Canada, then those who insist otherwise do not belong. Ms. Burie began her address to the Supreme Court with a ringing statement that this case was really about home and belonging. What does it mean for a Black person, Ms. Burie asked, to live in a place where racism and the legacies of slavery are routinely denied? At home, people use "the word."

The "racism" word. "How transformative is the power of the word," Ms. Burie observed. In places that are not home, its utterance has the power to bring down the full wrath of the justice system, to define who is reasonable and who is not, who is a good judge and who is not, and who belongs and who does not. Conversely, when it is acknowledged, the word "racism" has the power to make Canada home. It has the power to heal.[3]

While I would not claim that *R.D.S.* had the same kind of massive public educational impact on the lives of people of colour as the O.J. trial did, I do want to say that scars nonetheless remain. Lessons were taught and some of them were learned. Anyone of colour who is in a public role (and I count myself in this group), those few of us who are judges, lawyers, professors, teachers, politicians, in short, anyone of us working in the corporate, educational, judicial, or political elite, knows about the consequences of disputing the official story. We know now, if we didn't before, what happens when we dare to say that race matters. We have been warned. And this, no matter what the outcome of the decision itself, remains the enduring lesson of *R.D.S.*

It will surprise some that I begin so despondently, since the decision itself counts officially as a win. With Justices Lamer, Sopinka, and Major dissenting, six judges rendered a majority decision that Judge Sparks, a Black woman, did not exhibit a reasonable apprehension of racial bias when she observed that some police officers have been known to overreact when they come into contact with non-white groups. More than this, Justices L'Heureux-Dubé and McLachlin asserted unequivocally that the comments of Judge Sparks reflected "an entirely appropriate recognition of the facts in evidence in this case and of the context within which the case arose."[4] Judge Sparks' comments were not, as another member of the Court, Justice Cory, argued, "close to the line," unfortunate or unnecessary. Instead they were entirely appropriate. So why don't I feel at home? Why is this acknowledgement of the significance of naming racism by a majority of the Supreme Court still not enough to convey to me, a woman of colour, that the R word no longer separates the citizens from the non-citizens?

My unease with the decision in *R.D.S.* stems from the powerful lessons this case (the processes leading up to the trials as well as the trials themselves) offers people of colour about "the line" we must not cross. This is the line that Justices Lamer, Major and Sopinka all felt Judge Sparks crossed, the line that Justice Cory felt she came close to crossing, and the line that Justices L'Heureux-Dubé and McLachlin felt she did not cross. This line separates those who think race always matters from those who think it only matters, if at all, under highly limited circumstances involving specific individuals.

A commentator on the lower court trials, Richard Devlin, has offered what remains a useful beginning for thinking about the line and the claim that race matters.[5] Devlin suggests that the lower courts embraced a formalist position and rejected a realist one. In the case of the formalists, colour blindness holds sway and we are never to presume that racism is a factor to be taken into account, unless there are specific indicators that it is present. In the case of the realists, race matters and the possibility that racism has influenced how individuals think and act must always be considered. I suggest that colour blindness as revealed in the Supreme Court's responses to Judge Sparks' actions was more than simply a commitment to formal equality. I would describe colour blindness as a determined making of oneself as innocent, as outside of history, a wilful forgetting or what I described earlier as a will *not* to know. Further, with the exception of Justices L'Heureux-Dubé and McLachlin, The Supreme Court remained faithful to colour blindness. The question of whether people of colour can use the words of Justices L'Heureux-Dubé and McLachlin to name the bias of racist white judges arises. We can, but we should take note that colour blindness is always just around the corner waiting to reinstall innocent white subjects. And, the gains made towards taking race into account may not benefit racialized women because the paradigmatic form of racism that is acknowledged is the kind of racism directed at Black males.

PART ONE

MAKING INNOCENT SUBJECTS

Both lower courts in Nova Scotia allowed the appeal of the Crown and in so doing found Judge Sparks to have exhibited bias. Commenting on these decisions, Richard Devlin argued that these lower court decisions represented the triumph of colour blindness over contextualized judging. Distinguishing between formalists, who embrace colour blindness and "the assumption ... that each person is an individual and that racial identity (in the sense of skin colour) is an irrelevant consideration, unless its specific relevance can be demonstrated," and realists, for whom race matters and "racialization (in the sense of hierarchical social relations on the basis of race) is still an extremely important social factor and, therefore, that legal decision-making should always be sensitive to the possibility that race is a variable," Devlin concluded that the formalists prevailed at the lower courts in *R.D.S.*[6]

Something different occurred in the Supreme Court. There, the realists apparently won the day. That is to say, the majority decision reveals some endorsement for contextualized judging and thus for the position that race matters. It is important, however, to consider what colour blindness and contextualized judging mean for this court. Colour blindness, I would contend, as exhibited by the dissenting judges as well as some of those who ultimately decided there was no evidence of bias, is much more than a position advocating formal equality. Rather, it is a determined pursuit of white innocence, marked by considerable anxiety about the real meaning of white and Black bodies. Some of this anxiety survives even in the advocates of contextualized judging (Justices L'Heureux-Dubé and McLachlin).

The colour blindness approach espoused by Justice Major in dissent, and supported by Justices Lamer and Sopinka, is the same one articulated by the lower courts: there was no evidence presented at the trial that this particular police officer was motivated by racism. In observing that white police officers sometimes overreact when dealing with non-white youth, Judge Sparks was stereotyping police officers.[7] "Life experience is not a substitute for evidence," Justice Major opined, and "you can't stereotype police officers any more than you can stereotype women, children and minorities."[8] It is noteworthy, of course, that Judge Sparks is being accused by analogy of a misdemeanour as reprehensible as the stereotyping of society's most disadvantaged groups — women, children, and minorities. Relying on the same chain of equivalences (dominant groups = subordinate groups), Chief Justice Lamer also complained during the trial that the defence appeared to be arguing that the policeman had "some kind of hill to climb to demonstrate he was not racist."[9] Such strict scrutiny of police officers was clearly unacceptable, the honourable judge argued, because everyone can claim to be unfairly stereotyped; people of colour have no monopoly on racial stereotyping. The chief justice reminded the defence that he, too, was a victim of intolerance as a French Canadian. More significantly, asserting that the Chinese were tremendous gamblers (a statement he later denied by claiming that it was a hypothetical example[10]), both in his day as a lawyer in Montreal and at the present time, the Chief Justice wondered if he ought to apply what *he* knows about the Chinese whenever a Chinese person appeared before him. Once down this "slippery slope" of personal knowledge, he warned, the unthinkable — the stereotyping of people of colour by white judges — will start to happen.[11] Judge Sparks, by implication, is really leading us straight to racism against people of colour when she suggests that white police officers have been known to overreact when dealing with non-white populations!

If we are to link the formal logic of colour blindness in the decision to what was said by the dissenting justices during the actual trial, colour blindness begins to look less like formal logic and more like a language to support deeply held beliefs that racism does not exist. An insistence on formal equality (a white, French Canadian Supreme Court judge is the same as a Black youth in Halifax, Nova Scotia in an encounter with white police; Judge Sparks' knowledge of white police officers in Nova Scotia is the same as the Chief Justice's own knowledge of Chinese people's propensity for gambling), looks more like a *wilful* forgetting of social and historical context, not to mention of subject position. An uneasiness accompanies this heavy insistence on formal equality, an undertone of emotion, nothing empirically provable, but something that is present nonetheless in the frequent interruptions, analogies, and wild hypotheticals the dissenting judges put to the defence lawyers. Is this the unease that comes from knowing that once race is taken into account, and the stereotypes come tumbling down, what is left is the awesome fact of white supremacy? James Baldwin reminds white people: "If I am not who you think I am, then you are not who you think you are either. And that is the crisis."[12] Without gambling Chinese and emotional Black women partial to their own people and biased against white police officers, there would be no reasonable and impartial white men.

Not all members of the Supreme Court espoused colour blindness with the same degree of insistence as Chief Justice Antonio Lamer and Justice Major. However, even those who ended up voting to deny the

Crown's appeal and who concluded that there was no apprehension of bias, still relied on some version of colour blindness and betrayed the same anxiety to establish that race does not matter, except under highly specific circumstances. Justice Cory, (concurring with Madame Justices L'Heureux-Dubé and McLachlin), made a distinction between references to a social context based on expert evidence and tendered in a case like *Parks* (a case involving jury selection which I discuss below) and a case like *R.D.S.* where social context is being used to assist in determining credibility.[13] He concluded:

> In some circumstances it may be acceptable for a judge to acknowledge that racism in society might be, for example, the motive for the over-reaction of a police officer. This may be necessary in order to refute a submission that invites the judge as trier of fact to presume truthfulness or untruthfulness of a category of witnesses, or to adopt some other form of stereotypical thinking. Yet it would not be acceptable for a judge to go further and suggest that all police officers should therefore not be believed or should be viewed with suspicion where they are dealing with accused persons who are members of a different race. Similarly, it is dangerous for a judge to suggest that a particular person overreacted because of racism unless there is evidence adduced to sustain this finding.[14]

For Justice Cory, if Judge Sparks is off the hook, it is largely because the Crown also generalized when it submitted that there was no reason to suspect a police officer might be lying. To suggest that police are somehow different from others and never lie was, for Justice Cory, also an example of unacceptable group stereotyping. In spite of his overall assessment that Judge Sparks made her decision based on the evidence before her, Justice Cory finds Judge Sparks' comments "unfortunate,"[15] "troubling,"[16] "worrisome,"[17] "inappropriate,"[18] and "unnecessary."[19] Ultimately, concluding that the comments of Judge Sparks were "close to the line,"[20] Justice Cory is not far off from Justices Major, Lamer, and Sopinka in regarding race as irrelevant unless its relevance can be very specifically demonstrated.

To Justices L'Heureux-Dubé and McLachlin, race matters a good deal more than it does to their male colleagues. Instead of finding Judge Sparks' comments close to the line as did Justice Cory, they explicitly announce that the comments "reflect an appropriate recognition of the facts in evidence in this case and of the context within which the case arose — a context known to Judge Sparks and to any well-informed member of the community."[21] Relying on Jennifer Nedelsky's argument[22] that judging requires that we take the views of marginalised social groups into account, they proceed to elaborate that a reasonable person engaging in contextualized judging in this instance would have to take into account anti-black racism[23] and the Donald Marshal Inquiry which indicated that racism existed in the Nova Scotia Justice system.[24] In their reasons, Justices L'Heureux-Dubé and McLachlin write unequivocally that "a reasonable person is cognizant of the racial dynamics in the local community."[25] If this alone served as precedent, racial minorities would have gained a great deal.

If, however, these comments are then contextualized in terms of how the justices then go on to assess Judge Sparks, a little of their vigour is lost. Justices L'Heureux-Dubé and McLachlin advise us to remember that Judge Sparks delivered an oral judgment and that she was probably an overworked trial judge.[26] They note that she assessed the testimony[27] and the evidence[28] before her and that her comments were made in response to the Crown's submissions.[29] They clarify that Judge Sparks found a probable overreaction on the part of the police[30] but did not conclude that this overreaction was racially inspired.[31] While all of these paragraphs might be taken to weaken the central argument that race matters, in that they sound like the "mitigating circumstances" we ought to take into account to exonerate Judge Sparks, ultimately, their argument does return to a stronger position:

> While it seems clear that Judge Sparks *did not in fact* relate the officer's probable overreaction to the race of the appellant *R.D.S.*, it should be noted that if Judge Sparks *had* chosen to attribute the behaviour of Constable Steinburg to the racial dynamics of the situation, she would not necessarily have erred. As a member of the community, it was open to her to take into account the evidence as to what occurred against that background.[32]

Agreeing with Appeal Court Judge Freeman (dissenting from the lower court's decision), Justices L'Heureux-Dubé and McLachlin repeat his words that this case was "racially charged" from the start on account of its location and the race of the key players.[33] While this does not declare that racism is always a factor in such contexts, it directs us to consider how it might be operating.

PART TWO

CALLING WHITE JUDGES TO ACCOUNT

What, then, is the wider application of a direction from the two female justices of the Supreme Court that comes astonishingly close to making Canada home? The force of colour blindness from the other members of the Court gives me pause. It is not easy to forget the wilfulness behind their impulse to treat us all as the same, as though history and context did not matter. Neither is it easy to ignore the high anxiety that accompanied this performance of strict logic during the trial. Here I want to briefly explore how the words of Justices L'Heureux-Dubé and McLachlin might apply in cases of reasonable apprehension of bias when the judge whose impartiality is in question is white, and when what is at issue is his bias against, rather than for, Black men. I then want to anticipate some of the issues when the "race" in question is the race of racialized women.

ACCUSED BLACK MEN AND WHITE JUDGES

On November 15, 1993, a white, male, trial judge began hearing the case of Dudley Laws and Lawrence Motley, both Black men accused of transporting illegal migrants across the Canadian/U.S. border. The trial was a highly publicized one involving a well-known Toronto Black activist, Dudley Laws. It had all the ingredients of the "racially charged" environment noted in *R.D.S.* Mr. Laws is well-known for his activism on the issue of police accountability for the shootings of Black men and the case involved police wiretaps and the possibility that the police had deliberately entrapped Mr. Laws, one of their most vociferous critics. Before the proceedings could even commence, Judge Whealy, the presiding judge, rather unceremoniously demanded that male spectators wearing hats take them off. One individual (who later was identified as the Imam for prisons) who was asked on the first day to take off his hat or leave, protested that he was wearing a head covering for religious reasons. The fracas in the courtroom led to a formal ruling by Judge Whealy two days later. In this ruling he made clear that "a presiding judge not only has the authority but also the duty to oversee the demeanour, solemnity and dignity which must prevail in a superior court of law."[34] The judge noted that any highly visible groups must be barred from the courtroom. Recognizing that head coverings may be required in some religions, the judge was prepared to grant this right to major, recognized religions but warned that "self-proclaimed and unrecognized forms of religion or cults claiming to be religious" would receive limited protection under the Charter of Rights and Freedoms.[35] Subsequently, other men wearing the head covering were also banned. Since the religion in question was Islam (the world's largest religion), it is not difficult to see why the defence in this case would argue that the barring of Muslim men wearing headdress, all of whom were Black, indicates a reasonable apprehension of bias. On January 5, 1995, ruling again on the motion for an order for another judge, Judge Whealy again reiterated his position, denying the motion.[36] Michael Taylor, one of the men banned from the courtroom, filed a complaint against the judge with the Canadian Judicial Council (an interesting parallel to the Halifax Police Chief who complained to the Chief Justice of the Nova Scotia Trial decision about Judge Sparks). The Council decided that a single ruling by a judge was insufficient evidence to call for Judge Whealy's dismissal. The Canadian Human Rights Commission, with whom Taylor also filed a complaint, refused to hear the case because of judicial immunity. Ultimately, Michael Taylor's lawyer went to the Federal Court of Appeal to ask that the Commission be required to hear the case. A lawyer for the Attorney General argued that Whealy's judicial immunity was absolute and should not be subjected to a discrimination hearing by the commission. He further argued that Taylor could simply wait to resolve the issue at the appeal of the Dudley Laws case, a point disputed by Taylor's lawyer on the grounds that the appeal only concerns Law's rights as the accused and not Taylor's rights as a spectator.[37]

What is immediately a difference in the case of Michael Taylor is that it has not been possible to even air the issue of judicial bias given the great difficulty in getting any single legal body to hear the complaint. This in itself is instructive. Should the issue of Judge Whealy's bias ever be subjected to scrutiny, would it then be possible to argue that in dismissing Islam as a fringe religion, and finding one of its practices incompatible with dignity and decorum in a courtroom, Judge Whealy showed himself to be biased against male, Black Muslims?[38] Further, could it be argued that the judge brought to this case personal knowledge about world religions that was in fact stereotypical and revealing of his bias towards and limited knowledge of the religions practised by racial minorities? Could we point to the racially charged atmosphere (Black/police issues in Toronto) and say that Judge Whealy has a duty to acknowledge the racially charged nature of the case, the more so when he considers his duty to ensure that justice is done and is seen to be done? Barring Muslim skull caps from the courtroom can hardly indicate his sensitivity to justice being seen to be done.

With the words of Justices L'Heureux-Dubé and McLachlin, I believe such arguments can be raised with some chance of success when the cases involve Black men in Halifax or Toronto, and when it involves Aboriginal men in the West. They will not, however, be easy arguments to make. As the Laws and Motley trials indicate, the first problem is finding a place to make such arguments when the complaint is made against white judges. Further, neither Chief Justice Lamer nor Justice Allan McEachern of the BC Supreme Courts faced censure when complaints of racism were made about them. Indeed, in a situation of considerable irony, it was Justice McEachern who heard the complaint against Chief Justice Lamer.

There has been greater success in naming racism when the issue is the potential bias of jury members, although here again, lower courts have been less than enthusiastic. In the precedent-setting case *R. v. Parks*,[39] the Supreme Court concluded that in communities where racial bias was clearly extreme against the group to which the accused belonged, it was permissible to interrogate potential jurors in order to establish whether or not they were biased. Relying on *Parks,* in *R. v. Williams,* Madam Justice McLachlin, writing for the majority, concluded that an Aboriginal man accused of robbery and tried in British Columbia, did have the right to have potential jurors questioned about their attitudes to Aboriginal peoples. Overturning the lower courts, she wrote:

> ... there is an equation of being drunk, Indian and in prison. Like many stereotypes, this one has a dark underside. It reflects a view of native people as uncivilized, and without a coherent social and moral order. The stereotype prevents us from seeing native people as equals.
>
> There is evidence that this widespread racism has translated into systemic discrimination in the criminal justice system ... Finally, as Esson

C.J. noted, tensions between aboriginals and non-aboriginals have increased in recent years as a result of developments in such areas as land claims and fishing rights. These tensions increase the potential of racist jurors siding with the Crown as the perceived representative of the majority's interest.[40]

These statements are a clear acknowledgement that racism exists and can affect how juries think. It is important to note, however, that such ringing declarations that racism can and does exist rely on the accumulation of reports on systemic racism.[41] They also emerge after concerted efforts by anti-racist groups to name racism in the justice system.[42] Racialized women, for a number of reasons, generally have not been the focus of such texts and activities. One exception is the attention given to the murder of Helen Betty Osborne, an Aboriginal woman, by the commissioners of the Aboriginal Justice Inquiry of Manitoba. Here the commissioners note that Aboriginal women are the targets of sexual violence by white men in the remote Northern Manitoba community in which Osborne lived. They note too that Osborne's gender possibly contributed to the lack of outcry about her murder both from her own community and from the white community. Importantly, however, while the specific racism directed at Aboriginal women is noted, the commissioners do not then conclude that racism influenced the sixteen-year delay in bringing Osborne's murderers to justice.[43] When a case involves possible bias against racialized women, what would the Courts use to establish systemic racism and widespread community bias? The lack of "proof" of widespread racism against women of colour and Aboriginal women, in particular proof of the kind Courts prefer, namely statistics and "scientific" studies, remains a major barrier. It is to this aspect that I turn in the postscript.

POSTSCRIPT

RACE IN SCIENTIFIC DRESS

Throughout the writing of this comment, I repeatedly sought, and failed, to find a way to describe the subject position from which I experienced *R.D.S.* The personal knowledge of racism that I felt I brought to the case, knowledge acquired in my everyday life as a woman of colour who is an academic, could not be translated into the language this comment required. It seemed to have no place in scholarly argument. For instance, I was struck by two details more than any other and found them immensely believable and central, and yet I could only weave them into the comment in a postscript. First, R.D.S. is a young, Black man and a cousin of the youth, N.R., who was being arrested by the white officer. In R.D.S.'s version of events, he was trying to get the details of his cousin's arrest in order to go and tell N.R.'s mother what was happening. A woman, in the crowd of mostly young people under twelve that gathered, attempted to get the phone number of R.D.S. in order to tell his mother what was happening, but the police officer held R.D.S. in a choke hold and he could not respond. In the end, the first youth being arrested, N.R., gave the woman the phone number.[44] Second, the police officer in this case complained to his union and the police chief about Judge Sparks' comments. The Halifax Police Chief then publicly complained to the Chief Family Court Judge. A local newspaper was contacted. The newspaper sought access to the tapes of the transcript but Judge Sparks refused to grant access on the grounds that the transcripts were protected under the *Young Offenders Act*.[45] The Crown pursued its appeal on the basis of apprehension of bias with what appeared to be unseemly vigour.[46]

Taken all together, these two aspects of *R.D.S.* (the behaviour of the Black people in the story and the behaviour of the white people in decision-making roles) push many buttons for me, as I imagine they do for other people of colour. The youth's story about trying to get a message home is entirely familiar. This act of communal solidarity underscores that people of colour must look out for each other in a racially hostile world, and it specifically recalls the need to have community strategies for dealing with racist police who are so often beyond accountability.[47] The machinery that swung into action against Judge Sparks for calling attention to the operation of racism — the media, the judiciary, the civil service, is also all too familiar. The power of the dominant group, and the speed at which that power is exerted to penalize people of colour who name racism, are elements of the everyday experiences of many people of colour.[48] Yet something makes it difficult for the fully contextualized, historical meaning of these features of life in a racist country to enter the courtroom as things we know to be relevant to the case. The same "something" makes it difficult for me to argue that they must enter this article as *scholarly* and not personal knowledge and must help us to read the decision. Having been through the exercise of reviewing both the videotape of the trial and the decision, I wondered what would actually facilitate the entry of everyday and elite racism as facts in the courtroom. Could we, for instance, call upon the studies of everyday racism[49] to support the credibility of the story of R.D.S. that he was only trying to get a message home? Could we use the studies of elite racism[50] to show how quickly and efficiently the elite swung into action to call Judge Sparks to account, a showing of white group consensus? How many more Marshall Inquiries and Commissions on Systemic Racism will suffice to make the case that Canadians are racist and carry specifically organised racist responses into the courtroom? Can we draw on psychologies of prejudice, as American litigators have done, to argue that white stereotyping of Blacks is near inevitable in a racist society?[51] I think we can, but not without considerable opposition. It is clear that the ideas that give colour blindness its force, ideas of innocent white subjects without histories or present day privilege, block the naming of racism at a deep emotional level. I cannot easily forget the *demeanour* of several members of the Supreme Court as they pushed and pulled at whatever argument they were offered to make it fit into the small space of colour blindness. Dressing race up in scientific garb seems a weak strategy at best in the face of such denial.

The problems associated with naming racism in the courtroom are already large enough but when we add gender to the pot, the small ray of light offered by Justices L'Heureux-Dubé and McLachlin begins to fade even more. How do we prove that communities are racist towards women of colour, Black women, and Aboriginal women? When I think of the specific forms of racism women face, I wonder how we might scientifically argue that white jurors or white judges possess a number of stereotypical perceptions of us. While racialized women encounter some of the same obstacles in naming their realities in a court of law as do racialized men, obstacles I have summed up as the will *not* to know on the part of white people, our problems are also gender specific. We will need to talk, for example, of the sexual violence that is so central to the racism directed against women of colour and Aboriginal women. Bringing gendered racism to a Court's attention begins with expanding the paradigm of what constitutes racism. But complicating the stories of what racism is, talking about how ethnicity, class, colour, sexuality, ability and gender operate to structure it, requires a repertoire of well-known images and signs. Racialized women have generally had to choose from the images in circulation about the oppression of Black men or white women and these images, it goes without saying, are a limited number to begin with. After Rodney King, it is hard to argue that racism has other faces beyond the image of white policemen beating Black men, especially when this very egregious form of racism is in itself routinely denied. When courts have shown themselves receptive to feminist narratives, the kinds of studies and experts on which they rely have not generally paid attention to how race structures a woman's experience of gender oppression as well as her responses to it. For example, sexual violence directed against racialized women is routinely minimized and acknowledged only when our cultures and the men of our communities can be marked as barbaric and blamed for the violence.[52]

To communicate gendered racism to the Court, we will need a language of interlocking oppression where we can describe how the racism we experience has a different structure to it because it depends upon how female, racialized bodies are perceived and treated in this society. We will also need some of those scientific studies and Royal Commissions that quantify the systemic racism directed at us. For example, a detailed study of racism in the health care professions would bring to the surface the plethora of racist perceptions and treatment of racial minority women as nurses and nurses aides. Such a study would also mark the structural features of this site of racism, where an entire segment of the labour market is virtually structured to restrict the opportunities of racialized women. When a Black nurse gets to a courtroom to protest racism in employment, she is going to have to show that what happened to her happened to many other racialized women. If the experience of Judge Sparks teaches us anything, it is that we had better be prepared. Gendered racism is not an easy case to make to people who are so intent on taking themselves outside of history. The double legacy of *R.D.S.* for me is that while it offers a small ray of light that courts will acknowledge that race does matter, it also confirmed that to make it matter more often, we will need something more than a scientific study or two on the operation of racism in Canadian society. And racialized women will need even more.

NOTES

1. Toni Morrison, "The Official Story: Dead Man Golfing," in Toni Morrison and Claudia Brodsky Lacour, eds., *Birth of a Nation'hood* (New York: Pantheon Books, 1997), xxviii.

2. Ibid., xx.

3. *R.D.S. v. Queen*, File no. 25603, 10 March 1997. All subsequent references to comments made during the Supreme Court's hearing of the case refer to this source, the videotaped trial prepared for television (hereafter *Videotape*).

4. *R.D.S. v. Her Majesty The Queen and The Women's Legal Education and Action Fund, the National Organisation of Immigrant and Visible Minority Women of Canada, the African Canadian Legal Clinic, the Afro-Canadian Caucus of Nova Scotia and the Congress of Black Women*, File no. 25603, 10 March 1997, paragraph 30.

5. Richard F. Devlin, "We Can't Go On Together with Suspicious Minds: Judicial Bias and Racialized Perspective in *R. v. R.D.S.*," *Dalhousie Law Journal* 18, no.2 (1995), 408.

6. Ibid., 436.

7. *R.D.S.*, note 4 above, para. 19.

8. Ibid., paras. 13 and 18.

9. *Videotape*.

10. Dale Anne Freed, "Top Judge Accused of 'Stereotyping,'" *The Toronto Star*, 4 November 1997, A25. Citing the comments of Lamer J. during the trial of *R.D.S.*, the Chinese Canadian National Council lodged a complaint with the Canadian Judicial Council in Ottawa. Lamer J. wrote to the *Toronto Star* one day later explaining that he was using the Chinese example as a hypothetical. See Nicolaas Van Rijn, "Chief Justice Denies Attack on Chinese," *The Toronto Star*, 5 November 1997, A8. The judicial council investigating the complaint against Lamer made by the Chinese Canadian National Council concluded that judges must be free to use hypotheticals. Ironically, this decision was written by BC Chief Justice Allan McEachern, himself accused of racist remarks in his decision as the trial judge in the Gitksan and Wet'suwet'en lands claims case. "Top Judge Cleared of Misconduct — Judicial Council Acquits Lamer," *Vancouver Sun*, 24 January 1998, A7.

11. *Videotape.*

12. James Baldwin, "A Talk to Teachers" (1963), in Rick Simonson and Scott Walker, eds., *Graywolf Annual Five: Multicultural Literacy* (St. Paul: Graywolf Press, 1988), 8, cited in Lucy Lippard, ed., "Introduction," *Partial Recall* (New York: The New York Press, 1992), 43.

13. *R.D.S.,* note 4 above, para. 127.

14. Ibid., para. 132.

15. Ibid., para. 150.

16. Ibid., para. 151.

17. Ibid., para. 152.

18. Ibid., para. 153.

19. Ibid., para. 158.

20. Ibid., para. 152.

21. Ibid., para. 30.

22. Jennifer Nedelsky, "Embodied Diversity and the Challenges to Law," *McGill Law Journal* 42, no. 91 (1997).

23. *R.D.S.,* note 4 above, para. 46.

24. Ibid., para. 47.

25. Ibid., para. 48.

26. Ibid., para. 50.

27. Ibid., para. 51.

28. Ibid., para. 52.

29. Ibid., para. 53.

30. Ibid., para. 54.

31. Ibid., para. 55.

32. Ibid., para. 56.

33. Ibid., para. 58.

34. Her Majesty The Queen and Dudley Laws, *Ruling,* Ontario Court of Justice, Whealy, J., 22 November 1993, p. 1, para. 10.

35. Ibid., p. 5, para. 30 and p. 6, para. 5.

36. Her Majesty The Queen and Dudley Laws, Ontario Court of Justice, *Ruling,* Whealy, J., 5 January 1994.

37. Canadian Press, "Make Judge Go Before Rights Panel Court Told," *The Toronto Star,* 8 December 1997, A6.

38. Women wearing headdress were permitted to stay. The reasoning was that most civilized peoples believed that men must take off their hats as a mark of respect.

39. *R. v. Parks* (1993), 84 C.C.C. (3d) 353.

40. *R. v. Williams*, File no. 25375, 4 June 1998.

41. These include various Royal Commissions on Aboriginal Peoples, the Donald Marshal Inquiry and the Report of the Commission on Systemic Racism.

42. For example, the African Canadian Legal Clinic, Aboriginal Legal Services of Toronto and the Urban Alliance on Race Relations.

43. *Report of the Aboriginal Justice Inquiry of Manitoba*, vol. 2, *The Deaths of Helen Betty Osborne and John Joseph Harper.* Commissioners A.C. Hamilton and C.M. Sinclair (Winnipeg: Queen's Printer, 1991), 1–107.

44. *R.D.S.*, note 4 above, para. 67.

45. Devlin, "We Can't Go On Together with Suspicious Minds," 411.

46. Ibid., 429.

47. While writing this case comment, the *Toronto Star* ran a three-part series detailing cases where the police assaulted mostly poor people and people of colour and faced no disciplinary measures. See John Duncanson and Jim Rankin, "Above the Law," *The Toronto Star,* 30 November 1997, A1, A14. As well, Bill 105, the *Ontario Police Services Amendments Act* was passed which abolished the Police Complaints Commission and any other avenue of complaint to an external, civilian authority about police practices. Rosie Dimanno, "New Era for complaints against police," *The Toronto Star,* 8 December 1997, E1.

48. In her study of everyday racism, Philomena Essed documented the stories of over fifty women of colour. Many of these women made statements about the refusal of white people to hear stories of racism and their often hostile responses to those who told such stories. See *Everyday Racism,* translated from the Dutch by Cynthia Jaffe (Claremont, CA: Hunter House Inc., 1990). It is also noteworthy that the naming of whites as a group with power has often produced a near hysterical denial in the courtroom. For an example of this, see the reaction of Judge Allan McEachern to the suggestion that whites as a group have been dominant in the history of white/Aboriginal relations in British Columbia. Reported by Dara Culhane in *The Pleasure of the Crown* (Burnaby, BC: Talon Books, 1998), 136–137.

49. Philomena Essed, *Understanding Everyday Racism* (Newbury Park, CA: Sage Publications, 1993).

50. Teun van Dijk, *Elite Racism* (Newbury Park, CA: Sage Publications, 1993).

51. Cynthia Kwei Yung Lee, "Race and Self-Defence: Toward a Normative Conception of Reasonableness," *Minnesota Law Journal* 81, no.2 (December 1996), 462. Richard Devlin also discusses the sociological and psychological research that would support the notion that race is frequently conflated with

criminality. Devlin, "We Can't Go On Together with Suspicious Minds," 432.

52. See Sherene Razack, *Looking White People in the Eye: Gender, Race and Culture in Courtrooms and Classrooms* (Toronto: University of Toronto Press, 1998), chaps. 3 and 5.

CHAPTER 10

M. v. H.:
THE CASE FOR GAY AND LESBIAN
EQUALITY IN MARRIAGE AND FAMILY LAW

Martha McCarthy & Joanna Radbord

On December 9, 2004, the Supreme Court of Canada issued its advisory opinion in the *Reference re: Same-Sex Marriage*.[1] Our highest court affirmed that marriage for same-sex couples flows from the equality guarantee of the Canadian Charter of Rights and Freedoms. The meaning of marriage is not a frozen concept limited to heterosexual unions but has evolved to include the marriages of same-sex couples within its purview. Just as the Privy Council recognized women within the category of "persons" for the purposes of public office, despite centuries of exclusion from civil life,[2] the commitments of lesbians and gay men have now come to be recognized within the concept of marriage, despite a long history of denigration of same-sex relationships.

The *Reference* opinion has given the federal government the "green light" to proceed with equal marriage legislation. The proposed legislation, expected to pass in the spring of 2005, will have national effect and ensure that equal marriage is available to same-sex couples across Canada. Already, thousands of same-sex couples have valid legal marriages celebrated in the seven provinces and one territory that have litigated the issue. We were counsel to the Ontario and Quebec couples on the *Reference,* and counsel to the seven same-sex couples in the Ontario equal marriage case of *Halpern v. Canada (A.G.)*.[4] Throughout the equal marriage litigation, we argued that the case for equal marriage was easy. We said that the Supreme Court of Canada ruling known as

M. v. H. had already decided the issue. It seems judges have agreed with this analysis, as the common-law bar to the marriages of same-sex couples has been struck down as unconstitutional by court after court that has considered the issue. In celebration of what has been achieved, and in thanks to those who have brought us to this juncture, this chapter revisits the *M. v. H.* decision as the case which laid the foundation for equal marriage for same-sex couples.

IN THE BEGINNING ...

In 1992, when Martha was in her second year of law practice, a client walked into her office and changed her career. She told her the following story. She met her partner in 1980, while travelling with a group in Nepal. They started an immediate love affair, which continued when they returned to Toronto. In 1982, they moved in together and started their own business. They cohabited for the next ten years, sharing virtually every part of their lives, acquiring property together, pooling income and sharing expenses. Each year they celebrated October 15th as their anniversary.

They had just separated. The client had $5.64 in her bank account, no assets apart from a jointly owned country property, and no source of income apart from the jointly owned business. She took a few personal possessions with her, leaving behind all of the property that they had acquired together. When she went back the next day, the locks to both homes had been changed and when she phoned the business, it was identified under a new name. In addition, Martha was denied access to the business answering service and cut off from business contacts. The accountant told her that he was not authorized to give her information. Her partner had told her that day in a telephone call that she was not entitled to anything — that the law did not recognize her because she had been in a lesbian relationship.

It didn't take much to see that our client, on whose behalf we were both acting and who later came to be known as M. in the case of *M.* v. *H.,*[5] was discriminated against because of her sexual orientation. If she had been in an opposite-sex relationship, she would have had immediate access to family law remedies, and she could have obtained spousal support on an interim basis within weeks of separation. Little did we know that six years later we would argue the constitutional issue at a trial and an appeal, and that there would be more than fifty other judicial attendances in the case without M. ever receiving any relief from the financial stress of separation. Little did we know that, because the case was fundamentally so simple, this woman's struggle would result in a decision from the Supreme Court of Canada that contributed to achieving equality for gays and lesbians in Canada, culminating in the achievement of equal marriage.

On May 20, 1999, the Supreme Court of Canada released its decision in *M. v. H.* In an 8 to 1 decision, the Court struck down the opposite-sex only definition of "spouse" in section 29 of the *Family Law Act*[6] as contrary to the Canadian Charter of Rights and Freedoms, holding that "the exclusion of same-sex partners from the definition [of spouse] violates the equality rights guaranteed in s. 15 of the *Charter*" and "cannot survive any of the stages of review that comprise the s. 1 analysis."[7]

The *M. v. H.* decision was the next logical step in the development of Canadian family law. In the 1995 case of *Egan v. Canada*, Jim Egan and Jack Nesbitt, a gay male couple, challenged the constitutionality of the *Old Age Security Act* definition of "spouse." Under the Act's definition of "spouse," despite sharing their lives together since 1948, Jim Egan and Jack Nesbit were denied spousal Old Age Security benefits because they were not of the opposite sex.

While the Supreme Court of Canada unanimously recognized sexual orientation as a ground of discrimination, a majority of the Supreme Court of Canada determined that this treatment, while discriminatory, was constitutional.[8] Four justices held that there was no discrimination, and because sexual orientation was relevant to fundamental social norms and values, any discrimination would be justified.[9] Mr. Justice Sopinka, who wrote the swing decision, found that the legislation discriminated but stated that the government should be granted some time to respond to the widespread discrimination against gays and lesbians, because their claims to equality were "novel."

On the same day as *Egan*, the Supreme Court of Canada released its decision in *Miron v. Trudel.*[10] In that case, an unmarried opposite-sex couple challenged the definition of "spouse" under the *Insurance Act*. In contrast to *Egan*, the majority of the Supreme Court in *Miron v. Trudel* held that the differential treatment as between unmarried and married heterosexuals was discriminatory and could not be justified under section 1. Marriage was not a relevant marker for the legislature's purpose of reducing economic hardship after a family member had been injured. The "married" requirement was unconstitutional.

Despite the disappointing loss in *Egan*, these two decisions signalled that the Court was willing to question whether privileges should be associated with heterosexuality and marriage. In particular, a majority of the Court indicated that it would not tolerate discrimination against same-sex spouses indefinitely, and that it was constitutionally suspect to draw distinctions between unmarried and married opposite-sex cohabitees.[11] Whether by law reform or court challenge, these decisions confirmed that Canada was moving towards more equitable treatment of all intimate partners, be they married opposite-sex or same-sex cohabitees. This functional approach to family law was affirmed in *M. v. H.*

REACHING FOR SUBSTANTIVE EQUALITY

The *M. v. H.* decision had all of the hallmarks of a massive victory for equality. The language of the decision, following on the powerful drama of *Vriend v. Alberta*,[12] shows that the Supreme Court was embracing the notion of substantive equality for gays and lesbians. This should have meant the achievement of real and meaningful, contextually driven, discrimination-attacking equality. Substantive equality is the key to dealing with the intersections between race, gender and sexual orientation. A formal equality analysis will necessarily fragment persons as it seeks a dualistic comparison between the rights claimant and current rights holders. Substantive equality offers the thread of hope against discrimination that works synergistically, rather than additively. It can cope with the multiplicity of peoples' experience of privilege and oppression.

Formal equality is about treating "like" people alike and "different" people differently. The concept of sameness and difference is founded in biology, morality and tradition — the limiting frameworks founded in discriminatory thinking. Formal equality justifies segregation, concentration camps and the refusal to allow women to vote or to be senators. Since *Andrews v. Law Society*,[13] we in Canada have espoused to a higher promise of equality than the formal equality offered by the jurisprudence of other nations. Canadian courts have said that section 15 of the Charter promises a substantive approach to equality, focused on the effects of the impugned law on the disadvantaged group, from the perspective of members of the group. It demands that we step away from an us–them comparison, and instead situate the rights claimant in her larger social and political context and evaluate her claim from her own perspective.[14] The aim of substantive equality is to change the material conditions — the substance — of people's lives, so as to remedy *and* prevent discrimination. It attempts to ensure that law recognizes the inherent dignity of all persons.

Andrews is now twenty years old and, although we have always said that it promised substantive equality in law, it has apparently been easier to talk about it than to do it. We were supposed to have learned something from the transition from *Bliss* to *Brooks*.[15] (*Brooks* overruled *Bliss* and recognized that pregnancy discrimination was prohibited by the bar on sex discrimination.) However, our highest court has consistently struggled to apply a substantive equality approach. In particular, when the Supreme Court decided the (in)equality trilogy in 1995, it was split 5 to 4 in maintaining a substantive approach to equality.[16] The minority wanted to introduce a requirement that the distinction not be "relevant" to the benefit at issue. This was a formal equality approach with a new name, since the issue remained whether the rights claimant was relevantly the same or relevantly different from those persons who received a benefit. This division was sparked, no doubt, by the challenge to the definition of "spouse" under the *Old Age Security Act* by a gay couple in *Egan v. Canada*.

In *Egan*, the Court was so divided over its approach to equality rights and the justification of their infringement, that no one knew what the *Egan* decision stood for, except that the Court now disagreed about the fundamental test for equality law. Several unanimous equality decisions were released,[17] but the Court openly stated that it had agreed to disagree on the test for equality. Then something strange happened. The Court asked for a rehearing of *Law*, a woman's case about age discrimination for survivor pensions.[18] When the unanimous decision was released, the Court had agreed on an articulation of the equality test that appeared to endorse substantive equality, but in its effort to amalgamate all views on the bench, it retained vestiges of the relevance approach. Once again, minorities were left wondering whether the Court could practice what it was preaching. In *Law*, the Court had to define discrimination in the abstract, having found no discrimination in Ms. Law's case. *Law* focused on the effects of the impugned measure on the disadvantaged and one could hope that the Court had eliminated the idea that discrimination doesn't exist if the distinction is relevant to the purpose of the legislation.

M. V. H.: LIVING BETWEEN THEORY AND REALITY

In *M. v. H.*, the Court applied the reasoning in *Law* to find that section 29 of the *Family Law Act* gave heterosexual couples a right that it denied to gays and lesbians. This denial was economically damaging and unfair. Just as important, the Court also recognized the moral and societal implications of the refusal to grant gays and lesbians spousal and familial status. The message of exclusion, of being less worthy of protection and support, was unacceptable. It was demeaning and alienating. The government appealed to formal equality principles, relying on arguments about sameness and difference, rooted in biology and history and morality — the three pillars of discrimination. The government's arguments were rejected. Substantive equality seemed finally to apply in the context of sexual orientation discrimination. The Supreme Court of Canada's focus on equal respect and dignity held out the hope of actually changing the material conditions of people's lives.

M. v. H. was internationally significant. It was the first high court decision in the world to recognize the spousal status of gays and lesbians. It was about relationship recognition as opposed to, say, non-discrimination in employment, on an individual basis. The decision emerged in a context of limited relationship recognition internationally, with only formalistic Registered Domestic Partnerships (RDP) in some jurisdictions.[19] No high court had spoken of the equality rights of a same-sex spouse in anything like the Supreme Court's terms in *M. v. H.* Since *Andrews*, our high court and its equality analysis have been international leaders, an example to the courts of other nations. *M. v. H.*, and the marriage cases following immediately thereafter, have been enormously influential.[20] This leads to our second thought about the intersections between gender, race and sexual orientation. In all these areas, though we have accomplished much, there is much, much more to be done. Perhaps this sounds trite. But we can tell you that in *M. v. H.*, and in our practice since then, we have seen nothing but persistent contrast between the theoretical and the practical, between lofty case law and the lived realities of lesbians, on a daily basis.

Our client, M., spent years fighting for the right to apply to court for support without ever receiving any financial relief from the stress of separation. She won all of these landmark court decisions — some on the most minute level — without ever truly feeling any concrete sense of victory. She received no economic reward and no recognition, since she was too afraid of discrimination to be identified. Eight years after she began litigation, she sat in the Supreme Court having waived all of her claims including any claim to support, having been the catalyst to the ultimate in theoretical decision-making, and having listened to a judge make a joke about how she actually had forty-seven cents in another bank account that Martha hadn't mentioned.

There are many other clients who have experienced this gap between the Supreme Court of Canada's eloquent statements about substantive equality and everyday family law. For example, we represented a lesbian co-parent who had raised a child since his birth. She was denied all access upon separation, when the child was seven, by a judge who said he was not prepared to "experiment" with the child. We also represented an at-home mother who left her husband for a woman. She did this after the husband had insisted on bringing women home to have three-somes — something he lived to regret since she learned in the process that she was a lesbian. When the woman came to our office, she had in her possession a report from the Children's Lawyer's Office, which explicitly recommended custody to the father because she was a lesbian. A month later, a motion immediately removed her from the home and relegated her to the status of a parent with Saturday-only visitations, with the judge saying in open court that he had no problem with her parenting abilities — it was her "lifestyle" that he had a problem with. Martha cried in the cab that day on her way home from court. She felt totally disillusioned about the legal system and our accomplishments in *M. v. H.* Another family law lawyer in our office remarked, "You high-in-the-sky Supreme Court of Canada types, you think you've changed anything? Welcome to life in the trenches."

We could go on with relating stories that illustrate how *M. v. H.* is both the best and worst example of the contrast between theory and reality. While there are so many examples of the persisting inequality of gays and lesbians, there are also examples of many individuals who, in the simple dignity of their own lives, show us so much about courage and strength. We think of Egan and Nesbitt, the couple who first litigated a case of sexual orientation discrimination in the Supreme Court of Canada. We remember Matthew Shepard, the twenty-one-year-old student who was tied to a fence, crucified, set on fire and left to die, all because he was gay. We think of the 1999 Vermont marriage challenge, which ended just like *M. v. H.*, with the court finding discrimination but refusing to do anything about it, sending the matter back to the legislature to remedy.[21] Imagine if we had left segregation or the Person's Case to the legislature.[22]

One extreme example of the difference between rhetoric and real change lies in the legislation that has been enacted in response to *M. v. H.* In the Supreme Court of Canada decision, the Court stated that the constitutional violation could be corrected by amending the definition of "spouse" so that gays and lesbians would be included. The majority concluded that since there were other sections of the Act that would be effected by this immediate change, the legislature should have six months to fashion a constitutional response. In one of the last paragraphs of the decision, the Court wrote that the legislature should also consider a more comprehensive response in order to save the cost of litigating individual cases over and over again.[23] It was uniformly interpreted as demanding comprehensive legislative reform.

On October 27, 1999, we sat with our client M. in the Ontario legislature and heard Attorney General James Flaherty introduce *An Act to Amend Certain Statutes Because of Supreme Court of Canada Decision in M. v. H.*[24] We heard him say, "This bill responds to the Supreme Court of Canada decision while preserving the traditional values of the family by protecting the definition of 'spouse' in Ontario law … We are introducing this bill because of the Supreme Court of Canada decision."[25] In response to numerous challenges over the past two decades, Ontario has always argued that the term "spouse" need not include gays and lesbians, because "spouse" is inherently heterosexual. Lower courts have repeatedly rejected the argument and the Supreme Court dismissed it in *M. v. H.*[26] Rather than accept the ruling, Ontario responded with an alternative tactic: segregation of same-sex spouses under a new label, in order to "protect" the definition of "spouse" from the "taint" of gays, lesbians and bisexuals. There were no committee hearings nor consultation with the gay and lesbian community. The legislation was introduced and passed in forty-eight hours.

In most legislative provisions, unmarried opposite-sex couples are referred to as "spouses" and gays and lesbians are included as "same-sex partners." Where unmarried heterosexual couples are recognized as "families," gays and lesbians are referred to as "households." The primary exception is adoption legislation. Although the government claimed that its omnibus legislation was comprehensive,[27] in fact, it failed to correct the adoption statute in the same manner.[28] The only reasonable rationale for this omission is that the government wishes to denounce, or at minimum, deny the relationships between gay and lesbian parents and their children.

"SEPARATE BUT (UN)EQUAL"

"Separate but equal" nomenclature is rooted in a formal equality approach under which Ontario states that same-sex spouses are relevantly "unalike" to heterosexuals and so may have an appropriately different label. This approach completely misses the focus of substantive equality. Substantive equality is concerned with the effect of the differential treatment on the dignity of a disadvantaged group, situating the impugned legislation within a larger social and political context of disadvantage. In the current social context, it is clear that the segregated status of gays and lesbians sends a message that same-sex couples are a threat to the values of family. In fact, it was said outright in the legislature and in the press on several occasions: the Bill is designed to "preserve traditional values of the family by protecting the definition of spouse."[29]

To respond to the discriminatory purpose and effect of the *M. v. H. Act* we commenced a motion for rehearing before the Supreme Court of Canada. We drew on the analogy to the "separate but equal" analysis of *Plessy v. Ferguson*, which was overruled by *Brown v. Board of Education*.[30] And we cited a passage from the U.S. Supreme Court in *Brown*: "To separate generates a feeling of inferiority as to status in the community that may effect hearts and minds in a way unlikely to ever be undone."[31] The provincial government did not respond to any of our constitutional arguments nor address the effect or purpose of separate status for gays and lesbians. Instead, the attorney general made submissions on technical points, dealing with the nature of our supporting affidavits and objecting to our motion for an extension of time to file the extensive materials. The provincial government moved to strike out the affidavits that contained the voices of lesbians describing the effect of the legislation, and situating it within the larger social, political, cultural and historical context of discrimination, which they live on a daily basis. On May 25, 2000, with little fanfare and almost no media attention at all, the motion for rehearing was dismissed. No reason was given by the Supreme Court.

M. and the lesbian, gay and bisexual community wanted a decision from the Supreme Court that would signal a true commitment to ensuring substantive equality for same-sex spouses. There was no response.[32] Individual family law litigants continued to struggle in courtrooms across the country, seeking justice from a heterosexist legal system. For the sake of all those plaintiffs, and for all those who care about equality, we had hoped that the Supreme Court would denounce the Ontario government's segregated scheme and so make more meaningful the Charter's guarantee of dignity for all gay and lesbian citizens. Instead, a discriminatory regime of "separate but equal" was allowed to stand in a country that purports to respect the equality and freedom of all persons.

POSTSCRIPT: THE STRUGGLE CONTINUES

M. has seen lasting benefits to her legal struggle. In 2001, the federal government passed the *Modernization of Benefits and Obligations Act* as its response to the Supreme Court decision in *M. v. H.* The Act amended sixty-eight statutes to extend benefits and obligations to all conjugal couples equally, without categories organized on the basis of sexual orientation. Same-sex couples won access to significant benefits and obligations, including the protections of the Canada Pension Plan, the *Income Tax Act* and Old Age Security. Provinces amended their legislation to provide either the same treatment for all conjugal relationships (whether married or unmarried, same-sex or opposite-sex) or decided to provide equal treatment for all unmarried cohabitants, regardless of sexual orientation. These important legislative amendments were achieved in large measure as a result of M.'s personal battle.

More recently, the victory of equal marriage flows directly from the reasoning in *M. v. H.* Once the Supreme Court of Canada held that same-sex couples were entitled to equal respect and recognition at law, and rejected so-called biological imperatives and appeals to history and tradition as excuses for differential treatment, equal marriage for lesbians and gay men became inevitable. At the same time, we see again that high-profile court successes do not necessarily translate into practical victories. The Supreme Court of Canada's advisory opinion on the *Reference* did not make clear that equal marriage should already be available across the country. The Ontario and Quebec couples, and other interveners, supported the view of the Quebec Court of Appeal, that the issue of equal marriage had been decided on a final basis and the rulings of the appellate courts were binding across Canada, as a matter of federal common law but limited the effect of the ruling to those provinces and one territory in which court battles had been fought. This means that, unless and until legislation passes, litigation must continue province-by-province until equal marriage is available across Canada. It is ordinary gay and lesbian Canadians who bear the consequences of this lack of clarity in the law.

As well, governments have not yet amended their legislation to ensure that married same-sex couples have access to the same family law rights and obligations as other married couples. For example, a gay couple who reside and marry in Nova Scotia cannot obtain a divorce in the absence of a constitutional challenge. An Ontario lesbian couple would not be included in the *Family Law Act* protections with respect to their matrimonial home or equalization of their net family property, since the statute is drafted with heterosexist language. Absent legislative action and provincial statutes will need to be challenged, a process that is time-consuming and expensive. Again, ordinary gays and lesbians pay the price for the failure to achieve substantive equality in law.

Still, so much has been achieved since 1992, when M. was told by her partner that she was not entitled to anything. Gays and lesbians have significant access to the benefits and protections of law, and those remaining distinctions will be declared unconstitutional once challenged. Thousands of same-sex couples have celebrated their marriages with friends and family. All gays and lesbians feel more respected, treated more fully as citizens and persons. Canada's substantive equality jurisprudence remains an example for other nations. Thanks to M., the world has changed for the better.

NOTES

1. *Reference re: Same-Sex Marriage*, [2004] S.C.C. 79.

2. *Edwards v. Attorney-General for Canada*, [1930] A.C. 124.

3. As at December 22, 2004, the following decisions have established equal marriage for same-sex couples: *EGALE Canada Inc. v. Canada (Attorney General)* (2003), 225 D.L.R. (4th) 472, 2003 BCCA 251; *Halpern v. Canada (Attorney General)* (2003), 65 O.R. (3d) 161; *Hendricks v. Québec (Procureur général)*, [2002] R.J.Q. 2506; *Dunbar v. Yukon*, [2004] Y.J. No. 61 (QL), 2004 YKSC 54; *Vogel v. Canada (Attorney General)*, [2004] M.J. No. 418 (QL) (Q.B.); *Boutilier v. Nova Scotia (Attorney General)*, [2004] N.S.J. No. 357 (QL) (S.C.); and *N.W. v. Canada (Attorney General)*, [2004] S.J. No. 669 (QL), 2004 SKQB 434. See also Shawna Richer, "Gay Marriage Approved in Nfld.: Efford Meets with Church Leaders, Will Tell PM His Decision after Christmas," *The Globe and Mail*, 22 December 2004, A7.

4. *Halpern v. Canada (Attorney General)* (2003), 65 O.R. (3d) 161.

5. *M. v. H.*, [1999] 2 S.C.R. 3.

6. R.S.O. 1990, c. F-3.

7. *M. v. H.* at para. 137.

8. *Egan v. Canada*, [1995] 2 S.C.R. 513.

9. The minority approach to section 15 was adopted by Justices Lamer, La Forest, Gonthier and Major.

10. [1995] 2 S.C.R. 418.

11. More recently, and in a seeming reversal of the Court's approach in *Miron*, the Supreme Court upheld the constitutionality of a provincial property sharing scheme that applied only to married couples. After *Nova Scotia (Attorney General) v. Walsh*, [2002] 4 S.C.R. 325, it seems that some distinctions as between unmarried and married couples are permissible at law.

12. [1998] 1 S.C.R. 493.

13. [1989] 1 S.C.R. 143.

14. *Law v. Canada (Ministry if Employment and Immigration)*, [1999] 1 S.C.R. 497; *M. v. H.*

15. *Bliss* v. *Attorney General*, [1978] 92 D.L.R. (3d) 417 (S.C.C.); *Brooks vs.Canada Safeway Ltd.*, [1989] 1 S.C.R. 1219, 1989 Can III 96 (S.C.C.).

16. *Egan v. Canada* [1995] 2 S.C.R. 513; *Thibandeau v. Canada*, [1995] 2 S.C.R. 627; and *Miron v. Trudel*, [1995] 2 S.C.R. 416.

17. *Benner v. Canada (Secretary of State)*, [1997] 1 S.C.R. 358; *Eaton v. Brant County Board of Education*, [1997] 1 S.C.R. 241; *Eldridge v. British Columbia (A.G.)*, [1997] 3 S.C.R. 624.

18. *Law v. Canada* (see note 14 above).

19. See, Kees Waaldijk, "What Legal Recognition of Same-Sex Partnership Can Be Expected in EC Law and When? Lessons from Comparative Law," paper presented at the Legal Recognition of Same-Sex Partnerships Conference, King's College, London, UK, July 1–3, 1999. Currently, Denmark, Norway, Sweden, Iceland, Greenland, the Netherlands, Spain (Catalunga and Aragon) and France have RDPs.

20. Equal marriages for same-sex couples are celebrated in the Netherlands and Belgium, and the State of Massachusetts. In its equal marriage case, the Massachusetts Supreme Judicial Court in *Goodridge v. Department of Public Health* relied on the precedent of the Canadian equal marriage litigation, and our case law received mention in the U.S. Supreme Court decision striking down its criminalization of consensual sex between men in *Lawrence v. Texas*. On November 30, 2004, the Supreme Court of Appeal of South Africa (the highest court for non-constitutional matters with primary jurisdiction over the interpretation of legislation and common-law rules) relied extensively on *Halpern* in its ruling discrimination in marriage to be unconstitutional.

21. *Baker* v. *State*, (Supreme Court Docket No. 98-032) Filed 20 December 1999.

22. In *Edwards v. Canada* (A.G.), [1930] A.C. 124, the Supreme Court of Canada's decision to deny women status as "persons" was overruled by the Privy Council.

23. *M. v. H.* at para. 140, 141–143, 147.

24. S.O. 1999 (hereinafter the *M. v. H. Act*).

25. Legislative Assembly, *Ontario Hansard* (27 October 1999) at 1830.

26. See, for example, *Knodel v. British Columbia (Medical Services Commission)* (1991), 58 B.C.L.R. (2d) 346 (S.C.); *Veysey v. Canada (Correctional Service)*, (1990), 109 N.R. 300 (F.C.A.); *Dwyer v. Toronto (Metropolitan)*, [1996] O.H.R.B.I.D. No. 33 (Ontario Board of Inquiry [Human Rights Code]); *Leshner v. Ontario* (1992), 16 C.H.R.R. d/184; 92 C.L.L.C 17, 035 (Ont. Bd. of Inquiry); *Kane v. Ontario* (A.-G.) (1997), 152 D.L.R. (4th) 738; *Ontario Public Service Employees Union Pension Plan Trust Fund (Trustees of)* v. *Ontario (Management Board of Cabinet)*, [1998] O.J. No. 5075, 20 C.C.P.B. 38 (Ont.

Gen. Div); *Re Canada (Treasury Board-Environment Canada) and Lorenzen* (1993), 38 L.A.C. (4th) 29; *Coles and O'Neill v. Ministry of Transportation and Jacobson*, File No. 92-018/09 (October, 1994) (Ont. Bd. Inq.); *Canada (Attorney-General) v. Moore*, [1998] 4 F.C. 585 (T.D.).

27. Legislative Assembly, *Ontario Hansard* (27 October 1999) at 1830.

28. The *M. v. H. Act* did not amend the *Child and Family Services Act*, R.S.O. 1990, c.C.12 (*"CFSA"*) to include "same-sex partners." The legislature amended the stranger adoption provision by adding a new category of "any other individuals that the court may allow, having regard to the best interests of the child." Same-sex couples are given no more recognition or consideration than a group of strangers who wish to adopt a child. See the *M. v. H. Act*, section 6. The government did not amend the step-parent adoption provision of section 136 of the *CFSA* at all. It is uncertain whether same-sex couples will be able to rely on past adoption decisions like *Re K. and Re C.E.G.* In those cases, a declaration was granted that section 136 was to read "'spouse' means the person to whom a person of the opposite sex is married or with whom a person of the same or opposite sex is living in a conjugal relationship outside marriage." See *K. (Re)* (1995), 23 O.R. (3d) 679, (1995), 125 D.L.R. (4th) 653 (Ont. Prov. Ct.); *C.E.G. (No. 1) (Re)*, [1995], O.J. No. 4072 (Ont. Gen. Div.); and *C.E.G. (No. 2) (Re)*, [1995], O.J. No. 4073 (Ont. Gen. Div.).

29. Ontario Ministry of the Attorney General, Press Release, "Ontario Protects Traditional Definition of Spouse in Legislation Necessary Because of Supreme Court of Canada Decision in *M. v. H.*" (25 October 1999).

30. *Plessy v. Ferguson*, 163 U.S. 537 (1896); *Brown et al. v. Board of Education of Topeka et al.*, 347 U.S. 483 (1954).

31. *Brown et al.* at 494.

32. Because no reasons were given, we are left to speculate as to the reasons for the dismissal of the motion. It is likely that the Court felt it was inappropriate to address the issue by way of a motion for rehearing. There is no finding that the discriminatory scheme would pass constitutional muster.

BIBLIOGRAPHY

Abell, Elizabeth. "Black Writing, White Reading." In K. Appiah and H.L. Gates, Jr., eds., *Identities*. Chicago: University of Chicago Press, 1995.

Abella, Rosalie. "The Dynamic Nature of Equality." In Sheilah Martin and Kathleen Mahoney, eds., *Equality and Judicial Neutrality*, 3–9. Toronto: Carswell, 1987.

Acheson, Elizabeth, Mary Eberts, Beth Symes, and Jennifer Stoddart. *Women and Legal Action: Precedents, Resources and Strategies for the Future.* Ottawa: Canadian Advisory Council on the Status of Women, 1984.

Allen, Anita L. "Women and Their Privacy: What is at Stake?" In Carol Gould, ed., *Beyond Domination: New Perspectives on Women and Philosophy,* 233–249. Totowa, NJ: Rowman and Littlefield, 1984.

Ammerman, Nancy. *Bible Believers: Fundamentalists in the Modern World.* New Brunswick, NJ: Rutgers University Press, 1987.

Aoki, Doug. "Sex and Muscle: The Female Bodybuilder Meets Lacan." *Body and Society* 2, no. 4 (1996): 59–74.

Arnott, Jennifer. "Re-Emerging Indigenous Structures and the Reassertion of the Integral Role of Women." In Jane Arscott and Linda Trimble, eds., *In the Presence of Women: Representation in Canadian Governments,* 64–81. Toronto: Harcourt Brace, 1997.

Backhouse, Constance. "Lawyering: Clara Brett Martin, Canada's First Woman Lawyer." In Constance Backhouse, ed., *Petticoats & Prejudice: Women and Law in Nineteenth-Century Canada,* 293–326. Toronto: Women's Press, 1991.

—. "'Bitterly Disappointed' at the Spread of 'Colour Bar Tactics': Viola Desmond's Challenge to Racial Segregation, Nova Scotia, 1946." In Constance Backhouse, ed., *Colour-Coded: A Legal History of Racism in Canada, 1900*–1950, 226–271. Toronto: University of Toronto Press, 1999.

Bannerji, Himani. "The Paradox of Diversity: The Construction of a Multicultural Canada and 'Women of Colour.'" *Women Studies International Forum* 23, no. 5 (2000): 537–560.

Baxandall, Rosalyn, and Linda Gordon, eds. *Dear Sisters: Dispatches from the Women's Liberation Movement.* New York: Basic Books, 2000.

Beaman, Lori. "Collaborators or Resistors? Evangelical Women in Atlantic Canada." *Atlantis* 22 (1997): 9–18.

—. "Sexual Orientation and Legal Discourse: Legal Constructions of the 'Normal' Family." *Canadian Journal of Law and Society* 14 (1999): 173–201.

—. *Shared Beliefs, Different Lives: Women's Identities in Evangelical Context.* St. Louis, MI: Chalice Press, 1999.

Bell, Laurie, ed. *Good Girls/Bad Girls: Sex-Trade Workers & Feminists Face to Face.* Toronto: Women's Press, 1987.

Belleau, Marie-Claire. "L'intersectionalité: Feminisms in a Divided World (Quebec–Canada)." In Dany Lacombe and Dorothy Chunn, eds., *Law as a Gendering Practice*, 19–37. London: Oxford University Press, 1999.

Berger, Peter, and Thomas Luckman. *The Social Construction of Reality.* New York: Anchor Books, 1967.

Boswell, John. *Christianity, Social Tolerance, and Homosexuality: Gay People in Western Europe from the Beginning of the Christian Era to the Fourteenth Century.* Chicago: University of Chicago Press, 1980.

—. "Concepts, Experience and Sexuality." In Gary David Comstock and Susan E. Henking, eds., *Que(e)rying Religion: A Critical Anthology*, 116–129. New York: Continuum, 1997.

—. "Revolutions, Universals, and Sexual Categories." In John Corvino, ed., *Same Sex: Debating the Ethics, Science, and Culture of Homosexuality*, 185–202. New York: Rowman and Littlefield, 1997.

Bouchard, Josée, Susan Boyd, and Elizabeth Sheehy. *Canadian Feminist Literature on Law: An Annotated Bibliography / Recherches Féministes en Droit au Canada: Une Bibliographie Annotée.* Toronto: University of Toronto Press, 1999.

Boyd, Susan B. "Expanding the Family in Family Law: Recent Ontario Proposals on Same-Sex Relationships." *Canadian Journal of Women and the Law* 7, no. 2 (1994): 545–563.

—, ed. *Challenging the Public/Private Divide.* Toronto: University of Toronto Press, 1997.

Brooks, Dianne L. "A Commentary On the Essence of Anti-Essentialist in Feminist Legal Theory." *Feminist Legal Studies* II, no. 2 (1994): 115–132.

Bunch, Charlotte. "Lesbians in Revolt." In Barbara Crow, ed., *Radical Feminism: A Documentary Reader*, 332–335. New York: New York University Press, 2000.

Bunting, Annie. "Feminism, Foucault and Law as Power/Knowledge." *Alberta Law Review* 30 (1992): 829–842.

Bushby, Abby. "The Early Years: Sources of an Enduring Tradition. The Women's Law Association of Ontario 1919–1950." Paper presented at the 80th Anniversary Celebration of the Women's Law Association of Ontario, Toronto, Ontario, January 14, 2000.

Butler, Judith. *Gender Trouble: Feminism and the Subversion of Identity.* London: Routledge, 1990.

Canadian Press. "Make Judge Go before Rights Panel Court Told." *The Toronto Star,* 8 December 1997, A6.

Carby, Hazel. "White Women Listen! Black Feminism and the Boundaries of Sisterhood." In R. Hennessey and C. Ingraham, eds., *Materialist Feminism,* 110–128. London: Routledge, 1997.

Chunn, Dorothy, and Dany Lacombe, eds. *Law as a Gendering Practice.* Don Mills, ON: Oxford University Press, 2000.

Clark Hine, Darlene. "'In the Kingdom of Culture': Black Women and the Intersection of Race, Gender, and Class." In Gerald Early, ed., *Lure and Loathing: Essays on Race, Identity, and the Ambivalence of Assimilation.* New York: The Penguin Press, 1993.

Clarke, Cheryl. "Lesbianism: An Act of Resistance." In Cherríe L. Moraga and Gloria E. Anzaldúa, eds., *This Bridge Called My Back: Writings by Radical Women of Color,* 141–151. Expanded and Revised Third Edition. Berkeley, CA: Third Woman Press, 2002.

Cleverdon, Catherine L. *The Woman Suffrage Movement in Canada.* Toronto: University of Toronto Press, 1950.

Cohen, Martin Samuel. "The Biblical Prohibition of Homosexual Intercourse." *Journal of Homosexuality* 19 (1990): 3–20.

Colker, Ruth. "Bi: Race, Sexual Orientation, Gender and Disability." *Ohio State Law Journal* 56, no. 1 (1995): 1–67.

Comack, Elizabeth, ed. *Locating Law: Race/Class/Gender Connections.* Halifax: Fernwood, 1999.

Comack, Elizabeth, and Stephen Brickey, eds. *The Social Basis of Law: Critical Readings in the Sociology of Law.* 2d ed. Halifax: Garamond Press, 1991.

Corvine, John. *Same Sex: Debating the Ethics, Science, and Culture of Homosexuality.* New York: Rowman and Littlefield, 1997.

Cossman, Brenda. "Same-Sex Couples and the Politics of Family Status." In Janine Brodie, ed., *Women and Canadian Public Policy,* 232–244. Toronto: Harcourt Brace, 1996.

Countryman, L. William. *Dirt, Greed and Sex: Sexual Ethics in the New Testament and Their Implications for Today.* Philadelphia: Fortress Press, 1988.

Crenshaw, Kimberlé. "Demarginalizing the Intersection of Race and Sex: A Black Feminist Critique of Antidiscrimination Doctrine, Feminist Theory and Antiracist Politics." *University of Chicago Legal Forum* 139 (1989): 159–168.

—. "Mapping the Margins: Intersectionality, Identity Politics, and Violence Against Women of Color." In Kimberlé Crenshaw, Neil Gotanda, Garry Peller, and Kendall Thomas, eds., *Critical Race Theory: The Key Writings that Formed the Movement*, 103–122. New York: The New Press, 1995.

Culhane, Dara. *The Pleasure of the Crown*. Burnaby, BC: Talon Books, 1998.

Currie, Dawn H., and Valerie Raoul, eds. *Anatomy of Gender: Women's Struggle for the Body*. Ottawa: Carleton University Press, 1992.

Curtis, Denis E., and Judith Resnik. "Images of Justice." *Yale Law Journal* 96 (1986–87): 1727–1772.

Dale, Anne Freed. "Top Judge Accused of 'Stereotyping.'" *The Toronto Star*, 4 November 1997, A25.

Daniluck, Judith C. "The Meaning and Experience of Female Sexuality." *Psychology of Women Quarterly* 17 (1993): 53–69.

Dare, B. "Harris' First Year: Attacks and Resistance." In D. Ralph, A. Regimbald, and N. St. Amand, eds., *Open for Business: Closed for People*, 20–26. Halifax: Fernwood, 1997.

Das Gupta, Tania. "Political Economy of Gender, Race and Class: Looking at South Asian Immigrant Women in Canada." *Canadian Ethnic Studies* 26, no. 1 (1994): 59–73.

Davis, Angela. "Racism, Birth Control, and Reproductive Rights." In Marlene Gerber Fried, ed., *From Abortion to Reproductive Freedom: Transforming a Movement*. Boston: South End Press, 1990.

Davis, Kenneth C. *Administrative Law Treatise*. 2d ed. San Diego: K.C. Davis, 1984.

Dawson, T. Brettel, ed. *Relating to Law: A Chronology of Women and Law in Canada*. 2d ed. Toronto: Captus Press, 1998.

Dei, George. *Anti-Racism Education: Theory and Practice*. Halifax: Fernwood, 1996.

Dei, George, and Agnes Calliste, eds. *Power, Knowledge and Anti-Racism Education*. Halifax: Fernwood, 2000.

Devlin, Richard. "We Can't Go On Together with Suspicious Minds: Judicial Bias and Racialized Perspective in *R. v. R.D.S.*" *Dalhousie Law Journal* 18, no. 2 (1995): 411–446.

Doran, Chris. "Medico-Legal Expertise and industrial Disease Compensation: Discipline, Surveillance and Disqualification." In MacDonald, Gayle. ed., *Social Context and Social Location: New Struggles for Old Law*. Peterborough, ON: Broadview Press, 2002.

Duncan, Nancy, ed. *Body Space*. London: Routledge, 1996.

Duncan, Sheila. "Disrupting the Surface of Order and Innocence: Towards a Theory of Sexuality and the Law." *Feminist Legal Studies* II, no. 1 (1994): 1–28.

Duncanson, John, and Jim Rankin. "Above the Law." *The Toronto Star*, 30 November 1997, A1, A14.

Durham, Gigi. "The Taming of the Shrew: Women's Magazines and the Regulation of Desire." *Journal of Communication Inquiry* 20, no. 1 (1996): 18–31.

Edwards, George R. "A Critique of Creationist Homophobia." *Homosexuality and Religion* 18 (1989): 95–118.

Eisenstein, Zillah. *The Female Body and the Law.* Berkeley: University of California Press, 1988.

Ellington, Stephen, Nelson Trebbe, Martha van Haitsma, and Edward O. Laumann. "Religion and the Politics of Sexuality." *Journal of Contemporary Ethnography* 30 (2001): 3–55.

Elshtain, Jean Bethke. *Public Man, Private Woman: Women in Social and Political Thought.* Princeton: Princeton University Press, 1981.

Epstein, Debbie. *Changing Classroom Cultures: Anti-Racism, Politics and Schools.* Stoke-on-Trent, UK: Trentham Books, 1993.

Essed, Philomena. *Understanding Everyday Racism.* Newbury Park, CA: Sage, 1993.

Faith, Karlene. *Unruly Women: The Politics of Confinement and Resistance.* Vancouver: Press Gang,1993.

Ferguson, Kathy E. *The Feminist Case Against Bureaucracy.* Philadelphia: Temple University Press, 1984.

Fine, Sean. "Scales of Justice Tilt towards Power." *The Globe and Mail*, 6 November, 1993, A1.

—. "Different Styles on the Bench." *The Globe and Mail*, 25 October, 1993, A9.

Fineman, Martha Albertson, and Nancy Sweet Thomadsen, eds. *At the Boundaries of Law: Feminism and Legal Theory.* London: Routledge, 1992.

Foster, C. *A Place Called Heaven: The Meaning of Being Black in Canada.* Toronto: HarperCollins, 1996.

Foucault, Michel. *Discipline and Punish: The Birth of the Prison.* New York: Pantheon, 1977.

—. "Nietzsche, Genealogy, History." In Donald F. Bouchard, ed., *Language, Countermemory, Practice: Selected Essays and Interviews.* Ithaca, NY: Cornell University Press, 1977.

—. *Power/Knowledge: Selected Interviews and Other Writings, 1972–1977.* Edited by Colin Gordon. New York: Pantheon Books, 1980.

—. *The History of Sexuality.* Vol. 1, *An Introduction.* New York: Vintage Books, 1990.

Friedland, Martin. *A Place Apart: Judicial Independence and Accountability in Canada.* Ottawa: Canadian Judicial Council, 1995.

Gavison, Ruth. "Feminism and the Public/Private Distinction." *Stanford Law Review* 45, no. 1 (1992): 1–45.

Gilmore, Glenda Elizabeth. *Gender and Jim Crow: Women and the Politics of White Supremacy in North Carolina, 1896–1920.* Chapel Hill: University of North Carolina Press, 1996.

Goldman, Sheldon. "Reagan's Judicial Appointments at Mid-Term: Shaping the Bench in His Own Image." *Judicature* 66, no. 8 (1983): 335–343.

Grant, Isabel, and Lynn Smith. "Gender Representation in the Canadian Judiciary in Law Reform Commission of Ontario." *Appointing Judges: Philosophy, Politics and Practice,* 58–76. Toronto: Ontario Law Reform Commission, 1991.

Grillo, T., and S.M. Wildman. "Obscuring the Importance of Race: The Implications of Making Comparisons between Racism and Sexism (or other-isms)." *Duke Law Journal* (1991): 397–412.

Guest, D. "Social Policy in Canada." *Social Policy and Administration* 18, no. 2 (1984): 130–147.

Gupta, T. Das. "The Politics of Multiculturalism: Immigrant Women and the Canadian State." In E. Dua and A. Robertson, eds., *Scratching the Surface: Canadian Anti-Racist Feminist Thought,* 187-206. Toronto: Women's Press, 1999.

Hamilton, A.C., and C.M. Sinclair. *Report of the Aboriginal Justice Inquiry of Manitoba.* Vol. 2, *The Deaths of Helen Betty Osborne and John Joseph Harper.* Winnipeg: Queen's Printer, 1991.

Hans, James S. *The Fate of Desire.* New York: State University of New York Press, 1990.

Haraway, Donna J. *Modest_Witness@Second_Millennium.FemaleMan_Meets OncoMouse: Feminism and Technoscience.* New York: Routledge, 1997.

Harris, Mary B., ed. *School Experiences of Gay and Lesbian Youth.* New York: Haworth, 1997.

Helminiak, Daniel A. *What the Bible Really Says about Homosexuality.* San Francisco: Alamo Square Press, 1994.

Henderson, Elandria V. "The Black Lesbian." In Barbara A. Crow, ed., *Radical Feminism: A Documentary Reader.* New York: New York University Press, 2000.

Henry, Francis, Carol Tator, Winston Mattis, and Tim Rees. *The Colour of Democracy: Racism in Canadian Society.* Toronto: Harcourt Canada, 2000.

Hermer, Joe, and Alan Hunt. "Official Graffiti of the Everyday." *Law and Society Review* 30 (1996): 455–480.

Holland, Janet, Caroline Ramazanoglu, Sue Sharpe, and Rachel Thomson. "Power and Desire: The Embodiment of Female Sexuality." *Feminist Review* 46 (1994): 21–38.

Home, Peter, and Reina Lewis. *Outlooks: Lesbian and Gay Sexualities and Visual Cultures.* London: Routledge, 1996.

hooks, bell. *Ain't I A Woman: Black Women and Feminism.* Boston: South End Press, 1981.

Jeffrey, Leslie. "Sex and Borders: Gender National Identity and the 'Prostitution Problem' in Thailand." PhD diss., York University, 1999.

Johnson, Rebecca. "'Leaving Normal': Constructing the Family at the Movies and in Law." In Lori G. Beaman, ed., *New Perspectives on Deviance: the Construction of Deviance in Everyday Life,*163–179. Scarborough, ON: Prentice Hall Allyn and Bacon Canada, 2000.

Johnstone, Jill. *Lesbian Nation: The Feminist Solution.* New York: Simon and Schuster, 1974.

Kaminski, Elizabeth. "Lesbian Health: Social Context, Sexual Identity, and Well-Being." *Journal of Lesbian Studies* 4 (2000): 87–101.

Kay, F. N. Dautovich, and C. Marlor. "Barriers and Opportunities within Law: Women in a Changing Legal Profession. A Longitudinal Survey of Ontario Lawyers 1990–1996." Paper Presented to the Law Society of Upper Canada, November 1996.

Kellstedt, Lyman, and C. Smidt. "Measuring Fundamentalism: An Analysis of Different Operational Strategies." *Journal for the Scientific Study of Religion* 30 (1993): 259–278.

Kristeva, Julia. *"Stabat Mater."* In Diana Tietjens Meyers, ed. *Feminist Social Thought: A Reader,* 302–319. New York: Routledge, 1997.

Kwei Yung Lee, Cynthia. "Race and Self-Defence: Toward a Normative Conception of Reasonableness." *Minnesota Law Review* 81, no. 2 (1996): 367–500.

Lacey, Nicola. *Unspeakable Subjects: Feminist Essays in Legal and Social Theory.* Oxford: Hart Publishing, 1998.

Lahey, Kathleen A. *Are We "Persons" Yet? Law and Sexuality in Canada.* Toronto: University of Toronto Press, 1999.

Law Society of Upper Canada. *Bicentennial Report and Recommendations on Equity Issues in the Legal Profession.* Toronto: The Law Society of Upper Canada, 1997.

Laythe, Brian, Deborah Finkel, and Lee A.Kirkpatrick. "Predicting Prejudice from Religious Fundamentalism and Right-Wing Authoritarianism." *Journal for the Scientific Study of Religion* 40 (2001): 1–10.

L'Heureux-Dubé, Claire. "Stepping Forward, Stepping Back: Women's Equality at Century's End." Paper presented at the Massey College Symposium, Toronto, Ontario, March 3, 2000.

LeMoncheck, Linda. *Loose Women, Lecherous Men: a Feminist Philosophy of Sex.* New York: Oxford University Press, 1997.

Leonard, Leigh Megan. "A Missing Voice in Feminist Legal Theory: The Heterosexual Presumption." *Women's Rights Law Reporter* 12 (1990–91): 39–57.

Lippard, Lucy, ed. *Partial Recall.* New York: The New York Press, 1992.

Lorde, Audre. *Sister/Outsider: Essays & Speeches by Audre Lorde.* Freedom, CA: The Crossing Press, 1984.

Lowman, John. "Notions of Formal Equality before the Law: The Experience of Street Prostitutes and Their Customers." *The Journal of Human Justice* (1990): 55–76.

Makin, Kirk. "Lesbian Wants Court to Rehear Historic Case." *The Globe and Mail*, 8 April 2000, A8.

Mallen, Caroline. "Same-Sex Couples Granted New Rights." *The Toronto Star*, 28 October 1999, A7.

Mann, Patricia S. *Micro-Politics: Agency in a Post-Feminist Era.* Minneapolis: University of Minnesota Press, 1994.

Matsuda, Mari J., Charles R. Lawrence III, Richard Delgado, and Kimberlé Crenshaw, eds. *Words that Wound: Critical Race Theory, Assaultive Speech, and the First Amendment.* Boulder, CO: Westview, 1993.

MacDonald, Gayle. "The Body Inscribed, Described and Divided." Paper presented at a joint session of the Canadian Sociology and Anthropology Association and Canadian Law and Society Association meetings, Memorial University, Newfoundland, June, 1997.

—. "The Social Construction of Women's Sexuality as Deviant." In Lori Beaman, ed., *The Social Construction of Deviance*, 220–233. Toronto: Prentice-Hall, 2000.

—, ed. *Social Context and Social Location in the Sociology of Law.* Peterborough, ON: Broadview Press, 2002.

MacDougall, Bruce. "Silence in the Classroom: Limits on Homosexual Expression and Visibility in Education and the Privileging of Homophobic Religious Ideology." *Saskatchewan Law Review* 61 (1998): 41–86.

MacKinnon, Catherine. *Feminism Unmodified: Discourses on Life and Law.* Cambridge: Harvard University Press, 1987.

Martin, Sheila. "The Dynamics of Exclusion: Women in the Legal Profession." Paper presented at the Canadian Bar Association Conference, Toronto, Ontario, October 1992.

Matoesian, Gregory. *Reproducing Rape: Domination through Talk in the Courtroom.* Chicago: University of Chicago Press, 1993.

McClellan, R. "1,460 Days of Destruction." In R. Cohen, ed., *Alien Invasion: How the Harris Tories Mismanaged Ontario*, 91–111. Toronto: Insomniac Press, 2001.

McCormick, Peter, and Ian Green. *Judges and Judging: Inside the Canadian Judicial*

System. Toronto: James Lorimer, 1990.

McEachern, Allan. "Top Judge Cleared of Misconduct — Judicial Council Acquits Lamer." *Vancouver Sun*, 24 January 1998, A7.

McIntosh, Peggy. "White Privilege: Unpacking the Invisible Knapsack." *Peace & Freedom* (July/August 1989): 10.

McLaren, Angus. *Our Own Master Race: Eugenics in Canada, 1885–1945*. Toronto: McClelland and Stewart, 1990.

Miles, Angela. *Integrative Feminisms: Building Global Visions, 1960s–1990s*. New York: Routledge, 1996.

Miles, R., and R. Torres. "Does Race Matter? Transatlantic Perspectives on Racism after Race Relations." In V. Amit-Talai and C. Knowles, eds., *Re-Situating Identities: The Politics of Race, Ethnicity and Culture*, 24–46. Peterborough, ON: Broadview Press, 1996.

Minow, Martha. "A Feminist Reason: Getting and Losing It." In Katharine T. Bartlett and Roseanne Kennedy, eds. *Feminist Legal Theory: Readings in Law and Gender*. Boulder, CO: Westview, 1991.

Monture-Angus, Patricia. "Standing Against Canadian Law: Naming Omissions of Race, Culture and Gender." In Elizabeth Comack, ed., *Locating Law: Race/Class/ Gender Connections*, 76–97. Halifax: Fernwood, 1999.

Moraga, Cherríe L., and Gloria E. Anzaldúa, eds. *This Bridge Called My Back: Writing by Radical Women of Color*. Expanded and Revised Third Edition. Berkeley, CA: Third Woman Press, 2002.

Morgan, Cecelia. "Women, Gender and the Legal Profession at Osgoode Hall." *Canadian Journal of Law and Society* 11, no. 2 (1996): 19–61.

Morrison, Toni. "The Official Story: Dead Man Golfing." Introduction to Toni Morrison and Claudia Brodsky Lacour, eds., *Birth of a Nation'hood*. New York: Pantheon Books, 1997.

Mossman, Mary Jane. "Feminism and Legal Method: The Difference it Makes." *Australian Journal of Law and Society* 3 (1986): 30–52.

—. "The Paradox of Feminist Engagement with Law." In Nancy Mandell, ed., *Feminist Issues: Race, Class and Sexuality*, 180–207. Toronto: Prentice Hall, Allyn and Bacon, 1988.

Nedelsky, Jennifer. Review of *Inessential Woman: Problems of Exclusion in Feminist Thought*, by Elizabeth Spelman. *Michigan Law Review* 89 (1991): 1591–1607.

—. "Embodied Diversity and the Challenges to Law." *McGill Law Journal* 42, no. 91 (1997): 91–117.

Ng, Roxanne. "Racism, Sexism and NationBuilding in Canada." In C. McCarthy and W. Crichlow, eds., *Race, Identity and Representation in Education*, 50–59. New York: Routledge, 1993.

Nichols, Sharon L. "Gay, Lesbian and Bisexual Youth: Understanding Diversity and Promoting Tolerance in Schools." *The Elementary School Journal* 99 (1999): 505–519.

Noonan, Sheila. "Of Death, Desire and Knowledge: Law and Social Control of Witches in Renaissance Europe." In Gayle MacDonald, ed., *Social Context and Social Location: New Struggles for Old Law*. Peterborough, ON: Broadview Press, 2002.

Omatsu, Maryka. "On Judicial Appointments: Does Gender Make a Difference?" In Joseph Fletcher, ed., *Ideas in Action: Essays on Politics and Law in Honour of Peter Russell*, 176–187. Toronto: University of Toronto Press, 1999.

Omi, W., and H. Winant. "On the Theoretical Concept of Race." In C. McCarthy and W. Crichlow, eds., *Race, Identity, and Representation in Education*, 3–10. New York: Routledge, 1993.

Overall, Christine. "What's wrong with Prostitution? Evaluating Sex Work." In Debra Shogan, ed., *A Reader in Feminist Ethics*, 563–586. Toronto: Canadian Scholars' Press, 1993.

Pheterson, Gail, ed. *A Vindication of the Rights of Whores*. Seattle: Seal Press, 1989.

Pierson, Ruth Roach, Marjorie Griffin Cohen, Paula Borune, and Philinda Masters, eds. *Canadian Women's Issues*. Vol. 1, *Strong Voices*. Toronto: James Lorimer, 1993.

Pierson, Ruth Roach, and Marjorie Griffin Cohen, eds. *Canadian Women's Issues*. Vol. 2, *Bold Visions*. Toronto: James Lorimer, 1995.

Pothier, Diane. "M'Aider, Mayday: Section 15 of the *Charter* in Distress." *National Journal of Constitutional Law* 6, no. 3 (1996): 295–345.

Pratt, Marie Louise. *Imperial Eyes: Travel Writing and Transculturation*. London: Routledge, 1997.

Ramazanoglu, Caroline, and Janet Holland. "Women's Sexuality and Men's Appropriation of Desire." In Caroline Ramazanoglu, ed., *Up against Foucault: Explorations of Some Tensions Between Foucault and Feminism*, 239–264. London: Routledge, 1993.

Raymond, Janice. *The Transsexual Empire: The Making of the She-Male*. Boston: Beacon Press, 1979.

Razack, Sherene. *Canadian Feminism and the Law: The Women's Legal Education and Action Fund and the Pursuit of Equality*. Toronto: Second Story Press, 1991. Now available from Sumach Press, Toronto.

—. "Beyond Universal Women: Reflections on Theorizing Differences among Women." *University of New Brunswick Law Journal* 45 (1996): 209–227.

—. *Looking White People in the Eye: Gender, Race and Culture in Courtrooms and Classrooms.* Toronto: University of Toronto Press, 1998.

Rhode, Deborah. "The Women's Point of View." In Frances E. Olsen, ed., *Feminist Legal Theory II: Positioning Feminist Theory Within the Law,* 61–72. New York: New York University Press, 1995.

Rich, Adrienne. *Compulsory Heterosexuality and Lesbian Existence.* London: Only-Women Press, 1983.

Riley, Denise. *"Am I That Name? Feminism and the Category of 'Women' in History."* Minneapolis: University of Minnesota Press, 1988.

Ross, Howard. "Judicial Process Opened Up." *The Globe and Mail,* 29 April 1994, A5.

Russell, Peter H. *The Judiciary in Canada: The Third Branch of Government.* Toronto: McGraw-Hill Ryerson, 1987.

Satzewich, Vic, and Li Zong. "Social Control and the Historical Construction of 'Race.'" In Bernard Schissel and Linda Mahood, eds., *Social Control in Canada: Issues in The Social Construction of Deviance.* Toronto: Oxford University Press, 1996.

Schatzki, Theodore R., and Wolfgang Natter, eds. *The Social and Political Body.* New York: The Guilford Press, 1996.

Scroggs, Robin. *The New Testament and Homosexuality: Contextual Backgrounds for Contemporary Debate.* Philadelphia: Fortress Press, 1983.

Scrutton, T.E. "The Work of the Commercial Courts." *Cambridge Law Journal* 1 (1921): 6-20.

Shaver, Frances. "The Regulation of Prostitution: Setting the Morality Trap." Bernard Schissel and Linda Mahood, eds., *Social Control in Canada: Issues in the Social Construction of Deviance.* Toronto: Oxford University Press, 1996.

Shildrick, Margrit. *Leaky Bodies and Boundaries: Feminism, Postmodernism and Bio-ethics* London: Routledge, 1997.

Smart, Carol. *Feminism and the Power of Law.* London: Routledge, 1989.

Smith, Dorothy E. *The Everyday World as Problematic: A Feminist Sociology.* Toronto: University of Toronto Press, 1987.

—. *Writing the Social: Critique Theory and Investigations.* Toronto: University of Toronto Press, 1999.

Smith, Miriam. *Lesbian and Gay Rights in Canada: Social Movements and Equality-Seeking, 1971–1995.* Toronto: University of Toronto Press, 1999.

Smith, Patricia, ed. *Feminist Jurisprudence.* New York: Oxford University Press, 1993.

Spelman, Elizabeth V. *Inessential Woman: Problems of Exclusion in Feminist Thought.* Boston: Beacon Press, 1988.

Spender, Dale. *Man Made Language.* London: Routledge and Kegan Paul, 1985.

Stasiulis, D., and R. Jhappan. "The Fractious Politics of a Settler Society: Canada." In D. Stasiulis and N. Yuval Davis, eds., *Unsettling Settler Societies: Articulations of Gender, Race, Ethnicity and Class,* 95–131. London: Sage, 1995.

Tomasulo, Frank P. "'I'll See It When I Believe It': Rodney King and the Prison-House of Video." In Vivian Sobchack, ed., *The Persistence of History: Cinema, Television, and the Modern Event.* New York: Routledge, 1996.

Torczyner, J. "The Canadian Welfare State: Retrenchment and Change." In Robert R. Friedmann, Neil Gilbert and Moshe Sherer, eds., *Modern Welfare States: A Comparative View of Trends and Prospects,* 264–281. New York: New York University Press, 1987.

Valverde, Mariana. "'When the Mother of the Race Is Free': Race, Reproduction, and Sexuality in First-Wave Feminism." In Franca Iacovetta and Mariana Valverde, eds., *Gender Conflicts: New Essays in Women's History,* 3–26. Toronto: University of Toronto Press, 1992.

van Dijk, Teun. *Elite Racism.* Newbury Park, CA: Sage, 1993.

Van Rijn, Nicolaas. "Chief Justice Denies Attack on Chinese." *The Toronto Star,* 5 November 1997, A8.

Waaldijk, Kees. "What Legal Recognition of Same-Sex Partnership Can Be Expected in EC Law and When? Lessons From Comparative Law." Paper presented at the Legal Recognition of Same-Sex Partnerships Conference, King's College, London, England, July 1–3, 1999.

Wachholz, Sandra. "Confronting the Construct of Child Neglect As Maternal Failure: In Search of Peacemaking Alternatives." In Gayle MacDonald, ed., *Social Context and Social Location: New Struggles for Old Law.* Peterborough, ON: Broadview Press, 2002.

Walker, James W. St. G. *"Race," Rights and the Law in the Supreme Court of Canada: Historical Case Studies.* Toronto: Wilfrid Laurier University Press, 1997.

Warner, R. Stephen. *New Wine in Old Wineskins: Evangelicals and Liberals in a Small-Town Church.* Berkeley: University of California Press, 1988.

Webber, Jeremy. "The Limits to Judges' Free Speech: A Comment on the Report of the Committee of Investigation into the Conduct of the Hon. Mr. Justice Berger." *McGill Law Journal* 29 (1984): 369–406.

Weeks, Jeffrey, and Janet Holland, eds. *Sexual Cultures: Communities, Values and Intimacy.* New York: St. Martin's Press, 1996.

White, Frances E. "Africa on My Mind: Gender, Counter Discourse and African-American Nationalism." *Journal of Women's History* 2, no. 1 (1990): 73–97.

Williams, Joan C. "Dissolving the Sameness/Difference Debate: A Post-Modern Path

Beyond Essentialism in Feminist and Critical Race Theory." *Duke Law Journal* (1991): 296–323.

Wilson, Bertha. "Will Women Judges Really Make a Difference?" *Osgoode Hall Law Journal* 28 (1990): 507–520.

—. *Touchstones for Change: Equality, Diversity and Accountability: The Report on Gender Equality in the Legal Profession.* Ottawa: The Canadian Bar Association, 1993.

Wittig, Monique. "One Is Not Born a Woman." In Linda Nicholson, ed., *The Second Wave: A Reader in Feminist Theory,* 265–271. New York: Routledge, 1997.

Women's Legal Education and Action Fund (LEAF). *Equality and the Charter: Ten Years of Feminist Advocacy Before the Supreme Court in Canada.* Toronto: Emond Montgomery, 1996.

Wortley, S. *Perceptions of Bias and Racism Within the Ontario Criminal Justice System: Results from a Public Opinion Survey.* Toronto: Commission on Systemic Racism in the Criminal Justice System, 1994.

—. "A Northern Taboo: Research on Race, Crime and Criminal Justice in Canada." *Canadian Journal of Criminology* 41 (1999): 261–274.

Young, Iris. *Justice and the Politics of Difference.* Princeton: Princeton University Press, 1990.

Young, Lisa. "Fulfilling the Mandate of Difference: Women in the Canadian House of Commons." In Jane Arscott and Linda Trimble, eds., *In the Presence of Women: Representation in Canadian Governments,* 82–103. Toronto: Harcourt Brace, 1997.

LEGAL CASES CITED

Andrews v. Law society of British Columbia, [1989] 1 S.C.R. 143, 1989 CanLII 2 (S.C.C.).

Barbeau v. A.G. British Columbia (2003), BCCA 251.

Benner v. Canada (Secretary of State), [1997] 1 S.C.R. 358, 1997 CanLII 376 (S.C.C.).

Bliss v. Attorney General of Canada, [1979] 1 S.C.R. 183.

Brooks v. Canada Safeway Ltd., [1989] 1 S.C.R. 1219, 1989 CanLII 96 (S.C.C.).

Brown v. Board of Education of Topeka, 347 U.S. 483 (1954).

Catholic Civil Rights League v. Hendricks, 2004 CanLII 20538 (QC C.A.).

Dulmage v. Ontario (Police Complaints Commissioner) (1994), 21 OR. (3d) 356 (Ont. Gen. Div.).

Eaton v. Brant County Board of Education, [1997] 1 S.C.R. 241, 1997 CanLII 366 (S.C.C.).

Egan v. Canada, [1995] 2 S.C.R. 513, 1995 CanLII 98 (S.C.C.).

Eldridge v. British Columbia (Attorney General), [1997] 3 S.C.R. 624, 1997 CanLII 327 (S.C.C.).

Gomez v. Perez. U.S. 824 at 831 (1972).

Great Atlantic & Pacific Co. of Canada v. Ontario (Human Rights Commission) (1993), 13 O.R. (3d) 824 (Gen. Div.).

Halpern v. A.G. Canada (2003), 65 O.R. (3d) 161 (C.A.).

K. and B. (Re) (1995), 23 O.R. (3d) 679, (1995), 125 D.L.R. (4th) 653 (Ont. Prov. Ct.).

Kane v. Ontario (A.-G.) (1997), 152 D.L.R. (4th) 738.

Knodel v. British Columbia (Medical Services Commission) (1991), 58 B.C.L.R. (2d) 356.

Law v. Canada (Minister of Employment and Immigration), [1999] 1 S.C.R. 497, 1999 CanLII 675 (S.C.C.).

Leshner v. Ontario (1992), 16 C.H.R.R. D/184.

M. v. H. (1996), 132 D.L.R. (4th) 538 (Ont. Ct. Gen. Div.) (Epstein J.).

M. v. H. aff d (1996), 142 D.L.R. (4th) 1 (C. A.) (Finlayson J.A. dissenting).

M. v. H. aff d (1999), 171 D.L.R. (4th) 577 (Gonthier J. dissenting) (S.C.C.).

Masters v. Ontario (1994), 18 O.R (3d) 551 (Ont. Div. Ct).

Miron v. Trudel (1995) 2 S.C.R. 418.

Ontario Human Rights Commission v. Simpson-Sears, (1985) 2 S.C.R. 536.

R. v. Big M Drug Mart Ltd., [1985] 1 S.C.R. 295, 1985 CanLII 69 (S.C.C.).

R. v. Edwards Books and Art Ltd., [1986] 2 S.C.R. 713, 1986 CanLII 12 (S.C.C.).

R. v. Morgentaler (1974) S.C.J. No. 1 (QL).

R. v. Morgentaler, (1988) 1 S.C.R. 30, 1988 CanLII 90 (S.C.C.).

R. v. Morgentaler, [1988] 1 S.C.R. 30, 1988 CanLII 90 (S.C.C.).

R. v. Williams, [1998] 1 S.C.R. 1128, 1998 CanLII 782 (S.C.C.).

Re Canada and Lorenzen (1993), 38 L.A.C. (4th) 29R.S.O. 1990, c. F-3.

Ross v. New Brunswick School District No. 15, [1996] 1 S.C.R. 825, 1996 CanLII 237 (S.C.C.).

Thibaudeau v. Canada, [1995] 2 S.C.R. 627, 1995 CanLII 99 (S.C.C.).

Trinity Western University v. British Columbia College of Teachers, [2001] 1 S.C.R. 772, 2001 SCC 31.

Veysey v. Canada (Correctional Service) (1989), 44 C.R.R. 364.

Virend v. Alberta (1998) 1 S.C.R. 493.

CONTRIBUTORS

LORI BEAMAN (Ph.D., Sociology, University of New Brunswick) conducts research in the broad area of law and society, with specific attention to religious minorities and religious freedom. Overriding themes in her work include access to justice, power relations, surveillance, risk and governmentality. Recent articles include "Aboriginal Spirituality and the Legal Construction of Freedom of Religion"; "Sexual Orientation and Legal Discourse: The Egan Case"; "The Myth of Plurality, Diversity and Vigour: Constitutional Privilege of Protestantism in the United States and Canada"; and "Church, State and the Legal Interpretation of Polygamy" (forthcoming). In 1999 she published *Shared Beliefs, Different Lives: Women's Identities in Evangelical Context*.

DAINA Z. GREEN is a labour consultant and equity practitioner. She provides guidance in the development of anti-discrimination programs and policies to governments, unions, non-profit organizations and joint labour-management committees in Canada and abroad. Daina has developed and delivered diverse educational programs and is the author of training manuals currently used in Canadian workplaces. Trained as a social science researcher, she holds a Masters of Science degree from McGill University in Human Communication Disorders, and also works as a translator and interpreter in English, French, Portuguese and Spanish. She is a former co-cordinator of the Worker Education program of the International Council for Adult Education and currently administers the Humanity Fund of the CEP Union of Canada. She was the vice-chair of the board of directors of the Ontario Alliance for Employment Equity and is a long-time member of the Equal Pay Coalition.

AMANDA HOTRUM is a community based, anti-racism educator in Toronto. She has a Masters of Social Work with a specialization in social policy. She is currently an Investigation Officer at the Ontario Human Rights Commission.

BEVERLEY JACOBS is Mohawk, Bear Clan, from the Six Nations of the Grand River. She is married to Sheldon Cardinal, a mom to Ashley and a gramma to Nicholas and Tessa. She graduated with a law degree from the University of Windsor Law School and a master's degree in law from the University of Saskatchewan. She is the first Aboriginal woman to graduate with an LL.M. from the University of Saskatchewan. She opened her own law office at the Six Nations Grand River Territory in November 2003. In her work, she has focused on human rights issues, violations of Aboriginal women's rights, missing/murdered Aboriginal women, matrimonial real property, Bill C-31, residential schools, racism and health. She has taught at various educational institutions in Ontario and Saskatchewan, and as a public speaker has made numerous presentations across the country and internationally on issues affecting Aboriginal people and specifically Aboriginal women. She is the current president of the Native Women's Association of Canada.

REBECCA JOHNSON is an Associate Professor of Law at the University of Victoria. Her teaching interests are in the areas of constitutional law, criminal law, feminist advocacy, social/legal theory and law-and-film. Her research involves issues of interesectionality, and particularly the discourses and practices of power operating at the intersection of law and culture. Her current projects concern nursing mothers and the pub, and the relationships between reason, passion and the law in judicial dissent. She is the author of *Taxing Choices: the Intersection of Class, Gender, Parenthood and the Law* (2002).

JAN KAINER is an Associate Professor in the Labour Studies Program of Social Science at York University where she teaches in the field of labour relations. She has published on pay equity and on the implications of economic globalization on gender equality in the Canadian labour movement. She is the author of *Cashing In On Pay Equity? Supermarket Restructuring and Gender Equality* (2002).

ERICA LAWSON is a PhD candidate in the Department of Sociology and Equity Studies at OISE/UT. She holds a BA from Carleton University and an MA from OISE/UT. Her research focuses on Black mothers and daughters, health, and racism. Her work is informed by anti-racism theory and practice, Black feminist thought and indigenous knowledge. She is co-editor of *Back to the Drawing Board: African-Canadian Feminisms* (2003).

GAYLE MACDONALD, PhD, is Professor of Sociology at St. Thomas University. She is the editor of *Social Context and Social Location in the Sociology of Law* (2002) and the co-author, with Leslie Jeffrey, of a manuscript on sex-work in the Maritimes, currently with UBC Press. Her research interests included sexuality and the law, feminist jurisprudence, social control and the sociology of law.

MARTHA A. MCCARTHY is a partner with Epstein Cole LLP. She was called to the Bar in Ontario in 1991, winning the Silver Medal and the Family Law and Advocacy Prizes, and has practised family law since her call. She was counsel for M. in *M. v. H.*, which after eight years and a decision from the Supreme Court of Canada resulted in widespread amendments to include gays and lesbians as spouses in both federal and provincial legislation. In 2000, she commenced the equal marriage case *Halpern*, which resulted in the first decision in the country and internationally calling for immediate same-sex marriage, effective June 10, 2003. Martha later acted for the Hendricks couple in Quebec, and the Dunbar couple in the Yukon in cases that opened up equal marriage in those provinces as well. She was counsel to the Ontario and Quebec couples on the Supreme Court Marriage Reference and, just to complete the circle, was also counsel to the applicant in the first same-sex divorce in Canada. Apart from gay and lesbian equality issues, Martha's areas of specialty include the interaction of family issues with business organization and valuation, shareholders' remedies, marriage contracts, equality claims in family law, child representation and the effect of divorce on children. She is a Fellow of the International Academy of Matrimonial Lawyers and a frequent advocate, author and commentator on issues of gay and lesbian equality, and our evolving concept of family.

MARILOU MCPHEDRAN, C.M., LL.B., LL.M., LL.D. *(Honoris Causa),* founded and co-directs the International Women's Rights Project based at the University of Victoria Centre for Global Studies, and was appointed a Member of the Order of Canada in 1985 in recognition of her contributions to the successful grassroots campaign to strengthen protection for women and girls in the Canadian Constitution. She is a founding mother of the Women's Legal Education and Action Fund (1985), has chaired Canada's first task force on the sexual abuse of patients (1991) and co-authored *Preventing Sexual Abuse of Patients* (2004). Her research interests are in women's health and human rights generally, gender and governance specifically.

MARYKA OMATSU is the author of the award-winning book, *Bittersweet Passage: Redress and the Japanese Canadian Experience* (1992). She became Canada's first woman of Asian heritage to sit as a judge when she was appointed to the Ontario Court of Justice in February 1993. Presently, she presides over criminal trials in downtown Toronto. Before her appointment to the bench, Judge Omatsu was Chair of the Ontario Human Rights Board of Inquiry and an environmental lawyer representing Aboriginal peoples in provincial hydro and gas hearings. During the 1980s, she was counsel and a negotiator for the National Association of Japanese Canadians in their successful claim for compensation from the Canadian government for their internment, property confiscation and denial of civil rights.

RACHEL L. OSBORNE is a policy advisor in the area of educational governance. She is the former Equity Policy and Program Co-ordinator at the Law Society of Upper Canada. She has published and presented papers on the topics of violence against women in universities, sexual harassment, and exclusionary practices in legal education. She is currently on leave from her doctoral studies in sociology at York University.

JOANNA RADBORD is a lawyer with Epstein Cole LLP with a focus on family law and equality rights. Joanna worked extensively on *M. v. H.*, the first successful challenge to the heterosexuals-only definition of spouse. She acted as counsel in *Forrester v. Saliba*, a decision holding that a parent's transsexuality is irrelevant to a child's best interests. Joanna has been involved with the Women's Legal Education and Action Fund, appearing as its co-counsel in the spousal support variation case *Boston v. Boston* and serving on its factum subcommittee for *Little Sisters Bookstore v. Canada*. She was co-counsel to the eight Ontario and Quebec same-sex couples who won the freedom to choose civil marriage.

SHERENE RAZACK is Professor of Sociology and Equity Studies in Education at the Ontario Institute for Studies in Education/University of Toronto and has done groundbreaking work in the development of critical race theory in Canada. Her books include *Dark Threats and White Knights: The Somalia Affair, Peacekeeping and the New Imperialism* (2004), *Looking White People in the Eye: Gender, Race, and Culture in Courtroom and Classrooms* (1998), and the edited collection *Race, Space, and the Law: Unmapping a White Settler Society* (2002). She has also published articles on Canadian national mythologies and immigration policies of the 1990s, race, space and prostitution, and gendered racism.

CHARLES C. SMITH is currently the Equity Advisor to the Canadian Bar Association and Lecturer, Cultural Pluralism in the Arts, at the University of Toronto Scarborough. He has written several reports for the Canadian Bar Association focusing on accessibility and equality, including *Ten Years Into the Future: Where Are We Now After Touchstones for Equality?* As well, he has written broadly on anti-racism and racial profiling in policing and in national security for various equality-seeking legal organizations, including *Hamilton at the Crossroads:Anti-racism and the Future of the City—"Lessons Learned" from Community-Based Anti-racism Institutional Change Initiatives* (2003) and *Crisis, Conflict and Accountability: The Implications and Impact of Police Racial Profiling* (2004). Charles is also a published poet, playwright and essayist. He won second prize for his play *Last Days for the Desperate* from Black Theatre Canada. He has published poetry in numerous journals and magazines, edited three collections of poetry and published his own collection entitled *Partial Lives*.